ANARCHY AND COMMUNITY IN THE NEW AMERICAN WEST

Anarchy And Community in the New American West

Madrid, New Mexico, 1970–2000

KATHRYN HOVEY

UNIVERSITY OF NEW MEXICO PRESS ❖ ALBUQUERQUE

09 08 07 06 05   1 2 3 4 5

PRINTED IN THE U.S.A.

LIBRARY OF CONGRESS CATALOGING-IN-PUBLICATION DATA
Hovey, Kathryn, 1945–
Anarchy and community in the new American West : Madrid, New Mexico,
1970–2000 / Kathryn Hovey.
p. cm.
Includes bibliographical references and index.
ISBN 0-8263-3446-6 (alk. paper)
1. Madrid (N.M.)—History—20th century.
2. Madrid (N.M.)—Social conditions—20th century.
3. Community life—New Mexico—Madrid—History—20th century.
4. Madrid (N.M.)—Politics and government—20th century.
5. Anarchism—New Mexico—Madrid—History—20th century.
I. Title.
F804.M33H685 2005
978.9'56—dc22

2004027405

book design and type composition by Kathleen Sparkes
book is typeset using the Sabon family 10/14
display type is Latin 725

*To Dr. Vera John-Steiner, whose work on collaboration,
cooperation, and creativity has deeply informed
my own views on human potential;
her intellectual support remains invaluable.*

*To Mera Wolf, to Ken Hovey, and to my own grown daughters,
Tara, Meghan, and Karina; there are not ways enough to
thank you for your support. And to my sons, Joel, Shad,
and David, who remain invaluable friends.*

To Mark and Robert, for the space and the peaches.

*And to one other person, who knows
what his contribution was.*

Contents

$\_\mathcal{C} \mathcal{D}\_$

List of Photographs

All photographs were taken by the author during the spring and fall of 2000, using an old single-lens-reflex Pentax 35-mm camera set on auto focus and 400 ASA film.

Acknowledgments

This book is about a small fraction of the generation of people who reached maturity during the social revolutions of the 1960s in the United States. Yet the retreat that these disaffected folk found in northern New Mexico would not have existed but for the character of the place itself. Northern New Mexico shapes all those who live here for very long: Native American, Spanish settler, and Anglo entrepreneur have all been recast by the experience of this corner of the American West. Those who survive here have a quality of endurance; one does not manipulate and control the landscape and the forces of nature here, one acquiesces and endures. As the entire American West struggles to contain the twin forces of rustification and exurbanism, it is my deepest hope that places like this—short on easily exploitable resources but long on breathtaking beauty and solitude—will endure as well.

This work was conceived and done as part of the requirements for a Ph.D. in sociology, completed at the University of New Mexico in the summer of 2002. The dissertation was published under the title *Coalminer's Stepdaughter: A Study of Fragility and Sustainability in Madrid, New Mexico*. No one accomplishes such a task alone, and I have been greatly blessed to have had the mentorship of the four committee members who dedicated time and energy to make this project a reality; my work would have never reached fruition were it not for the involvement of Dr. Jane Hood, Dr. George Huaco, Dr. Richard Wood, and Dr. Mark Gottdiener. I count myself doubly blessed because throughout a long and occasionally difficult graduate career these mentors remained friends as well.

Dr. Richard Wood spent untold hours suggesting revisions—revisions that made this text readable; any remaining errors or mistakes of judgment are mine alone. Our many substantive discussions of the material and his coordination as dissertation chair were always accomplished in a truly corroborative manner.

Dr. Jane Hood contributed greatly to my research goals as well as to the clarity of many substantive issues throughout this work. Very special thanks for the innumerable conversations and moments of encouragement.

Many years ago Dr. George Huaco reintroduced me to social theory and the joy of a life of the mind. Without his influence over the years, I would not have done this work at all.

Dr. Mark Gottdiener has provided intellectual stimulation and a grounding in contemporary urban theory. With his help and understanding, I was able to stay focused on important issues beyond the needs of the moment.

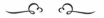

Preface

I started this research with a set of very naïve research questions: what had drawn the people who resettled Madrid to the old ghost town, how had they managed to create a community starting with such meager resources, and what did the community look like after thirty years of rebuilding. Although I never lived in Madrid during the 1970s, I was living in Santa Fe at the time the Ducks arrived in the village, and I had been attracted to the area myself. I was of the same generation as the young people who moved to the village, and share many of their political and lifestyle leanings—albeit without adhering to the belief in the liberating quality of drugs. Later, through a serendipitous series of acquaintances, I met Joe Huber in the course of running a business in Albuquerque, where I had settled in 1974. He always invited everyone he met to come and visit "his hometown," and I was given his guided tours through the town on two occasions—when it was still pretty much a ghost town, although there were a few people like the Ducks and August living there. Therefore I was familiar with the reconstruction of the village by those folks from my generation who drifted out from the mainstream culture to become the group I have called "the resettlers," and familiar with Huber's grand hopes for his hometown. I remember the excitement among my more footloose friends when Huber sold the town and some of them took advantage of the opportunity for a life outside the big city of Albuquerque.

The inspiration for studying Madrid came from several sources: a long-time interest in company towns and the industrial paternalism that controlled the lives of their workers right down to the types of housing available—I had worked for years in the building and architectural trades, so the built environment retains its fascination for me; a sense of disquiet over the disappearance of social protest in the wake of the conservative turn in America following the death of the Great Society programs under Lyndon Johnson; and simple curiosity about what had happened to those few people whom I had known who had settled in Madrid and were part of its rebirth. So while I never got to live directly in the village—even during my research—I had been conscious of this counterculture attempt at building a lasting community from the village's beginnings. By the time I engaged in the observation stage of the research, the rents in the village were as high as in Albuquerque, necessitating the caretaking arrangements "out on the land" that enabled my entry into the village as a member of the larger Madrid community rather than as an outsider.

The methods used for this research were patterned after the classic University of Chicago School's community studies and the contemporary participant observation study of inner city urban gangs, *Islands in the Streets*, by Martin Sanchez Jankowski (1991). I originally planned on doing a combination of participant observation and intensive interviewing to collect the data about Madrid's resettlers, and, in fact, thought that the community was small enough that a census of the village's population might be possible. I was eventually able to use observation and interviewing as my main research tools, but I discovered very early into the project that there were several difficulties with my initial plan. The first stumbling block was the nature of the community itself—the suspicion and paranoia underlying social relations made entry into the village difficult. I spent one whole year commuting to Madrid from Albuquerque, talking informally with people in the coffee shop, the general store, and the tavern, and observing the interactions between the locals and the tourists. One shop owner and later arrivee considered herself to be one of the village's unofficial historians; she was sympathetic to my research and allowed me to help in her shop and to assist her with her many personal needs—she was one of Madrid's quasi-sheltered individuals; she eventually felt threatened by the community's lack of social support systems and returned to her family home out of state. Helping Shirley created a legitimate reason for me to be in the village, and began breaking down the suspicion on the part of the residents that I was one of two things: that I was either a federal agent or a *National Inquirer* reporter—neither one a good basis for developing the kind of rapport needed for serious research.

After this first year, when there seemed to be no increased harassment of locals by various law enforcement agents, I was able to begin more intensive interviewing. I had found during this exploratory period that few of the original resettlers—those who bought from Joe Huber or immediately after the land rush—survived in the community or surrounding countryside. None of the people whom I had known was there either, although a few resettlers remembered my old friends. In keeping with the serendipitous nature of Madrid, the first real break in establishing a tie to the community came through a chance meeting as part of my classroom teaching at the University of New Mexico, which brought me into contact with Sam Duck, the first of the thirteen resettlers I was able to interview in depth. Sam no longer lived in Madrid, and was one of the first of the Ducks to leave after the water system was installed by the county, but he maintained extensive photo albums of his life in Madrid and graciously provided over six hours of taped interviews about his experiences as a member of the first group of hippies to rent from Huber before the town was sold.

From these two friendships, I was eventually able to build a base of trust among residents to begin more coordinated observations and interviews in the village. Being befriended by Sam proved to be a key piece of cultural capital among the resettlers, for virtually all of them had known the Ducks. When the opportunity came up to form a partnership with one of the later arrivees and to live out in the country on land belonging to another sympathetic shop owner, the difficulties of interviewing and community participation were greatly reduced. Now I had a legitimate reason to sit in on planning meetings, MLA meetings, and other community events, and, since I was always observed taking copious notes everywhere I went, I was asked by two organizations to become their secretary.

Once the initial difficulties of entry into the village were reduced, the work of finding and interviewing the remaining resettlers began. It had become obvious that these were the folks who had set the cultural agendas for Madrid, so in spite of their reduced numbers in the village, they were the targeted group for intensive interviewing and I made every effort to reach as many of these people as I could. I had only one refusal by an original resettler, so out of the eighteen people known by current Madroids to be still in the area, I was able to interview thirteen, leaving only four people with whom I was never even able to become acquainted. Most of the folks granted at least two-hour taped interviews, and all but two of these folks were always available for informal chats or conversations about current events in the village. True to form for Madrid, only three of these interviews took place in people's homes; the rest were outside or in shops and studios. The intensive interviewing of resettlers was done in accordance with the University of New Mexico's Institutional Review Board's guidelines as approved for this research (#9825–0003), and descriptions if individuals and pseudonyms were chosen to minimize the ability of anyone outside of the village to recognize any particular persons. Participant observations continued throughout the time I was conducting the interviews with resettlers, and—once settled into village life—I was able to be present in town while doing the routine activities of everyday life. My work as a teacher took me out of town for the three years I lived there, but I was there enough to keep in close touch with the pulse of unfolding events.

Another way in which I became involved with village life was through participant activism, and this was useful but dangerous (in terms of research) in such a small town. I worked actively on the greenbelt proposal, with the village library, and with the town's historical society as well as volunteered with the first Lady Amvets Thanksgiving Day dinner and other small things as the occasion arose. This participation gave me excellent access to how decisions were—or usually were not—arrived at within these groups, but for the small library and historic society one more active, committed member could sway the direction of what action was taken. I eventually had to excuse myself from such deep involvements due to time constraints. I would have remained in the village had it not been for the length of the commute—a drain on both my time and on natural resources.

Overall, for three years I lived a life very close to that of many of those original resettlers and later arrivees about whom I have written; had I lived in the village, where life is a bit easier, or had I not lived in the surrounding neighborhood at all, I would have had no insights into the real difficulties faced by those who choose a life away from the amenities of urban life. It would have been much harder to understand the immense effort that it took to take a ghost town and turn it into a unique but viable place in which to live; and it would have been much easier to see the outward appearance of a laid-back lifestyle as the manifestation of a lazy and indolent life given over to the hedonist pursuits of pleasure and the concomitant refusal to grow up and accept responsibility by working for corporate America. Likewise, if I had only observed and interviewed the folks in Madrid and not actively participated in the tendrils of organizational efforts that occurred during those three years, I could not have seen the depth to which my generation's countercultural threads still inform the everyday workings of village life.

Beyond these direct methods of gathering data, I interviewed many people involved with institutional powers beyond the village, such as highway engineers, water experts, and neighborhood activists from the nearby vil-

lages to triangulate information about Madrid itself as well as the issues
of exurban sprawl that affect the entire region around Madrid. I have
attended countless community meetings (most of them outside Madrid),
county zoning hearings, citizen protest meetings over mining and land use
issues, and monthly meetings of the various tourist booster groups active in
the area; for three years I participated in as many of these as time permit-
ted. This combined information, in conjunction with my twenty-year background in architecture and the building trades, provided a solid backdrop
against which to place Madrid's attempts at self-definition and survival—
or perhaps better to say Madrid's attempts at ignoring the reality of the
encroaching outside world, as the villagers continue to believe their unique-
ness can be protected by lack of water and a few meager greenbelt and open
space efforts.

All participant-observation studies share a common weakness; the
findings from this type of research are focused through the lens of the
observer. Every person from Madrid would have a slightly different picture of the village; mine is only one of many stories that could be told. While
I have discussed at length the excesses of individualism among some of my
generational cohort in Madrid, there are two threads that I hope remain
clearly expressed in the text. One is that while we are perhaps a *self*-ori-
ented generation, the counterculture participants who form the core of this
study were not materialistic narcissists; we expressed our *self*-centeredness
in other ways. The second is that beneath or beyond this *self*-ness, there was
a deeply felt need to find a way of living that was outside of the hypocrisy,
exploitation, and commodification of the dominant society. If an ethical way
of living through socially just and economically sustainable means has not
completely been achieved in Madrid, it has certainly not even been attempted by most of the people in mainstream American society. I have tried to
be a faithful conduit for documenting this other, often forgotten side of the
counterculture movement of the late 1960s and 1970s.

There is one person whom I interviewed for this research whose work
and life need to be noted, although he is not directly a part of Madrid. I will
call him Father Mike, the parish priest at the church in Cerrillos. Father
Mike is a Franciscan, an order dedicated to working with the poor, and he
has been a rural parish priest for his entire working life. He was in his mid-
seventies when we met and still conducted mass every Sunday in Cerrillos,
then drove over a treacherous road to Gallisteo to perform mass at the

church in this small village. He also managed the historic chapel at Golden and performed mass there once a year.

What struck me during our time together was the degree to which this man and his beliefs represented the polar opposite of so many folks of my generation—in and out of Madrid. Called by faith, Father Mike attended to the needs of the people he served, whether or not they had ever served the church in any way. He officiated at many a hippie funeral at the little cemetery at Madrid that dates to the coal-mining era, including baby Anna's. Although he wondered out loud to me about how men and women could live together so casually and change partners so easily, when asked to come to administer the last rights to a local Madrid woman dying of cancer he came without hesitation. This devotion to a calling larger than himself was so striking, especially in contrast to the *self-ness* of the people I was studying (and, indeed, my own self), that I will never think of Madrid without thinking of Father Mike, and wonder at the intersection of such different worlds.

Note: As the book goes to print, I feel obligated to pass on to the reader that Father Mike has since retired from active service due to ailing health; sadly, the village of Cerrillos is without a parish priest for the first time since the church was built.

CHAPTER ONE

The American West
Its Importance to Madrid

*American social development has been continually beginning
over again on the frontier. This perennial rebirth, this fluidity
of American life, this expansion westward with its new opportunities, its continuous touch with the simplicity of primitive
society, furnish the dominating American character.*
—Frederick Jackson Turner,
"The Significance of the Frontier in American History"

*Some of the Sioux who charged Custer at the Little Bighorn
would later charge him nightly in [Buffalo Bill's] . . . Wild
West. Indians who fought whites in Cody's Wild West would
return to the Dakotas to fight whites for real during the culmi-
nation of the Ghost Dance troubles that led to the slaughter of
the Sioux at Wounded Knee in 1890. Buffalo Bill would step
off the stage during both the Custer Campaign and the Ghost
Dance to serve as an army scout, each time incorporating
aspects of his experience into the show.*
—White and Limerick,
The Frontier in American Culture

The American West is a palimpsest of images, icons, and metaphors, symbolic currencies that resonate with people throughout the world. It is a
medium of semiotic exchange that is borrowed, distorted, reinterpreted,
and commodified; each generation uses the West for its own purposes, leaving its interpretations as another layer of this history. Mythic stories of
expansion, conquest, and triumph generated from the western frontier (it is
argued) created the American character, and the symbolic spaces created
through the frontier experience provided (it is still argued) an escape from
discontents with civilization, even for those destined never to experience the

West firsthand. In fact, America is a land of forever final frontiers, one receding into history as the next one appears, awaiting our arrival. For earlier generations, the West and its frontier were proof positive of American exceptionalism and American innocence, both ideologies justified through creation myths in which European emigrants, as benighted innocents, engaged in either the pastoral settling of empty lands or the heroic routing of barbarians (White and Limerick 1994; Truettner 1991). Today the West maintains an aura of mystery, a sense of unending space, unlimited opportunities, and unfettered freedoms, long after the cooptation of the physical space by Euro-Americans.

When Frederick Jackson Turner decided that the space of the American frontier was closed after 1890, he set the precedent for more than sixty years of concern about the potency of the American identity, about the loss of America's exceptionalism and Americans' ability to renew their democratic strengths by trial and error in the crucible of the wilderness. This sense of Eden lost informed not only the general public but academics as well, as we will see later. Yet while some pondered the effects of the closed frontier, other Americans continued to expand and utilize the frontier imagery to inform new types of adventures, new associations, and new ways of living. At the same time, Western frontier iconography became commodified, infused with the manipulative power of advertising, as what was once a lived experience became a road show. As we see from the epigraph above, the postmodern experience of fragmented, commercialized reality was at home on the frontier, and the easy slippage from fantasy to reality has been part of the American West for a long time. In Madrid, New Mexico, this shifting between fantasy and reality is an everyday event.

Figure 1.1 is emblematic of contemporary Madrid: this "Kodak moment" blends past, present, and future Madrid into a single existential moment and captures the exploitation of the reconstructed past by present tourist enterprises. The reality of the past lies underfoot; the ground is covered with coal slag along the main street.

Frederick Jackson Turner had used the census figures from 1890 to define the frontier as any place with fewer than two people per square mile, but as the West became increasingly more settled, other types of narratives appeared. As Patricia Nelson Limerick suggests, this "closing" has always been more symbolic than real: when the tourist discovers the quaint folks living in formerly despised places, and when the outlaws begin earning their

FIGURE 1.1. *The Museum and Engine House Melodrama Theater*

living as photo-ops, the frontier is "museumized" rather than closed. But this closing can be a very ephemeral event, for "[l]et the car break down in the desert, let the Indians file a lawsuit to reassert an old land claim, and . . . the frontier is suddenly reopened, and the whole question of beginnings and endings becomes unsettled again" (White and Limerick 1994, 74). The city of Santa Fe is a case in point, increasing its urbanized land area by 80.7 percent in the last fifteen years while increasing its population by 41.4 percent, making it the fifth least-dense metropolitan area in the country and thereby expanding the urban-rural interface into what many had considered the modern frontier of "open space" (McDonald 2001).

This pivotal point between the frontier and the civilized, between past and future, center and the margins, and authenticity and tourist venue is exactly where Madrid, New Mexico, finds itself in today's landscape. This is not a historical anomaly, but rather that Madrid has been at this juncture before and that understanding these past histories is crucial to comprehending Madrid's place in the contemporary West. For while the village may have been a near ghost town for twenty-five years, the past is part of the future in Madrid as it is throughout the region.

Long-Distance Links to the Past

Global economies are not exclusively the child of the twentieth century, nor
are the Euro-Americans the only peoples to utilize the open spaces of the
West as a frontier. Because the history and prehistory of the region continue to play an important role in the lives of twenty-first-century dwellers, we
need to look at these older uses of Madrid as connections to the present,
physically and symbolically. Pueblo Indians continue to fight for their rights
to maintain ancient sacred sites throughout the region; prehistoric mining
areas have become county open spaces; free-ranging cattle still wander the
roads; corporate moguls engage in extractive industries; movies about "the
old west" are filmed in the area; and a few people carry on the ancient work
of hand digging turquoise out of the hills.

The region has been altered by extractive industries dating back at least
two thousand years (Harbottle and Weigand 1992). The turquoise from
Mount Chalchihuitl in the Cerrillos hills probably supplied the gem used
throughout the Mesoamerican precontact period. The mine there is large (130
feet deep and 200 feet wide), and no other ancient site can account for the
quantity of turquoise used by the ancient peoples of Mesoamerica. Adolph
Bandelier (in Northrop 1975) reported that in the century before the Spanish
conquest the Tano people working the mines in the Cerrillos area guarded
them jealously, for they prospered from the trade in turquoise with their
Mesoamerican neighbors; by 1892, the American Turquoise Company operated the famous Tiffany Mine on a nearby hill, extracting the highest propor-
tion of gem-grade turquoise in America, valued at over two million dollars (in
1915 dollars). One mining historian claims that no modern turquoise mine
exists that is not laid over the workings of a prehistoric site. Ancient and modern mine sites pockmark the entire region, shadowy (and sometimes dangerous) evidence of the extent to which humans have altered and exploited this
landscape (Pogue 1970 [1915], 52–55, 97–104; Northrop 1975, 39–52).

Prehistory and history still play themselves out in these hills just to the
north of Madrid. For example, a 1910 report in a mining journal documents
a heist by Santo Domingo Pueblo Indians occurring at the Tiffany Mines, in
which one Native American,

> after leaving a guard of about 16 warriors at the mouth of the
> shaft, descended the 125-foot shaft by means of a rope, ascending

with some of the much sought for stone. Efforts have been made by Santa Fe officials to capture some of the band. . . . The Indians still claim the turquoise mines from which their forefathers took turquoise centuries ago . . . (quoted in Northrop 1975, 54)

Claims of buried riches still entice prospectors and treasure hunters to this area, and there are few legends that endure with such strength as those of lost Indian and Spanish mines—of vast hordes of gold and silver covered over during the Pueblo Revolt or other troubles—if only they could be found again. The trade in lost legends and lost paradises waiting to be redis-covered is largely grist for the real estate industry today. As Chris Wilson has documented in his work on Santa Fe, many modern migrants to the region are amenity seekers and retirees looking for a Tahiti in the desert, and they construct their own myths of paradise using bits and pieces of these old dreams of glory (1997). Few newcomers came to the Southwest with as complicated a mission as the Spanish conquistadors in the sixteenth cen-tury; none would ever again see the landscape of scattered, independent, rel-atively self-sufficient defensible villages that wrested a simple but sustainable living from the arid land.

The Historic Record: Hispanic and Early Anglo Occupation of the Area

The impact of Spanish and later Anglo American occupation of the New Mexico territory continued this prehistoric legacy of mineral extraction and population movements at an accelerated rate of resource use and exploita-tion. Viewing this early historic contact through the writings of late-twenti-eth-century historians makes it clear that the already complex prehistory settlement and resource use patterns of the area in and around north-cen-tral New Mexico became even more complex after the Spanish conquistador Coronado first explored the territory in 1540. More than fifty years later, in 1598, Don Juan Oñate led an expedition of six hundred colonists along with their seven thousand head of livestock from the colony at Santa Bárbara, New Mexico, to San Juan Pueblo at the confluence of the Rio Chama and the Rio Grande (thirty miles north of present-day Santa Fe) and founded the colony of San Gabriel. The fabled stores of gold and silver that drew the colonists to the territory never materialized, leaving the Pueblo

Indians as the only exploitable resource in the region. The Native Americans quickly became a valued commodity fought over by both the Spanish clergy and the Spanish civil authorities. Both the clergy and the government saw the indigenous peoples as a source of cheap labor, but for the padres the Native Americans also provided souls for the work of God. The Spanish expropriation of the labor and the subsistence agricultural products of the native peoples, along with European diseases and armed conflict between the two peoples, soon reduced the Pueblo peoples to a fraction of their precontact population. As documented by Steve McDowell (1990, 19–41), Marc Simmons (1988, 65–76), and Chris Wilson (1997, 21–23), between Oñate's settlement in 1598 and the Pueblo Revolt of 1680, the estimated population of 100,000 Puebloans, inhabiting perhaps 135 towns, had dropped to 20,000 people, and led to the abandonment of at least 80 pueblos.

The Pueblo Revolt of 1680—the only successful regaining of conquered territory by indigenous peoples in North America—provided only a short hiatus from Spanish domination, for when Spanish rule was reestablished in 1695 under Don Diego de Vargas, the colonial population expanded rapidly, soon outnumbering the Native Americans. New villages were founded all along the Rio Grande and its tributaries, and while Santa Fe (founded in 1610) remained the capital, Albuquerque (founded in 1706) completed a string of villas from El Paso to the north country. The new colonial government brought with it the realization that some degree of coexistence (rather than continual coercion) was the only way to survive in this isolated territory, and peasant farmers began sharing a subsistence lifestyle with native peoples. But the colony offered little worth defending. It was geographically remote; its mountains had yielded little precious metal compared to the riches of Mexico and neighboring Arizona; "and in general it was too rugged, too impoverished, and too deficient in marketable resources to warrant any kind of aggressive development" (DeBuys 1985, 61–62). That is still not a bad way to describe large portions of northern New Mexico today. Supply wagons from Mexico could be as infrequent as every three or four years, depending on the ferocity of the Apache raiders; New Mexico's main purpose became not belonging to any of Spain's enemies, especially the French or the British (McDowell 1990, 4; Simmons 1988, 43–44, 82–85). So marginal had New Mexico become by the mid-eighteenth century that Spain was reluctant to send even essentials like metal tools or firearms along the Camino Real, for Spain expected its colonies to be at least self-sufficient (if not profitable), and the cost of provisioning such a remote, unproductive area was seen as a drain on the Crown. There remained only two justifications for maintaining the colony in the late seventeenth century: as a bulwark against feared French expansion from the Mississippi, and to placate the Church, still intent on converting the Native Americans (DeBuys 1985, 63–65). The fear of French expansion was halted with the ending of the French and Indian Wars in 1763 and the temporary ceding of the Louisiana territory by France to Spain, extending the Spanish empire to the Mississippi (Simmons 1988, 81).

The French were not the only power in the arena. After 1740 British and American traders supplied arms to the Indians (for their own divisive purposes), especially the Comanches who often traded and raided in the Spanish territory. By 1776, because of the reluctance of the Spanish government to supply its own people with the necessities of frontier life, the settlers and the Puebloans were buying their guns from the much better equipped Comanches (DeBuys 1985, 64–65). International colonialism replaced the turquoise trade as a force of competition, and violence, continual population shifts, and migrations continued to dominate the region.

Some Puebloans left the Rio Grande area for the western plains as a result of Spanish colonial population pressure, joining the Plains Indians in their migrations. Other groups, like the Apache and the Comanche, moved into northern New Mexico or began having a much stronger presence than in the pre-French and pre-British colonial contact era. Soon the Americans would add their own settlement agenda to the pressures pushing Plains Indians into the Spanish territory. As these Native American groups moved into New Mexico, they upset the recently reestablished balance of power in the region. Some Native Americans worked for the Spanish as scouts and auxiliaries; others had a less peaceful agenda, as when the Comanches decided to destroy Pecos Pueblo in the late 1700s. Epidemics of smallpox and other European diseases, sometimes coming in ten-year cycles, could reduce the population of a pueblo by 25 percent with each cycle, forcing the abandonment of many communities, as happened at Pecos Pueblo. Stragglers from these devastations would migrate to the next closest viable pueblo that was part of their kinship structure (DeBuys 1985, 57–58).

While Spain struggled to control its northern boundary, international events once again changed the fate of New Mexico and her peoples. Napoleon seduced Spain into returning the Louisiana territory to France in 1803, then promptly (and against the agreement) sold the area to America. Once again in the territory fact blended into fiction, as Spain, still fearing for the safety of its silver mines in Mexico, continued the prohibition against trade with or trespass by foreigners for fear of invasion down nonexistent waterways. Spain mounted two unsuccessful attacks on the Lewis and Clark expedition, failing largely because of Spanish ignorance of the geography of their own northern boundaries (Burns 1999). But before long, intrusions like Zebulon Pike's 1806 expedition pierced the enforced solitude of Santa Fe and the surrounding northern area. Although unknown to Pike and later American merchants, small caravans had been bringing minuscule amounts of much desired trade goods to the northern region since 1739, when two Frenchmen had dared to cross the plains with mercantile goods for the settlers at Santa Fe (Simmons 1988, 80, 96–99). Chimera-like fairy tales of wealth, after all, had lured the conquistadors north, and Spain's fear of losing the vast buffer zone protecting the material wealth in Mexico had maintained her presence in the area. Thus the real physical distance and the politically enhanced isolation had separated the place and its people from deep allegiance to the Crown, and had isolated its settlers and natives from knowledge of the larger world. This isolation had also brought a sense of mystery, intrigue, and suspicion about the region, a sense that would (in less than three generations) be exploited by those hoping to capitalize on the make-believe world of tourism. So, although considered marginal to the main thrusts of empire for Spain, France, and Great Britain, the territory nevertheless was a site used and exploited by those who themselves were marginalized in the process of conquest.

Long before Anglo settlers came to northern New Mexico, international forces beyond the control of natives and settlers alike determined the quality and nature of life in the region, and the pre-Anglo New Mexican frontier looks more like the unsettlement of a space than the settlement of new territory. With these interpretations in mind, it is hard to see the "American West as a pristine landscape, a place that acted like the best aspirin on the worst headaches of civilization" (Limerick, quoted in Klett 1992, 9). The Spanish colonial population growth, in fact, created headaches for its own administrators, and points to two other threads from New Mexico's early history that are still playing themselves out today.

While nineteenth-century historians like Frederick Jackson Turner would see the ever-expanding settlement of frontier spaces as renewal, the opposite view—of the frontier as a site for losers, misfits, barbarians, and even outlaws—has an equally long history. The second strand is that of

resource depletion, and that also has its roots in the Spanish colonial period. In 1751 the governor of New Mexico, Velez Cachupin, described the
people who were being given the land grant for Las Trampas: "there is not
[in Santa Fe] land or waters sufficient for their support, neither have they
any other occupation, trades, or means of traffic, excepting agriculture and
the raising of stock" (DeBuys 1985, 68). The twelve families receiving the
grant had been living in the Barrio de Analco, south of the Santa Fe River,
a settlement composed of "simple, unlettered people." Twenty-five years
later, Fray Dominguez described Las Trampas, now sixty-three families
strong, as "a ragged lot, but there were three or four who have enough to
get along after a fashion. . . . Accordingly, most of them are low class, and
there are very few of good, or even moderately good blood" (DeBuys 1985,
68). As historian Patricia Nelson Limerick has commented, the West has
always been a dumping ground for civilization's unwanted commodities,
from Indians to nuclear waste: "the West displays the ongoing legacy of conquest in everyday life" (Limerick 2000, 23–26). For centuries, poverty of
land and of people has competed with the images of resources beyond measure in this part of the frontier. The lure of riches and space without limits
ensured that these competitions would not be peaceful.

Conquest and violence continued to mark the territory as Ute, Navajo,
Apache, and Comanche nomads preyed upon the Hispanic and Puebloans
alike. In 1776, while Fray Dominguez was surveying the territory for Spain
and documenting settlements like Las Trampas, he found that nearly every
family of Hispanics mourned a relative lost to these raids, and whole villages
and ranches had been ruined and their flocks destroyed. From 1598 until the
defeat of Geronimo in 1886, the area was under constant siege, and "[n]o
town was so large as to be completely secure from raiders; no traveler ever
left home without wondering if he would ever see it again" (Simmons 1988,
6–9). Insecurity was such an everyday phenomenon that it structured the lives
of settlers and was passed on from one generation to the next. Some have
speculated that this frontier hardship forged among the settlers a sense of
fatalism and an inner stoicism that enabled them to endure the isolation and
poverty of Spanish colonial New Mexico (Simmons 1988, 6–9). Without
arguing this historical point, it is obvious that many current residents of rural
northern New Mexico, renegade outcast and regular citizen alike, share
something of this ancient belief system and endure contemporary uncertainties with a similar attitude.

Everyday life for the colonial Spanish and Native American populations in the New Mexico territory underwent another conquest with the opening of the Santa Fe Trail in 1821, concurrent with the Mexican Revolution that finally freed Mexico from Spanish domination. Yet the region remained a backwater without even a printing press until one was hauled over the Santa Fe Trail in 1834 by two merchants, Josiah Gregg and Jesse B. Sutton (Rittenhouse 1975). According to William DeBuys, the territory was without other seeming necessities such as metal plows or sawmills, much less luxuries like a college (1983, 100). The continued inability of the Mexican territorial government to satisfy the demands of its own people resulted in a nearly successful uprising in 1837 of citizens and Pueblo sympathizers, known as the Chimayo Rebellion. Consequently, when the American army colonel Stephan Watts Kearny marched into Santa Fe in 1846 and declared the territory part of the United States, there was little organized resistance. After two years of hostilities and a payment of fifteen million dollars, the Mexican American War settled the political ownership, if not the cultural priorities, of the newly acquired United States territory (McDowell 1990, 47; Simmons 1988, 112–13). Even the American Civil War, in which the new territory participated, failed to bring the region into mainstream American culture. The extreme poverty of the Hispanic Americans in northern New Mexico shielded them from larger effects of the Anglo economy, for they had little money with which to buy the new things sold by Anglo traders. They had no schools and only scant interest in schooling, so the English language was slow to penetrate their mountain valleys. And they had no hunger for Anglo customs or ideas, for however poor they were in material things, they had a rich sense of their own authenticity. They were rooted in time, in tradition, and in place (DeBuys 1985, 121).

Yet again, extra-territorial forces worked to reshape traditional lives in the newly acquired territory, for while the material culture of the new conquerors was beyond the reach of most, the Church was not. Two years after the Treaty of Guadalupe Hidalgo ended the Mexican rule over New Mexico, the ancient fears that the French would expand into Spanish territory were realized in the person of French-born bishop Jean Baptiste Lamy, installed in the new archdiocese of Santa Fe in 1850. For the preceding three centuries the closest bishop had been in Durango, Mexico, nearly a thousand miles to the south. Lamy took over an area of almost a quarter of a million square miles, with perhaps sixty-five thousand people, served by only nine secular priests. Lamy looked not to Spain but to France for his cultural inspirations, and his brand of progressivism was not appreciated by conservative Hispanics and Pueblo people, as he attempted to outlaw their indigenous practices. Lamy, unlike the Franciscan Spanish clergy, took no pleasure in the poverty and backwardness of the frontier area he had come to serve; he established the first hospital, the first orphanage, and the first college in Santa Fe, pushed for free public schooling, and participated in replacing wagon ruts with railroads (McDowell 1990, 48–49; Simmons 1988, 139). The railroad allowed northern New Mexico to join marginality with industrialism, the twin forces that rewrote the physical and social landscape of the region once again. The railroad and the American army finally brought an end to the Indian raids and allowed the Hispanic population to expand further into the countryside, away from defensible centers. While allowing for the expansion of the traditional pastoral and subsistence farming practices into newly accessible markets, the railroad simultaneously brought industrial relations, company towns, and large-scale emigration of wage laborers to the area.

Industrial Relations Come to Madrid and the West

Throughout the West, not just in northern New Mexico, the railroad was the pivotal player in the development of extractive industries and the claiming of "unsettled" land for the benefit of remote corporate owners. Railroads left an enduring legacy, the remains of which can be seen all over the West in towns like Madrid. In an irony of history, the gold and silver riches that had lured the conquistadors to the area were indeed under their feet, had they but had better technology, better luck, and less trouble with the Native Americans. There are conflicting reports in the historical literature, but most sources indicate that the Spanish operated many mines in New Mexico before and after the 1680 uprising. One legend claims that the roof of Chalchihuitl at Cerrillos collapsed in 1680, killing many Puebloans working underground as slaves, and that this tragedy triggered the Pueblo Revolt (Northrop 1975; Pogue 1970).

The Spanish and Mexican mines were worked for the glory of God and the Crown, as well as for individual profit, but northern European capitalism was nonexistent in the Spanish territories. Nevertheless, reports documenting deposits of silver, copper, lead, sulfur, turquoise, and salt were sent to the government in New Spain from the 1620s onward. Mining of silver, gold, and salt was taking place by 1630. These activities were interrupted by the Pueblo Revolt in 1680, and legends of lost mines—such as the gold, silver, and copper mines reputed to have been worked by Franciscan friars in Taos worth "several millions of dollars" and covered over by the Indians so future generations could not rediscover them—only served to spur more prospecting in the territory after the reconquest in 1692. One such tale concerns a Captain Madrid, who sought to reopen his father's lead mine near Cerrillos for the manufacture of bullets, but found it had been covered over by the Indians (Northrop 1975).

Placer gold mines were known in the Ortiz Mountains (known as the Old Placers District), and Spanish-era smelters have been found throughout the area. The Santa Rita copper mine was worked by the Elguea family from Chihuahua starting in 1804. In 1828 the largest gold strike west of the Mississippi up to that date was found in the San Pedro Mountains, fifteen miles south of Madrid, from which sprang the town of Golden. By 1883 Golden comprised twenty-two stores, one hundred houses, and as many as five thousand inhabitants. The mines were producing forty to fifty tons of ore per day, valued at $250 per ton. By 1942, the New and Old Placers mines had produced four million dollars of gold, about 25 percent of the total placer gold yield in New Mexico. It was assayed at 92.5 percent gold (Northrop 1975). Industrial gold mining continues in the San Pedros, although today Golden is nearly a ghost town. While Madrid itself produced no gold, the coal mines there enabled electrical generation, and Madrid's electricity was even sold to mine operators across the Rio Grande in the Jemez Mountains for a brief period in the 1880s.

As with all extractive industries, whether Spanish, Mexican, or American, the profits went elsewhere, usually leaving the local people and the landscape more impoverished than before. The boom and bust nature of resource exploitation in the West left many such abandoned towns. But the history of Madrid as a coal camp was slightly different from the boom and bust nature of so many hard rock mining towns. Coal, after all, was the motive force of the Industrial Revolution.

Madrid as a Coal Camp

The area around present-day Madrid had been settled in the early 1800s by a branch of the Madrid family, which as we have seen had been active in New Mexico before the Pueblo Revolt. Coal, which the Indians had used only for medicinal purposes, is still readily available from seams at the surface of the earth in the Madrid area. By 1835, the area was producing small amounts of the fuel that supplied the gold mines at the nearby communities of Cerrillos and Dolores, as well as the smelter located at San Pedro, at the southern end of the Ortiz Mountains. Each miner worked his own claim, digging with hand tools and carrying out his production on his own back, or, if he were wealthy enough, on the back of his burro (Motto 1973). The miners (and sometimes their families) lived in rock or adobe huts scattered about the hills, the remains of which can still be seen on many of the back roads in the region.

It was the railroads' unceasing demand for more bituminous coal to feed its steam engines as westward expansion closed the frontier that brought the Ortiz Mountain region from hand coal production to industrial mass production in the space of a few years. This area became known as the Cerrillos District Coal Field, named after the then-thriving community of Cerrillos, three miles north of Madrid. There were three coal-producing canyons, Miller Gulch, Waldo Gulch, and Coal Gulch. By an accident of nature, Coal Gulch is one of the few places in the world where both bituminous and anthracite coal are found in the same bedding planes. The railroads used bituminous for their steam engines, but coke ovens (coke was necessary for making steel) required anthracite, and anthracite is found in only two other places in the United States: Colorado and Pennsylvania. At one time, Waldo, New Mexico, had fifty coke ovens, and the area's anthracite was shipped to at least eight surrounding states as well as to a smelter in El Paso, Texas. Because of its dual production capacity, Madrid had the oldest producing coal mine west of the Mississippi.

In 1892, four investors incorporated as the Cerrillos Coal Company bought lots and leases at Coal Gulch from a larger holding company operating at Waldo, built a small settlement, intensified the work at the mine, and renamed the site Madrid after the original settlers in the area. The buildings from this era form the core of the present-day village; many are refurbished and lived in, others still bear witness to the hard life in the mining camps. Some of the houses had been brought from another camp, having been cut into three pieces, put on rail cars, and reassembled in Madrid. In a few of the derelict houses these seams where the houses were put back together are still clearly visible, as few attempts were made to disguise the cuts.

By 1893 the Cerrillos Coal Company was processing both types of coal and shipping the ore out by rail. In 1896 the Cerrillos Coal Company, through a series of complicated lease buyouts, came under the ownership of Colorado Fuel and Iron (CF&I), part of Rockefeller's industrial behemoth. Rockefeller was the biggest operator in the four-state region. CF&I operated the mines until 1906, when a fire in one of the largest bituminous shafts proved inextinguishable, and the entire operation was shut down without warning either to suppliers or to workers. During this period, the mines at Madrid produced approximately five hundred tons of coal a day. Forty years ago the U.S. Bureau of Mines estimated that there were 50 million tons of anthracite and bituminous coal left untouched at Madrid, but economies of scale and an altered consciousness about land use make it impossible to extract. The beds are tilted in two directions, twenty degrees to the east and then slightly to the north; the seams are narrow, twenty-four to forty inches high, restricting the output even with the advent of electric mining machines (Melzer 1976).

The closing of the Madrid mines by CF&I in 1906 left one Albuquerque retailer without a source of coal to sell his customers. George Kaseman, one of the founders of Albuquerque's First National Bank, decided to buy the operating leases from CF&I and began operations there the same year, rather than find another supplier. He named his endeavor the Albuquerque and Cerrillos Coal Company, and ran the operations out of Albuquerque from 1906 to 1919. He did little to improve the working or living conditions for the miners. Typical of mining camps, the shacks had no baths, no indoor toilets; few had running water, none had electricity, and all relied on coal stoves for heating and cooking. The boarding houses (probably three) were for single miners, and they had electricity and shower facilities in the basements. The only other buildings with electricity were the company's operations buildings (now part of the museum). The only telephones in town were in the company headquarters, and all incoming and outgoing calls went through the Cerrillos exchange, facilitating company control over the lives of the miners and restricting union organizing (Huber 1963; Melzer 1976: Motto 1973).

Before the turn of the century, a few miners built homes in the village (as had been customary before industrialization), but as with most mining camps, under CF&I the bulk of the housing was provided by the company. Kaseman's onsite manager, Oscar Huber, who would become a key figure in Madrid's later history, described why this was so, using the language of industrial paternalism popular in the early 1900s:

Miners were more or less of an itinerant group and generally without finances ... if the mines were to work this was about the only
class of help available, so somebody had to provide a place for
them to live and finance them until such time as they produced
coal ... If anyone had suggested at this time that a miner purchase
his own home the miner would have thought it ridiculous, and the
company, of course, wanted to maintain the town as a unit which
they controlled. (Letter from Oscar Huber, 17 June 1962, quoted
in Allen 1966, 50–51)

There was nothing unusual about this living situation; Madrid was in conformance with the standards of the day. In Madrid, a typical rent for this
type of housing in 1916 was two dollars per room per month, including coal
for cooking and heating. Fifty cents per month was added on for each electric drop in the house. This compares to a range of rents in Wyoming and
Colorado during the same year of between five dollars and eighteen dollars per month, (Allen 1966, 87). Madrid was a middling town, with only
the anomaly of its coal types to make it stand out from any other, and its
lower rents reflected the lower productive capacities of its coal fields.

Some improvements were made into the second decade of the twentieth century: shacks were wired with a single bulb in each room (again an
industry standard); there was a Catholic church (now a private residence);
a school for first through fourth grades; a company doctor who treated all
the residents, including pregnant women—unusual in coal camps of the day
(some of the equipment survives in the museum); a company store with a
small post office (the company store is still one of the most substantial buildings in the village and houses a variety of shops, including the original soda
fountain); and, to supplement the company store, a mail-order house
(Motto 1973). Mining has always been a temporary arrangement in the
West. These distinctive communities, created by the profit motive, have been
described by one writer as transient, tough, and highly insular. These are
places modeled after mobile-home parks rather than New England towns
(Hyde, in Wrobel and Steiner 1997, 110).

Kaseman ran Madrid as an absentee landlord until 1919, when he
installed Oscar Huber as resident manager. Huber had come to Albuquerque in 1914 from Kansas City, Kansas, and had commuted daily to Madrid
by rail. Tiring of the commute, he asked Kaseman to let him live in the

village with his wife and three children. Huber never left. When Kaseman was killed in an oil field explosion in 1938, Huber leased the operations at Madrid. Then, in 1947, he bought the operating leases and the remainder of the site from various railroad interests, assuming sole ownership and landlordship of the town he had managed since 1919. It was commonly said that Madrid was a company town, and Oscar Huber was the Company (Motto 1973). When Oscar passed on in 1962, his son Joe inherited the mines, the town, and the relationships established by his father during the previous forty-three years.

Like all single-enterprise towns, the coal mines at Madrid were the life support for the miners; their fortunes existed in an intricate and unpredictable web of resource availability, national markets, and competition from other sources of energy. What made Madrid slightly different from most western mining operations was the fact that the owner's lifeblood was also so closely tied to those same fortunes. Neither Huber nor Kaseman before him had national or international aspirations; they hoped to maintain at best a regional labor and commodity market edge. In 1928, production peaked at 87,148 tons of anthracite and 97,562 tons of bituminous coal. In that year, 725 miners were employed in the mines (Motto 1973). Yet, even during this time of maximum exploitation of the natural resources, the men would listen for the five o'clock whistles to see which mines would be working the next day. Miners at Madrid, as in other mining camps, often hired out as agricultural laborers during slack times. When times were really desperate, as they were during the Depression, they resorted to county welfare (Melzer 1976, 14–15). Huber, along with most mine owners, offered scrip in lieu of part of the men's paychecks, and this practice became a powerful tool to keep the men working Huber's mines instead of migrating to more lucrative sites.

Scrip could usually be redeemed only at the company store (or at a severely reduced rate if there were another store around), and Huber posted men at both ends of town on paydays to keep track of who went out of the village to purchase goods. These folks were not outright blacklisted, but a record was kept of how many times this happened (field notes 1999). Scrip was combined with a line of credit at the company store that was essentially a system of industrial debt peonage. This practice was explained by Joe Huber:

> The Madrid Supply Company [the company stores] was a
> business in itself, serving two good purposes. First it permitted

the employee to accumulate something and enjoy it, thus making
him a better and happier employee. It was also felt by the Coal
Company that an employee indebted for such a luxury would
work harder, thus raising the coal production. In my opinion, it
worked very well for all concerned. I personally feel well qualified
to say that I know what I am talking about, for it was myself that
sold the automobiles for 25 years. I might add one thing here in
saying that it was quite a help for a salesman to be furnished with
information that a certain employee should be pushed to purchase
an automobile. (Huber 1963, 8)

At one time, Madrid had one of the highest per capita car ownerships
in the United States, and car ownership became a symbol of high status
among miners, even though they often only had enough gas money to drive
up and down Madrid's main street. There was a car club, composed mostly of miners, whose members donated time to building and repairing the
unpaved roads off the main street so that there would be more places accessible to their cars (Melzer 1976, 20). Of course they were all Chryslers from
Joe's dealership; anyone bringing a car in from outside Madrid was threatened with the loss of his job—and thereby his house as well (field notes
1996). Fig. 1.2 is a photograph of the Company Stores today.

Huber adopted many other paternalistic schemes in his attempts to keep
a reliable labor force in his town. There were Fourth of July Parades, a community Easter egg hunt, and famous Christmas displays that were nationally recognized. Continental Airlines rerouted its flights for the month of
December to allow passengers to view the lights that filled the entire valley. All of these activities were coordinated through the Employees' Club,
the dues for which (seventy-five cents a month) were deducted from the miners' pay. Huber and the mine foreman ran the club, kept the books, and
made the decisions; the miners and their families got to donate their free
time and hard work in addition to their dues. Huber kept a census of all the
children in town, making sure that each one received presents at Christmas
and Easter. Huber easily justified this type of social control. For example,
when writing about the Fourth of July, he explained:

Our people stay home before the Fourth and get ready and after
the Fourth because they are tired and have had all the excitement

FIGURE 1.2. *The Company Stores today. One of the original Christmas displays is visible on the roof.*

they want for sometime, whereas if they left here to celebrate they would stay away until after all their money was spent.... We would [then] have to take care of them until they could again produce. (Melzer 1976, 40)

In spite of what would seem outright coercion on the part of the Hubers, the miners from this era remember the 1930s as the best years of their lives. One miner recalled that he loved working underground; there was never any worry about the weather and the work was always the same (field notes 1999). Richard Melzer documents that they remember the unity created by the Employees' Club and did not see it as exploitative paternalism. They remember the town as a place of social and racial equality, "in spite of the fact that 70% of the miners were Mexican, 15% were Anglo-American, 10% were Slavic or Italian, and about 5% were Black." As to the hardships, no one felt better than his neighbor because "the majority of the miners lived in similar houses, had similar jobs, had similar belongings, and suffered similar deprivation" (Melzer 1976, 39).

FIGURE 1.3. *The former Chrysler dealership.*

Figure 1.3 shows the former Chrysler dealership, once owned by Joe Huber, now a combination of residences and shops.

Throughout the West, the coming of World War II was the death knell for small operations like Huber's: men left the mines in favor of higher paying war employment in California, or they entered the service, and the population of Madrid rapidly dwindled. A ban on night lighting put an end to the Christmas displays, and until recent times the town was not prosperous enough to support such events. In all of Santa Fe County, there were only 216 men employed in mining in 1941, and this number sank to 82 in early 1945. Even an exclusive contract to supply coal to Los Alamos National Labs during and after the war could not keep the mines going, for labor shortages made fulfilling the contracts difficult. When Los Alamos chose natural gas over coal in 1954, Huber closed the mines and dismissed the last of those who lingered on (Melzer 1976, 39–40). Only the couple running the Mine Shaft Tavern and Huber's watchman, Frank Ochoa, and his family remained in the town on a full-time basis. When I met Joe Huber in the mid 1970s, he was living in Albuquerque but visiting Madrid nearly every day, offering anyone who would come a tour through the old mines—for a small fee, of course. The town was essentially deserted, the buildings long abandoned to the weather and the pack rats. The first job one of the earliest resettlers had was collecting the dollar fee for touring the "museum."

Madrid's Ties to the Industrialization of the West

While the railroads were the instrument that brought mass industrial relations to the West, it was the availability of nonrenewable energy sources, like coal, that underwrote this transformation. Early millworks relied on water power, and could not command the level of exploitation of human and natural resources that came with later technological developments. For instance, at its maximum in the 1850s, the millworks at Lowell, Massachusetts, employed 6,500 operatives; by 1901, Rockefeller's Colorado Fuel and Iron owned thirty-eight mining camps in the West (including Madrid), employing 75,000 operatives (Mulrooney 1989, 11), more than tenfold the manpower. The utilization of fossil fuels both required and accelerated the exploitation of the West, and sites like Madrid would have remained backwaters but for their natural resources.

In both form and content, Madrid followed the dominant trends of the era of the robber barons and the Gilded Age, yet there are interesting twists and anomalies to the place that telegraph through history to the contemporary community and that today play a self-conscious role in the culture of the village. These similarities and contradictions relate to specific areas: (1) the forms of industrial housing provided at remote mining sites, including the limited but yet salient ability of workers to exercise some control over their housing; (2) Huber's patterning of Madrid after the "model" company towns fashionable at the time; (3) the continuities and ironies of a company town that was built on maximizing social control through both brute force and cultural constraints and that then became the refuge for dissident counterculture settlers hoping to live without social controls. Most current residents of Madrid are familiar with their town's industrial past and appreciate both the connections to the past and the ironies of their own occupation of the site.

Housing

Housing in company towns has a long history, a history in which Madrid participates. Welsh and English coal mining and mill towns of the early 1800s were the forerunners of the company towns; row houses and tenements provided by the owners created a captive, submissive, yet mobile labor force, perfectly suited to the uncertain conditions of mining extractive resources. "A housed labor supply," according to a 1917 U.S. Department of Labor report, "is a controlled labor supply" (quoted in Mulrooney 1989, 9). In the West, as everywhere that mining and milling appeared, the industrial process mass-produced workers accustomed to relocating, to granting paternalistic authoritarian rights to a managerial elite, and to re-producing themselves in the next generation by sending their children to work under the same conditions experienced by the parents (McHugh 1988; Hahn and Prude 1985). We have seen that both Hubers used the con-trol housing gave them over their workforce. In this respect, Madrid was no different from any other coal camp.

As documented in a 1920 U.S. Coal Commission report, coal camps in the West commonly had a high percentage of foreign-born miners, and owners excelled at using ethnic differences to keep miners from organiz-ing unilaterally (Allen 1966, 103). The allocation of housing areas in the coal camps was generally by ethnic group, but with an interesting twist. It was assumed that native whites, Germans, Irish, Scottish, and Welsh were more "inclined" toward advancement in the mines and were therefore the most productive workers. These groups were given the best of the miners' shacks for housing. Eastern and Southern Europeans, however, remained in the lower status occupations, thereby qualifying for only the most minimal housing. Wages were set by the company to reflect the worth of the coal deposits; rents and charges for other housing amenities like electrical drops were in turn based on the wages miners earned. These expenses were figured into the level of housing the company was willing to provide its workers. Throughout the coal camps, anthracite miners were provided with better housing than bituminous miners, reflecting the greater value and scarcity of the former resource. Additionally, "the rules and regulations governing occupation of workers' houses were so numerous that the companies' influence extended into the home as well as the workplace . . . the town became the embodiment of the company. . . . Over time, these traits formed the core of a distinct coal company town ideology" (Mulrooney 1989, 9–10, 117–20). Huber was typical in exploiting this ideology for his own benefit.

Housing in Madrid was also typical for coal camps, as documented in a 1920 U.S. Coal Commission investigation of housing throughout the entire U.S. coal industry. This report found that 95 percent of company housing was of wood construction, with over two-thirds finished only with weatherboards on the exterior and no sheathing; composition paper was used for roofing on two-thirds of the houses; foundations were usually of posts with no permanent foundations; most had porches; fully half had exposed wood for interior finishes and only 38 percent had interior plaster; under 14 percent had running water and fewer than 3 percent had bathtubs and indoor toilets; only two-thirds had electricity or gas; and slightly fewer than half of the company towns had any kind of community water system (Allen 1966, 78). Rents reverted to the company; and the company charged for each light bulb and each bushel of coal used for light and heat; in fact, real estate was a second revenue stream for mine owners (Margolis 1999, 182). As can be seen in the picture of the unrestored miners' shacks (figure 1.4), this is exactly the type of housing stock and infrastructure that the 1970s resettlers of Madrid utilized in their re-creation of the town. The new settlers continued the pattern of renting from the company, in the person of Joe Huber, who was still finding a way to profit from his real estate.

Figure 1.4 is of the unrestored miners shacks that have been moved to the south end of Madrid. Housing was routinely moved around to suit the changing needs of mining towns. This impermanency was facilitated by the lack of permanent foundations or plumbing. The house second from the left is the only one partially finished and is occasionally rented out.

Little has been documented about the segregation of housing along racial divides in Madrid during the Huber years; I did, however, record a story of the use of African American workers to do the most dangerous jobs in the mines. During one of the Fourth of July festivals (described in more detail in chapter 4), two families from the Huber era returned to Madrid for "Old-Timers Day." One of the miners, now in his eighties, recounted the use of a young black man to ride on the front of the coal cars to ensure there were no obstacles on the tracks that would derail the cars. He, not the coal, was considered expendable.

The historic record is clear, however, on another aspect of life in Madrid that I touched on earlier; exploited though they seemed to have been, the miners enjoyed the town and generally thought well of Huber's stewardship (Melzer 1976). Huber provided paint for every house, miners were encouraged to have a garden with a picket fence surrounding it, and the main street had elevated boardwalks, making walking to the stores easier (Motto 1973). Fragments of the boardwalk can still be seen south of the ballpark, and pick-

FIGURE 1.4. *Derelict miners' shacks.*

et fences still appear on the occasional house on the main street of Madrid today. But the form and architecture of company towns were also constrained by complex cultural expectations, not all of which stemmed from the utilitarian needs of capitalism. These constraints tied Madrid to the larger processes industrializing the West. Just as colonial peoples had been caught up in complex forces beyond their control, so too were the latest conquerors of this place.

The row houses acceptable to early mill workers in Wales and England were not readily accepted as American industrial housing. The 1841 publication of Andrew Jackson Downing's *The Theory and Practice of Landscape Gardening* established the desirability of detached, single-family homes for even the most modestly employed, especially if one wished to rise above the miserable masses of industrial workers and enter the middle classes (if only symbolically). Such housing reinforced the Jeffersonian ideals of property ownership and citizenship, and these ideals of home ownership were appropriated by both the industrialists and the workers. Advances in construction techniques such as cheap balloon framing, dimensioned lumber, and the mass production of fasteners enabled the production of housing along factory lines, lowering the costs and making such housing more widely affordable. The thousands of plan books generated by Downing's examples, which were widely circulated among vernacular builders, raised expectations among workers—even those who did not own their dwellings. Mill and mine owners in remote sites were obligated to provide housing or they would have no labor, but labor brought with it the cultural expectation of a detached (or at the least a semi-detached) house with its own yard; in the West—where land was cheap—this is largely what the owners provided. We have seen how the Hubers both used and conformed to these ideologies in operating Madrid.

Model Company Towns

A more powerful set of expectations for industrial housing came from the development of model company towns, created by utopian architects and planners who wished to recapture the agrarian ideal in miniature by providing better housing for the labor force. Idealized communities such as Frank Lloyd Wright's Greenacres and Ebenezer Howard's Garden Cities offered mass-produced housing set in idyllic semi-rural settings, with gardens and open space separating work from home. The concept was designed to give industrial workers the same advantages enjoyed by the middle classes—fresh air and the illusion of space and freedom, thus giving workers fewer reasons to unionize. These prototypes were so far removed from the reality of life in most company towns as to be laughable, and it is doubtful that other than in Pullman, Illinois, few industrialists ever embraced these concepts wholeheartedly. However, in spite of their unrealistic idealism these plans had a great deal of currency in their day, and the appeal to anti-union sentiment was a strong motivating force for American capitalists. Nor were these movements restricted to America.

Between 1889 and 1910, nine international industrial (company) housing conferences and exhibitions were held in Europe in response to threatened government intervention in the affairs of private business, sanitation reforms being of primary concern. At the Colombian Exhibition in Chicago in 1893, models of the best available company housing and even whole company towns were laid out for inspection; American model villages consistently won first and second places (Gardner 1984, 93, 110–12).

There is no documented evidence to date that Oscar Huber was explicitly aware of these movements, but Melzer (1976) has shown that Huber was constantly in touch with other coal camp owners in order to stay one step ahead of union organizers. Scytha Motto (1973) wrote about the model-town nature of the reforms that Huber brought to Madrid after the neglect of the absentee landlord, Kaseman. Conversations recorded in my field notes also support Huber's manipulation of his labor force through the amenities of the built environment. We have seen firsthand that both Oscar and Joe Huber felt the best way to control their workers was through subterfuge and debt peonage. So it is not unreasonable to suggest that these model industrial town images may well have provided at least a backdrop to the way Madrid was managed and maintained under the Hubers.

Even the use of such culturally acknowledged forms of manipulation and inducements could not isolate Madrid from the reality of its resource base, however. Coal production in Madrid, as documented above, peaked in 1928, but for New Mexico coal mining reached its zenith in the decade of the 1900s, employing approximately twenty thousand people. In contrast, Wyoming's coal boom lasted until 1920 and employed over thirty thousand. Furthermore, the steady increase in the demand for coal ended in 1921 when overproduction and underconsumption began to plague the industry. Natural gas and fuel oil replaced coal as primary energy sources, and even coal operations switched to natural gas (Margolis 1999, 176–78, 192). By 1938, when Oscar Huber acquired Madrid, coal production had already become a declining economic activity in the West. The marginality that so typified New Mexico's colonial era has never really been overcome.

As noted above, World War II temporarily increased the demand for coal, but at the same time encouraged the young men to leave the camps; many men never returned to such hard and uncertain labor when given the opportunity for better paying work in the postwar factories. Many former employees from this era who worked the mines at Madrid followed the regional pattern and settled in California (Madrid Old-Timer's List). By 1944 the use of mechanical miners—equipment whose remains can be seen in the Mining Museum at Madrid—replaced the independent hand miner, and employment in coal mining continued to decline until 1968, when scares over nuclear power reduced the use of atomic energy as a fuel source. The waves of immigration feeding America's industrial revolution had long since ceased, the foreign-born had been acculturated into American life, unions achieved some solidarity against corporate owners, and, above all, "the private automobile ended the company town as a total institution and miners like everyone else were free to live one place and work in another"

(Margolis 1999, 196). The company coal mining town passed from reality into the romance of the American West.

That Madrid took longer to enter that terminal decline was due to its contract with Los Alamos, as noted above, for which Madrid provided the fuel for the Manhattan Project and other related nuclear defense activities, in an odd blending of old and new extractive industries.

Continuities and Ironies

During its heyday as a coal camp, Madrid was no different from other company coal towns in terms of its overt use of force to preserve the right of the owners to control its labor force. And no amount of symbolic amenities could fully mask the true nature of power in industrial relations. Trouble-makers and strike sympathizers were summarily evicted by the town marshal (always a company man, never an elected official); widows or those whose husbands were too ill or injured to work were evicted immediately. Once again, the past and the future collide in Madrid: the contemporary village has a self-appointed marshal who is paid a small stipend by the landowners' association to patrol the streets and maintain a "presence" for the merchants; he also delights in posing for photo-ops with the tourists. The Madrid Landowners' Association, as detailed later, is the successor to Joe Huber's ownership of the town. The irony here is that the mercantile elites of a counterculture community are paying a private person to pose as a legitimate law enforcement officer to give the impression that the town has more structure than it really has. The art of impression management in Madrid has changed its face, but not its presence in the village.

The ersatz sheriff does not hide the alternative nature of present-day Madrid any more than the neatly painted houses and picket fences masked the true utilitarian nature of the town as a coal camp. Nor could Huber's paternalistic capitalism obscure the separation of managers and the professional elite from the miners and operatives. Madrid was dominated by the tipple at one end of town and the breaker at the other; these huge structures that cascaded down the mountainside were for separating the raw ore into coal for shipment by railcar to other sites. Gates at either end of the town could be locked to prevent union agitators from gaining entry—the remnants of the gates and the breaker survived into the 1970s. Timbers from the breaker can be found in many newer homes in the area, sometimes recycled into cabinets or other fixtures. The miners' shacks were clustered in the less valuable spaces,

FIGURE 1.5. *The former Huber residence, foreground. Note the other legacy from the coal camp era of Madrid's history—the huge tailing pile of slag from the mines in the background.*

separated from the area known universally in coal camps in the West as "Silk Stocking Row" (Margolis 1999, 176–78, 180–81), located along Madrid's main street (see figure 1.5 and 1.6).

During the mining era, these homes were for the merchants, the camp doctor, and other upper-level managers. These structures today in Madrid serve a mix of business and residential uses, and partly recreate the separation between employer and owner, as I will detail in a later chapter.

The striking difference between Madrid and most company towns of the era was, of course, that the Huber family both owned the town and lived there. Joe Huber had grown up in the town and inherited it when his father died. He was intimately acquainted with every building and piece of machinery in the place. After twenty-five years of unsuccessful attempts at selling the town as an industrial site, he tolerated the presence of the counterculture settlers as his best hope of revitalizing the village while still making a profit from his real estate. Madrid's remoteness appealed to some of the 1960s generation who were seeking exactly this type of setting. Yet no matter how marginal

FIGURE 1.6. *Former manager's home, now a private residence.*

or remote this site remained, events emanating outside the region were once more redrawing the social and physical landscape of the area.

I have briefly traced how New Mexico's prehistoric trade routes linking her to Mesoamerica were subsumed under the colonial Spanish frontier, which in turn was supplanted by the mass production of the frontier as a place for resource extraction and individual renewal. The threads that link these very different histories together are ones of cultural and physical marginality and enforced self-sufficiency, attributes common to frontier areas everywhere. For Madrid as a particular site in the West, the coming of the industrial production of coal built on the remoteness and difficulty of life experienced by Puebloan and Spanish peoples. Mining also brought industrial relations and a new form of individual self-sufficiency.

Miners as a whole exhibited an ideology well suited to free labor markets—each miner felt free to take his tools and skills and go anywhere there was paying work (Mulrooney 1989). The reality that these freedoms were greatly curtailed by the power of the owners to set wages regionally, to blackball dissident workers and union organizers, and to build company towns designed with excruciating levels of social control seems not to have dimmed their ideologies for a moment. This legacy of industrial individual-ism was to give way to a new layer of people bringing with them yet anoth-er variant of individualism, one based not on the desperate needs of scarcity and survival but rather built on the material successes and excesses of the industrial era. In the resettlement of Madrid by counterculture advocates in the early 1970s, we see the juxtaposition of the economies of production and the economies of consumption. The industrial era produced such excesses that whole towns were created and abandoned nearly overnight, at great social and ecological costs. Yet the remnants could be reused by a succeeding generation that had not known true material want. That these places exist—and exist in opposition to the cultural homogenization of postindustrial capitalism—is what Madrid symbolizes today.

Contemporaneously, the industrial era's metaphors of the West as a place of renewal and as a safe haven from the crime of the city still operate with ferocious consequence. The Jeffersonian ideals echoed by utopian planners are now the common language of real estate agents selling a bit of the Old West to those who still dream of unlimited space and freedom. But Frederick Jackson Turner was also right: the frontier is closed. All new settlement takes place at the expense of some other group or ecologically fragile species. This reality, too, is a link among past, present, and future in the West.

Symbolisms and Continuities

Huber ran this ad in the *Wall Street Journal* in the spring of 1954:

ENTIRE TOWN
200 houses, grade and
high school, power house,
general store, tavern,
machine shop, mineral
rights, 9000 acres,
excellent climate, fine
industrial location.

$250,000

Over the next twenty years, Huber had from three to five buyers for his property but all the deals fell through. His real estate agent, Jim Mocho, discovered an old subdivision plot for the site previously filed with the county of Santa Fe. Mocho convinced Huber that the town could be sold in parcels. In February 1975, Joe put the remaining 150 standing buildings up for sale, starting with the folks who had already settled there, giving them credit for their sweat equity. Joe gave Jim Mocho a year's exclusive contract to sell the town. Jim felt it would sell in six months; Mocho remembers that the entire town was sold in six weeks. Huber financed some of the sales himself. Many of the shacks sold for as little as $1,500 or less, and if the down payment was a problem, Huber would lend that to the prospective owner also. He reserved certain buildings for those folks he thought would best use them, and worked deals on many homes and businesses. He insisted on a set of restrictive covenants (written by Jim Mocho) that all new owners had to sign, and established the Madrid Landowners' Association to enforce the regulations. These covenants were to maintain the village's model company town architectural heritage: they prevented large-scale businesses and mobile homes or other temporary dwellings, and encouraged home-based arts and crafts industries that fit well with the new residents' emphasis on locally produced, small-scale handcraft enterprises. Huber maintained his presence in the town's activities until his death in the 1980s, sometimes joining in the Christmas celebration for the village children (Melzer 1976; field notes 1998; interview 2002).

The changes undertaken by the counterculture generation that began renovating the ghost town are but the latest in the long series of occupations and uses of the area. The ultimate irony, of course, is that with the help of the man who carried out the social control mechanisms of the past, a company town became a haven for outlaws, renegades, and counterculture folks. And other parts of the past remain alive in Madrid and the West, with equally surprising results. As a one historian of U.S. Western history writes,

> People from the Philippines, people from Senegal, people from Thailand, people with plenty of reasons to resent the frontier and cowboy diplomacy inflicted on their nations by our nation—many of them nonetheless grew up watching Western movies and yearning for life on the old frontier and the open range.
>
> As a mental artifact, the frontier has demonstrated an astonishing stickiness and persistence. It is virtually the flypaper of our mental world; it attaches itself to everything—healthful diets,

FIGURE 1.7. *Real estate dreams: a portion of this land, at the north end of Madrid, became part of the town's open space to protect it from exurban development.*

space shuttles, civil rights campaigns, heart transplants, industrial product development, musical innovations . . . a mental and emotional fastener that, in some very curious and unexpected ways, works to hold us together. (Limerick 2000, 91–92)

Symbolically, the frontier and the West are still with us, even as we push our housing developments and our urban lifestyles farther into the wilderness. Madrid (and other small defiant communities like it) stand as a contested space in this arena, neither rural nor urban, neither wild nor tamed. The analysis that follows will demonstrate how critical the myths and symbols of the frontier and its space remain in the twenty-first century. The symbolic and physical place that is Madrid continues to carry on the centuries-long tradition of being a marginally located battlefield over which extra-territorial forces wage their contests. Figure 1.7 is indicative of this ongoing conflict.

The presence of a nationally prominent real estate agency at the northern edge of Madrid is indicative of the onrush of development that is transforming rural places throughout the West by commodifying the area's marginality and wildness so the newly wealthy can experience the wilderness from a safe vantage point. In the succeeding chapters I will show that this ongoing transformation of space needs to be understood at several levels, because it is not only at the level of real estate dealings that space is being contested. Fissures are deepening between those residents who wish to take advantage of increased global trade and those who wish to remain in isolation. In what once seemed a place of unending space, the protection of the village from encroaching exurban development has been left to county authorities—authorities few trusted in the past; what was once open space is now *open space*, defined by county ordinance as off-limits to development. As these transformations continue, the village ethos of "live and let live" without boundaries and without definition is being codified into a specific and ordered set of expectations over access to space, over who can profit from the uses of space, and over who can make moral claims over the meaning of that space.

CHAPTER TWO

Constraints and Promises for the Future in the West

The future ain't what it used to be.
—"A Guide to Community Visioning,"
Oregon Visions Project

In the 1960s and 1970s, towns like Aspen, Crested Butte, and Park City made the transition from dying mining town to booming ski town. As resort operators harvested another natural resource, snow, they needed cheap labor to manage the snow and the tourists who came to ski on it. At first, locals filled the need, but as skiing became a national pastime, labor had to be imported. As large corporations like Vail Associates and Marriott bought up interests in ski resorts, service workers came increasingly from outside the region. In Colorado and Utah, young Hispanic workers fill low-paying jobs in the restaurants and hotels surrounding ski mountains. Most of the work is seasonal, with employees coming in for the winter season and leaving for the summer—not at all dissimilar to the patterns in the fur and hide trade and in the coal-mining industry.

The intensity of the boom created another problem. As wealthy tourists bought up land houses for vacation property, real-estate values skyrocketed, making it nearly impossible for local people to remain in their own communities
—David M. Wrobel and Michael C. Steiner, *Many Wests*

The area around Madrid is not the only community in the West in which real estate speculation, development, and tourism have replaced extractive industries and ranching as the dominant economic activity. Throughout the region, promises of a home on the range in the wide open spaces are still a powerful pull, and the legacy of conquest continues as exurban overspill and amenity seekers threaten Santa Fe County and its historic villages in a similar manner to other communities in the West. But the exploitation of the land is nothing new to the region, nor are the conundrums that accompany contemporary growth patterns without historic precedent. A comprehensive history of the ecology of the area is well beyond the goals of the present book, but the limitations imposed by the landscape and the history and culture of its peoples must be considered here, as well as the role played by government agencies and their legal agendas. Powerful interest groups defend and exploit all of the former, and communities themselves play an emerging role in attempting self-definition and self-preservation. All of these forces must be put into a perspective that illuminates the village of Madrid's role in this complex web of constraints and possibilities. The success the symbolic role the West has played in providing the American consciousness with a space for renewal and reinvigoration now threatens the very environment upon which the myths were predicated.

The Spanish were the first to overuse the land's capacity for renewal. Oñate's seven thousand head of livestock brought with the conquest of New Mexico in 1598 had grown to over 100,000 grazing animals by the 1750s. By the late 1880s there were five million sheep and one and one-quarter million cattle reported on New Mexico ranges (Scurlock 1998; DeBuys 1985, 219–20). The American conquest of the territory brought with it clear-cutting of millions of acres of forests to feed the railroad and mining industries. This clear-cutting denuded the already overgrazed land, lowering water tables and rendering useless traditional native and Spanish irrigation techniques. The Anglo culture imposed a different set of definitions concerning land use and the communal good, and different concepts about the future use of space in the West. These differences continue to deepen as the West's wide open spaces become subdivided into vacation and trophy home sites.

The salient issues for Madrid's survival are reproduced throughout the West and have deep implications for the resistance of communities everywhere to the homogenizing forces of transglobal capitalism. Here, I will concentrate on four areas: (1) the conflicted role of government—federal, state, and local; (2) the historic and enduring ecological constraints on continued resource exploitation and population sustainability; (3) the powerful dialectic between individual property rights defended by our legal system and the tragedy of the commons; and (4) the organizational abilities of grassroots and local government entities to address these issues. This chapter will explore the surrounding matrix within which all local sites struggle for identity and survival.

The Role of Government (Federal, State, and Local) in the Culture of the West

The frontier of the American West has never been as unfettered as our national consciousness would like to remember it. Today, approximately 85 percent of the land in the state of New Mexico is under the administration or caretaking of federal or state agencies. This 85 percent is partitioned out among the National Forest Service, the Bureau of Land Management, the State Land Office, the Department of the Interior (trust lands of Native Americans), the Corps of Engineers (waterways and dams), and the Department of Defense (military reservations and testing grounds); this leaves only approximately 15 percent of the state open for private exploitation. The townsite of Madrid is part of several old mining claims, some dating to the mid-1800s, and is part of lands that the Santo Domingo Pueblo people consider their traditional area. Madrid, as were virtually all mining towns, was underwritten by the U.S. government's largess toward corporate exploitation of the region's resources. To ignore the role of the government—particularly the federal government—in the creation of the myth and reality of the West is to fail to understand the palimpsest that is the American West.

Historical Relations

The U.S. government inherited a mosaic of private and community land grants and land claims from the Mexican government by the Treaty of Guadalupe Hidalgo in 1848, which spelled out clearly that Spanish and Mexican grantees would retain their rights. Native American Pueblo lands, as defined by the Spanish Crown, were included in this settlement. Neither group was to find much solace under the new government, however, and land grant activists and Native Americans still bring suit against various government agencies to reclaim portions of their lands that they feel have been taken unjustly. The core of these contemporary conflicts is a clash of cultures that the Treaty of Guadalupe Hidalgo was designed to mediate. These conflicts are not trivial: witness the Sandia Pueblo's recent suit to reclaim the western face of the Sandia Mountains to maintain access to ceremonial sites—over the objections of two high-priced real estate developments. It was one thing for President

Jackson in 1832 to recommend that all public lands (in the West) be given away free to the states, territories, and individuals as a means of populating and taming the "wild" West (Turner 1993 [1893], 78–79), but quite another when frontiersmen ran headlong into prior claims to the land in the New Mexico Territory of 1848.

The best lands in the Spanish land grant areas were those where the relative concentrations of populations had kept the settlers comparatively free from Indian attack; these areas contained the choicest grazing, the best water, and sizable stands of timber. The U.S. government sent a series of surveyors general to the new territory between 1854 and 1891 to bring the land grant claims into conformance with the English-speaking laws, a process that was to honor the existing land grants. But the office was understaffed and underfunded (and the first surveyor general did not speak Spanish) and was kept busy documenting unclaimed land, so that only 22 of 212 claims were resolved, leaving more than thirty-five million acres of New Mexico's most fertile areas in limbo for thirty-seven years. A cabal of wealthy Hispanos and Anglos were able to concentrate their landholdings at the expense of poorer folk, resulting in "[t]he concentration of New Mexico's best real estate in the hands of a few wealthy men [and] producing a similar concentration of economic and political power. . . " (DeBuys 1985, 174, 169–70). Little has changed in New Mexico.

The process of Manifest Destiny—so quickly claimed by governments and frontiersmen alike, was based on a Euro-American paradigm of "usefulness." As DeBuys writes, the "Indigenous New Mexicans found their subsistence-oriented management of the region's resources questioned by the Anglo government." A lieutenant with an early U.S. survey crew stated what would become common currency for Anglos dealing with the Native American and Hispanic populations: "the shiftless Mexicans could not take advantage of the wealth the land offered," and he declared that "New Mexico is far superior to any other [lands] west of the Mississippi." The land grants, many of them community grants entitling every member to common access to grazing, forest, and water resources, were the stumbling blocks to progress. The lieutenant's suggestion was "to buy up all those claims at a good round sum and throw the land open to settlement under the homestead laws" (quoted in DeBuys 1985, 160–65).

But this was not to be the legacy of the intermountain West. As Limerick has pointed out, most of America's public domain lands are in the West.

"The Western states followed another track entirely [instead of privatiza-tion]—in part because the aridity, or sometimes the elevation, of much Western land made it unsuitable for conventional Anglo-American econom-ic development and in part because the federal government made a mas-sive swing toward permanent ownership of the public domain, beginning with the creation of the forest reserves in 1891" (2000, 23–26). As the U.S. government began placing the common lands (and thus the minimal wealth of many Hispanic communities) into the public domain, only those commu-nities with enough money to bid on grazing rights could use the land. Subsistence agriculture in most northern New Mexican settlements became something only the women and children engaged in, as the men went to work as sheepherders and cowhands for large Anglo ranchers and traveled with the herds. Other U.S. government policies supplanted traditional cul-tural patterns in the region: corporate mining, such as took place at Madrid, replaced the individual or family miner; railroads were given huge parcels of land throughout the West to dispose of as they wished, which was usual-ly for profit; corporations were encouraged to clear-cut forests for railroad ties and mining timbers, denuding large sections of northern New Mexico and subjecting the area to severe flooding. Individualism and self-reliance (or at best reliance on the immediate family) replaced reliance on an entire community for resources and support (Atencio 1989), thus further impov-erishing Hispanic and Native American families who were often deeply embedded in more communal traditions. The federal government's role in supporting private profit on public lands was thus at odds with 250 years of communal subsistence living.

The U.S. government shaped the industrial development of the West at the same time that it was shaped by it. The rapid industrialization of America following the Civil War required the coal and other natural resources avail-able on its public lands. This economic exploitation of the West was accom-plished with massive government support of corporate profits, yet it engendered a sense of self-sufficiency in western migrants that disguised the underlying dependencies. The extractive industries (including ranching) "have created a relationship with the federal government different from that in parts of the West that have more varied economies..." Furthermore, these economies "created a distinctively unrooted culture that combined hyper-individualism with industrial processes and boom-and-bust economies that severely limited personal control." Communities such as Madrid were built for profit, not for sustainability, and today, as 150 years ago, "the entire region has experienced tension between traditional extractive industries that bored mountains out and tore them down and the tourism that worshiped the mountains" (in Wrobel and Steiner 1997, 110, 95–96).

When the counterculture settlers of the 1970s came west looking for refuge from the excesses of materialism produced by the industrial era, they were in part recreating the myth of the West as the hope of the future and in part exploiting its past accomplishments. They brought with them a sense of hyper-individualism similar to that experienced in the coal and timber camps, but while they appeared as unrooted as the miners and lumberjacks before them, this generation of migrants hoped to escape the relationships of exploitation and social injustice brought by modernity. The counterculture movement's participants had an equally complicated relationship with government as had earlier settlers—using government allotments while claiming self-sufficiency and independence from authority. They differed, however, from earlier migrants in attempting to establish sustainable lifestyles built on non-market relationships. Alternative lifestyle advocates remaining in Madrid today find themselves surrounded by tourists who come to look at the aging hippy generation as much as to enjoy Joe Huber's "fine industrial location."

Today   .

Today in northern New Mexico such historically privileged occupations as mining, timbering, and ranching are opposed by diverse coalitions of interest groups, some of whom are only in the region because of the very exploitation of the landscape they now decry; other groups have simply changed products. Many ranchers have decided that growing cattle is not as profitable as growing houses, and opposing such developments has remained fraught with difficulty, for reasons I will explore below. Examples of this broad spectrum of conflicts abound, and include (but are hardly limited to) the following:

> [T]he Rio Grande Chapter of the Sierra Club is promoting new
> rules for mining as of this writing in order to curtail gravel mining
> to preserve the "quality of life" of the suburban gentry, even
> though the product is essential to new roadbed base courses and
> residential construction. Banning gravel pits locally may mean

having aggregate hauled longer distances, creating more air pollution and traffic congestion, and simply shifting the environmental costs to someone else's neighborhood.

The village of Cerrillos (Madrid's nearest neighbor) worked with a coalition of Santo Domingo Pueblo Indians, urban transplants, and real estate interests to successfully defeat a gravel mine on its northern periphery proposed by J. R. Hale Company, in spite of the offer of jobs for the local economy and over the objections of some in the area for whom mining is still a family enterprise.

The annexation of an 8,046-acre master planned development to the village of Edgewood, south of Madrid, will include three resort hotels, two golf courses, some commercial development, and 4,023 homes—an instant community of approximately ten thousand people where previously a few dozen cattle grazed. In chapter 7 I will explore the theoretical implications of growth and its oppositions, as growth is *the* defining element of the contemporary West, and Madrid sits in the middle of it.

Madrid's formerly isolated space as a ghost town, harboring the misfits and renegades of the counterculture era, is now a stage for water wars, real estate development, and local governments' attempts at promoting and protecting the sustainabilities of human and ecological resources.

The Conflicted Role of Government

The real estate industry is not generally thought of as an extractive industry, but private development at whatever scale it occurs removes space from the public sphere and places it in private hands—especially in the West where so much land has been held in the public trust and left undeveloped. This changing landscape of space is not lost on old and new residents of the area of this study. Throughout these changes, the role of the state (federal, state, and local governments) remains ambiguous. Some factions of each promote growth while others work for sustainability and controlled population expansion.

A current example, of hundreds that could be cited, was the attempt by the U.S. Fish and Wildlife Service, acting in consort with private conservation groups, to put enough water in the Rio Grande in the fall of 2001 to save the silvery minnow—an endangered species. This action was deeply opposed by cities, farmers, and ranchers along the river and by other conservation groups who wanted the water for other agendas and other endangered animals. The minnows did receive their temporary reprieve, but at a cost to the sandhill cranes who got mired in the mudhole left behind when the waters were diverted for the minnows. Issues relating to human populations are even more complex but exhibit the same difficulties of apportioning the common good among competing groups.

Most state and local governments have, until very recently, been pro-growth advocates, boosting their local economies in order to lure new businesses and tax revenues to their regions; this advocacy has increasingly been in opposition to some of their own electorate, who prefer slow or no growth when such growth threatens their own neighborhood stability (Gottdiener 1977; Davis 1992). An attempt at more coordinated efforts at dealing with growth issues is occurring in the County of Santa Fe. Here a county government initiative has given local communities a unique opportunity for self-definition. Patterned after the Oregon initiative (see the opening epigraph to this chapter), it has been an ongoing process since the mid-1970s, when growth was perceived to be only an irritant to the city of Santa Fe, not the looming disaster it appears today. At that time, the 2 percent growth every year of the "City Different" was thought acceptable, although aspects of it needed to be managed and controlled (Santa Fe County Planning Department 1975). The *Santa Fe General Plan Report (SFGPR)* acknowledges that the fates of the city and the county of Santa Fe are linked; unfortunately, this remains a recognition only at the planning level, because unlike two other city/county urban growth areas in New Mexico (Dona Ana County and the city of Las Cruces, Bernalillo County and the city of Albuquerque), there is no joint governance plan between the city and the county. Generally speaking, that means what is prohibited or controlled in terms of development in the city of Santa Fe simply gets pushed into the county areas, threatening the ability of both city and county to control quality of life issues.

In terms of what is important for the nexus of growth vs. defensible space for county residents, including those in Madrid, the 1975 *SFGPR* document contained the following imperatives for the county's future: (1) to encourage growth away from and outside of Santa Fe; (2) to encourage industries that did not require a large imported labor force; (3) a recognition that more growth often benefits outside conglomerates [the Wal-Marts] at the expense of local family businesses. "The size of the pie will grow, but not the size of each piece" (Santa Fe County Planning Department 1975).

In 1972, in order to prepare the *SFGPR*, the county had done a survey of its resources (Santa Fe County Planning Department 1972). This survey had found that (italics are my own comments):

- The rural areas would carry the bulk of new growth.
- Only the central part of the county was suitable for dense rural development as the southern part (south of Madrid) was not well watered and "it is debated whether to allow low density residential lots or should [the area] remain grazing land."
- "Existing villages need protection of their historic character, their agriculture and open land." *By 2000 any agriculture left in the historic villages was of a token nature at best.*
- Around Madrid, mining, ranching, and railroads were major employers but now there was little to support local employment, and Madrid is listed as a ghost town, along with Kennedy, Dolores, Hyer, Venus, Waldo and San Pedro.
- There was recognition of the long-term potential for either scenic or mineral wealth in the Madrid-Golden areas, as the Cerrillos Coal Field contains all of the estimated reserves in the state of New Mexico. *Note the lack of recognition that mining and scenery do not mix well; however romantic old mining towns might seem, working ones do not appeal to tourists.*
- Continued viability of the rangeland for cattle raising is questioned; 70% of such land may need restoration [as of 1967]. *Note that this even contradicts the above statement about the viability of ranching in the southern part of the county. While this research report emphasizes the large percentage of rangeland that needed restoration in 1967, yet as late as 1964, 80 percent of the county's agricultural products still came from the livestock industry. Such disconnects between what county planners know about resource bases and their ability to influence the direction of economic activity illustrate part of the problem for contemporary communities.*

Another disconnect between the time this planning research was done and today is the presence of two new exurban subdivisions built within the last five years in southern Santa Fe County—Paa-ko and San Pedro Creek

Estates—providing housing in the $325,000 to $1,000,000 range; this is in a state where the individual median income (at $18,734) is 23 percent below the national average (2000 U.S. Census, table QT-3, U.S. Department of Commerce, n.d.). The developers of San Pedro Creek Estates, Campbell Farming, have carved their subdivision from part of the former Campbell Ranch, a cattle-raising enterprise in the southern part of Santa Fe County, the same part of the county that the planners in 1975 thought would suffer a lack of water. Paa-ko and San Pedro Creek Estates are adjacent to each other and directly across Highway 14 from another proposed development by Campbell Farming: the three-hotel, two-golf-course planned community of ten thousand people mentioned above. These developments are about ten miles south of Madrid. At the present writing, this latest development is caught up in complicated legal challenges, but land sales and construction are ongoing. Whichever way the development goes, it points to the two most serious issues for local governments to come to grips with in the West: water and uncontrolled growth in the private sector. I will examine each separately before moving on the next section.

Water

First, the water issue: no topic in the West or in New Mexico will draw a line in the sand faster than the mention of water and its availability. You will find developers and boosters on one side, slow-growth and no-growth advocates and various shades of environmentalists on the other. The 1972 county reconnaissance survey found that the aquifers were already being mined (more being pumped out than is replenished by natural sources) and that wells in the county might have to be extended five hundred to one thousand feet, the cost of which would cause many homeowners and even whole villages to abandon their investments. By the year 2002, the meteorological predictions that entire regions of the West would be in a severe drought are now everywhere in evidence, thus further depleting the ability of the land to recharge the aquifers at a time of increasing residential development. This development did indeed take place in the county areas, as the planners had predicted, meaning that hundreds of new private, unmetered, and unregulated wells tap a diminishing resource.

The West's legal traditions complicate water rights issues. Water rights are separable from the land, just like mineral rights, and they are considered on a first-come, first-served basis, regardless of who owns the land on top of the water or who has the greatest need. Because they are severable from the land, water rights can be sold and transferred; this is how cities like Albuquerque can maintain their growth, by buying up agricultural water rights elsewhere in the basin, retiring the farms, and "transferring" the water to Albuquerque users. This virtual "paper water" is assumed to be representative of the "wet water" available in the real aquifer (these are the terms used by the hydrologists, not my invention). Water rights not used for three years (farmers who no longer irrigate, for instance) can be lost to thirsty municipalities such as Albuquerque. Some alternative suggestions for managing this resource in the *Santa Fe County Reconnaissance Survey* were as follows:

1. Continue to mine the resource and let the devil take the hindmost [*in other words, business as usual*];
2. The cities of Española and Santa Fe could serve the surrounding rural areas from their Rio Grande surface supplies—but those water rights may not be available [*several pueblos and traditional Hispanic communities claim rights to this river water*];
3. Severely limit or stop the growth in either or both the county and the city of Santa Fe.

Deeming none of these measures feasible, the report continued by recommending county zoning be done by availability of water to sustain development—but warned that sources will still be depleted in 125 years [now 100 years]; or, require developers to prove they have a hundred-year supply of water for their developments. The latter is seen only as a holding action in hopes of some technological fix in the future; the natural aquifer will still be depleted in one hundred years. The report emphasized that even these measures will only protect the overall Rio Grande basin, not particular local communities. These measures are largely in place now; development density zones are mapped for the entire county, determining how much of what kind of growth can take place specific to the underlying aquifer, and developers must have a hydrologist's confirmation of a hundred-year water supply before approval of new projects. Still growth continues at the urban fringes throughout the county.

The grim reality recognized by local government in the early 1970s— just as Madrid was being resettled—was that available water resources had reached a point of no return. Many counterculture settlers advocated "living lightly off the land" and "leaving a lighter footprint on the earth," ethics more friendly to the area's fragile resource base. But neither they nor local governments have found a way to expand those philosophies to the majority of developers, who still depend on the myth of unending resources in the West to legitimize continued growth.

The Private Sector

The second dilemma for the county government and planners—which cannot be truly separated from water—is the lack of knowledge over the intended development of privately and corporately held lands. Planners simply lack information about what key decision makers are doing in a free market economy made up of individual (usually corporate) actors maximizing their profits. The lack of governmental ability to control the future of its own resources is properly the subject of a following section, but the frustration evident in the county planning documents as far back as the mid-1970s illustrates the constraints inherent in the historic position of governments to watch over the general welfare of the public without a definition of whose general welfare is being protected.

In the area surrounding Madrid, New Mexico, as elsewhere in the West where competing cultural and economic interests have collided, growth issues are complex, involving water, the feasibility of maintaining some semblance of historic subsistence agricultural livelihoods, water, tourism, economic development, and the overall ecological sustainability of the entire region to support continued population growth. In the absence of any clear mandate to protect one interest over any other, communities and interest groups can sometimes find a niche in which to protect their own resources. Unlike city neighborhoods undergoing urban renewal agendas, these niches have occasionally allowed remnants of older lifestyles to continue, in part because of the power of the symbolic West to convince new settlers that some parts of the past must be maintained for the region to maintain its appeal and its separation from the urban congestion that pushed them to move in the first place.

The parts to be maintained are very selective, as we have seen above, and reflect the incompatibility of residential suburbs with the older extractive industries. Since the early 1900s, fleeing urbanites have found the corridor along the Rio Grande—with its quaint communities and subsistence agricultural traditions—to be the ideal mix of settlement and wilderness.

The pastoral *gemeinschaft* appearance of these settlements belies the true fragility of the landscape to support even the eighteenth-century Hispanic population, much less continued growth. The *Santa Fe County Reconnaissance Survey*, quoting from a 1964 New Mexico State University Agricultural Experiment Station Report (#184), showed the precarious nature of the traditional subsistence economy:

> Farms are so small that it is not simply a question of a man buying his neighbor's farm or half of it to make his total operation viable, as is being done in some areas. In this region [Santa Fe County], it is a question of consolidating several small tracts for which no legal title may be available.

Yet it is just these small agricultural enterprises with their mosaic of fields and small-scale operations that continue to reinvigorate the symbolism of the West as an escape from massive urban developments.

In the mid-1970s over two-thirds of the irrigated farms in Santa Fe County were less than ten acres in size, with unclear titles stemming from the land grant imbroglio, and only yielded half the income considered the break-even point by economists (Santa Fe County Planning Department 1972). While recently transplanted urbanites found confirmation of their images of idyllic rural lifestyles in these settings, the local population suffered continued economic marginalization.

But it is not these types of landholdings that frustrated the county planners back in 1972; it was the unknown intents of large-scale development interests. With 48 percent of the county's 1,909 square miles held in state or federal government hands and unavailable for planners to regulate, the large amount of land held in private or corporate ownership removes even more of the landscape from regulatory oversight. Much of this latter category of land is held not for immediate development but for speculation. To give an example of how real estate speculation inflates prices while adding neither to productivity or usable public lands: land south and east of the city of Santa Fe known as the Simpson Ranch was sold for $18 an acre in 1927; for $50 an acre in 1950; AMREP (the developer of Rio Rancho on Albuquerque's west side) bought part of this acreage in the same year for $134 an acre, and sold 6,000 acres of that parcel [still largely undeveloped at the time] for $1,000 an acre in 1971 (Santa Fe County Planning Department 1972).

Planners can only guess at what private and corporate owners are going to do with their land, but the "bandwagon effect of one successful development [is seen to increase] the future profits for all others"; land sales without construction "takes large tracts out of farm production or out of public access," marginalizes traditional farming even more by increasing land values through speculation; and puts in jeopardy the ability of existing communities to cope with expansion when it does happen for during the interim they are taxed as undeveloped land (Santa Fe County Planning Department 1972). The research findings were that "If all the land being considered for development were in fact developed, the undeveloped parts of the county would become a major metropolitan area. While many would be housed, there would not be jobs to support growth" (Santa Fe County Planning Department 1972). And, of course, the pastoral charm of rural northern New Mexico would resemble that of Los Angeles.

The final proposals of the survey planners are worth quoting at length, because some of their fears for the future have happened and because some of their proposals for local action have been taken and have impacted Madrid:

> Without the active implementation of land-use policies by local government, low density residential development probably will locate anywhere within this prime development sector, with random development leapfrogging over underdeveloped parcels. There are, however, alternative forms for development. One is concentrated development either at existing villages or new towns. . . . A second is to distinguish within the prime development sector the location of higher density areas from lower density holding zones. This would allow a logical sequence of private development and of the extension and maintenance of public facilities particularly roads. Another is to plan for large areas of open space in and near the prime development sector and, in particular, to maintain until further study all land now owned by any government body. *Some BLM and State land may have the opportunity for considerable dollar sales because they are advantageously located in the sector of expected future population growth but, because they are so crucially located, these lands may be best used for open space green belts."* (Santa Fe County Planning Department 1972; italics mine)

As indicated in italics, even though land is held in trust by various federal and state government agencies, such set-asides are not sacrosanct and can be sold or traded to private developers. Planning staff and the local governments to which they answer often have no idea of pending deals between developers and other government entities, adding to the unknown elements in managing resources for the common good. One such example occurred in Madrid's neighboring community of Cerrillos, where a private developer threatened to take large portions of Bureau of Land Management land in the nearby Cerrillos Hills—the site of the turquoise mines discussed in the previous chapter—and create a large residential subdivision in the hills overlooking the tiny historic village. Community activists got wind of the deal and, working in conjunction with sympathetic county officials, were successful in having much of the proposed development site set aside as the first Santa Fe County Park. Madrid also has benefited from this combination of activists and local government intervention, as I detail in a later chapter.

The *Santa Fe County Reconnaissance Survey* established the need for this type of procurement of public space by the county, and this need was codified into Santa Fe County's first General Plan, the second edition of which was passed in the mid 1990s and to which development in the county is supposed to conform. The current edition of the General Plan recognizes the need for open space and greenbelts to protect the county's historic villages and also to ensure enough undeveloped land to provide watershed and airshed recharge areas. I was told by one planner that the county planners considered such areas to be the county's infrastructure, just as critical as roads, bridges, and other public amenities. But, as the planners indicated in the *Santa Fe General Plan, 1975*, a planning document—even one based on reasonable assessments of human and ecological resources—is no guarantee of successful management of those resources. I will explore below the two other critical areas that impact the future of sustainability in northern New Mexico, the long-standing ecological constraints and the problematic legal fixes to development dilemmas.

The Enduring Ecological Constraints

The Long View

The pastoral history of this region of New Mexico upon which so much of its tourism and amenity real estate growth depends has been idealized as a static system of human communities living in harmony with nature. As with other myths about the West, the reality of this much-worked-over land does not hold up well to scrutiny. Native American groups mined extensive holdings in the Cerrillos Hills, as mentioned in chapter 1; tailings piles dot the hills from precontact times. Hispanic pastoralists brought cattle, sheep, goats, and horses to the New World, leading to the devastation of the meadows and riparian environments; commercial ranching continued this trend. Trapping throughout the intermountain West brought species to the brink of extinction.

The first environmental law in what was to become New Mexico—a six-year moratorium on trapping beaver and otter in the Rio Grande—was passed by the Mexican government four years after the opening of the Santa Fe Trail to American commerce. The entire southern half of the Sangre de Cristo mountain range [the eastern edge of the Santa Fe basin] was trapped out for beaver during those years. As many as eight thousand beaver may have been taken between 1821 and 1825, compared to a 1967 estimated population of six thousand beaver in all of New Mexico (DeBuys 1985, 97–98). While the beaver have made a partial comeback, the last verified sighting of an otter in New Mexico was in the Gila watershed in the 1950s (Rich Beausoleil, New Mexico Game and Fish Department, personal communication; Polechla 2000).

Before the coming of the Americans and their capital-intensive ranching and farming methods, the population of Hispanic settlers pushed the limits of the resource base. As we have seen in the opening chapter, the poorer populations sought out the more marginal lands, as even by the eighteenth century the well-watered grazing lands were taken. Charles Loomis, in his classic Depression-era study of northern New Mexican villages, found extensive overgrazing in the high mesa lands in the Pecos [east of Santa Fe]; once the grass cover is gone, the wind and rain quickly take their toll. Writing in 1939,

> Reports of studies completed and others in progress on the Pecos
> Watershed repeatedly point out that the depletion of the grass
> cover had added tremendously to the flood damage along the
> Pecos River during the last two or three decades. . . . The early
> economy of San Miguel County was one of abundance. Land
> was available and could be had for either the asking or the taking.

Temporary depletion of the grass resource invoked little more
hardship than moving livestock to another proximate area or
spreading it over a wider base. Little thought was given to the
fact that some day the soil might be impoverished or exhausted.
(Leonard and Loomis 1941, 11–12)

When Loomis lived with the Hispanic agrarians in the 1930s, their subsistence existence was "Definitely submarginal," and he found the population
was beyond the capacity of the land to sustain subsistence agriculture.
Loomis further observed that in the village he studied, typical of many in
northern New Mexico at the time,

[y]oung men and women leave . . . for the CCC and the NYA
camps. The older people are not concerned about the new
tendency on the part of a few young men to leave . . . [and] regard
such a move as advantageous because it alleviated the pressure of
population at home, and feel the movement should be encouraged
as much as possible. (Leonard and Loomis 1941, 60)

What harmony with nature existed was short-lived in the fragile watershed areas of the region, and even the Hispanic farmers and ranchers
depended somewhat on outside markets for their sheep and wool. DeBuys
further documents the interrelationships between water, land, and human
use of these resources; it was population pressure in the villages that pushed
every area into production. Only severe winters gave the land a rest from
grazing. In areas as widely separated as the Rio Puerco [on Albuquerque's
west boundary] to the Rio Galisteo [east of Santa Fe], deforestation for mine
timbers and railroad building denuded tens of thousands of acres, causing
the rain runoff to scour the arroyos wider and deeper. This deforestation
lowered the water table and made irrigation impossible, destroying fields
and grazing lands. Much of this building was done in a mania of competition in the second decade of the twentieth century to build a narrow-gauge
railroad through New Mexico before the Panama Canal could be finished,
in the hope of preempting the national and international trade—largely for
the benefit of those outside the territory (DeBuys 1985, 216–33). As in colonial times, the marginality of northern New Mexico failed to protect its peoples and its natural resources from exploitation by outsiders.

The Contemporary Growth Situation[1]

The 1972 projection by county planners in the *SFGPR* that the city of Santa
Fe's population would be seventy thousand and that the bulk of the growth
would be in the county areas was partly accurate. The city of Santa Fe has
added more land to its area than population, however; a Brookings Institute
report published in 2001 showed Santa Fe as the fifth least-dense metro area
in the country, pushing more people into the county while preserving the
thematic presentation of the "City Different" (McDonald 2001; Wilson
1997). The 2000 U.S. census shows the city's population at 62,203, while
the county's population growth has been exponential. Starting with a population of 53,756 in the 1970 U.S. census, the county grew by 40 percent
through the 1970s, 31 percent through the 1980s and again in the 1990s.
The U.S. census in 2000 showed a county population of 129,292, keeping
its rank as the third most populated county in the state, behind Bernalillo
(556,678), and Dona Ana (174,682), and before San Juan (113,801).
During these same years, the state of New Mexico's population increased
by 28 percent during the 1970s, 16 percent during the 1980s, and 20 percent during the 1990s, and in the 2000 U.S. census was at 1,819,046. As a
wider comparison, the whole United States population grew by 11.5 percent in the 1970s, 9.8 percent in the 1980s, and 13 percent in the 1990s
for a total population of 281,421,906 (U.S. Department of Commerce
2000, Population of Counties by Decennial Census: 1900–1990). The mythic pull of the American West had lost none of its power.

The growth in the county follows the predictions made in the planning
documents from the 1970s: developments leapfrog wherever land is available;
this is in spite of the county's following through on many of its guidelines for
controlling growth. These measures include: (1) less dense developments are
encouraged in water-scarce areas; (2) the designation of existing communities
(both historic and contemporary) as areas that can write their own zoning
codes to define and maintain their boundaries and individual characters; (3)
establishing the precedent at Madrid and neighboring Cerrillos of buying large
amounts of land to preserve the open space around the villages; and (4) requiring developers to document water sustainability for up to one hundred years

---

[1]Information in this portion of the text not provided with citations comes from
the author's fifteen years of work in the field of architecture, from interviews
with hydrologists and state engineers, and from extensive notes from planning
and visioning meetings attended for the last six years in the four-county area.

for their projects. Through these measures county officials and community residents hope to stave off the kind of growth that has gone on all around them in the county. But these measures, helpful though they may be in small ways, may not be strong enough to truly protect the rural environment from the onslaught of ever-more people. The threat, or opportunity, depending on how growth is viewed, is showing no signs of stopping.

At the present writing, the biggest regional threat to Madrid in particular does not come from the urban overspill from the city of Santa Fe. It comes from the southern part of the county, the same part cited twice above as being unsuitable for rapid growth due to water shortages but which has nevertheless expanded its residential base rapidly. This expansion threatens Madrid, ten miles to the north of these developments along State Highway 14, because growth demands roads, and roads bring even more growth. At present, the road leading north from east-west Interstate 40 to Madrid is four lanes wide only as far as the turnoff to the ski basin in the Sandia Mountains; the rest of the distance to Santa Fe (about twenty miles) it is a two-lane blacktop road. Projected growth along this existing corridor has already been the focus of two public meetings held to determine the feasibility of a high-volume state road that would link the East Mountain communities south of Madrid to the other major interstate highway, north-south I-25. To quote one of the local papers about this issue:

No more important issue exists for East Mountain residents, for such a road will alter the pace, pattern and dynamic of growth not just in the East Mountains but throughout a four-county region. Because residences follow highways, and businesses follow residences, such road will shift the focus of development to the northwestern sector of the region. North 14 would probably have to become a highway as far north as Golden or Madrid, and possibly all the way to Santa Fe.... While change creates new opportunities, it also threatens present values that we hold dear. What is clear is that this road will alter the area forever. (*Independent*, August 30–September 5)

Any widening of New Mexico 14 through Madrid would destroy the town, as the historic buildings line the road with barely enough room for walking; there is no obvious way to build a bypass around the village, either, as it is in a narrow valley. At present, there are four county-maintained roads that connect I-25 and NM 14 between Albuquerque and Santa Fe; they are poorly maintained gravel roads with few improvements. Improvements will put even more pressure on existing landowners closer to Madrid to sell out to the next highest bidder as land prices continue to increase. Without question, whatever route is chosen for a new paved road around the Sandia Mountains linking the eastern areas to the interstate corridor, it will be the site of intense development. The population pressure from such development will impact Madrid and the other communities to the north, as—even without such incentives—the Rio Grande corridor is the primary location for dense development due to its existing infrastructure, transportation routes, mild climate, and relatively level landscapes.

Yet the critical resource of water is in no larger supply in this part of Santa Fe County than it was in the 1970s when the planners began voicing concerns about its depletion. Estimates by the principal water suppliers (private for-profit corporations, in this case, not municipalities) indicate that the current well levels are dropping at an average of 3.5 feet a year, making even present growth unsustainable (*Independent*, August 30–September 5). Water may eventually be imported from Canadian rivers to feed the insatiable demand for growth in the intermountain region. The residents of Madrid argue that they are protected from such growth by their historic lack of potable water; the reality of their situation may be much different.

The extension of the urban into the rural as a settlement pattern in America is nothing new; Henry Binford's 1988 study of Boston from around 1815 to the 1850s documents that the pattern was well established long before the suburban explosion following World War II. I have discussed in chapter 1 the similarly long history of the symbolism of the single-family home as the embodiment of middle-class ideals. These initiatives fit with the country's founding ideologies of Jeffersonian yeoman farmers—if farming per se was not possible, the next best thing was ownership of a home surrounded by at least a small greensward. After the closing of the frontier at the end of the nineteenth century, the Country Life Movement reinvigorated the Enlightenment's ideals of good spaces producing good citizens. Good spaces were to be found in the country or as close to it as you could get (Bailey 1913; Bowers 1974; U.S. Senate 1909; Schnatt 1969). America has historically been primed for defending country living as part of the mantle of individualism and democracy, and those with investment dollars and development expertise have not been lax in capitalizing on these ideologies for private gain.

In response to urban sprawl, a relatively new breed of neotraditional developers have been designing suburban small towns where residences, commercial centers, and civic institutions like churches and schools are within walking distance of each other. Each town is surrounded by greenbelts from other developments and from regional urban centers. Seven years ago there were too few to count; by 1999 there were one hundred existing neotraditional towns, with two hundred more in the planning stages, including Mesa del Sol on the south edge of Albuquerque (Padgett 1999). This "new suburbanism" is countered by the "new urbanism"; the clustering of workplaces and new or restored housing around transportation hubs, with the hope of reducing individual dependence on the automobile (Firestone 1999). While these types of developments attract considerable numbers of urban dwellers, the appeal of moving to the country and having a ranchette of your own in the West continues to feed exurban growth in western states like New Mexico.

I find that a story in the local Taos newspaper, *Horsefly*, puts a better human face on the effects of sprawl in rural areas than statistics and prognoses. Taos is a small city north of Santa Fe best known for its Pueblo Indians, D. H. Lawrence, and Mabel Dodge Luhan. Sixty-seven percent of Taos County families earn less than $25,000 yearly, compared to mean annual family incomes of $38,779 for New Mexico and $49,507 for the United States as a whole (U.S. Department of Commerce, 2000 U.S. Census, table QT-3). Being a rural county with virtually no industry save ranching and tourism, 66 percent of Taos County's revenues come from property taxes, which have increased every year for the past fifteen years, quadrupling between 1985 and 2000. Newcomers pay upwards of $400,000 for homesteads in the Taos area, while—in spite of escalating property taxes for locals—enjoying property taxes that are often less than one-third of those in their former locales.

While the following is a fictional account, it could be anywhere in New Mexico or the West. The *Horsefly*'s fictional newcomer, Kristin, finds that her delight in the economies of owning land in Taos soon gives way to anger, for Kristin discovers that Rosa, next door, paid far less in taxes than she did for property of equal or more value. In order to address such feelings and to keep up with the increasing cost of sprawl, the county reappraises property

values to be at 85 percent of current market value. Rosa's property, formerly at $115 an acre for dry agricultural land, is reassessed at the going sub-
division market value of $45,000 per acre. Rosa's house, a four-room adobe
that has housed her family for six generations, jumps from an assessed valuation of $10,000 to $80,000, and her yearly taxes from $67 to $5,827.
While Kristin has seen her land value spread out more evenly—even rationally—over all the landowners in the county, the fictional Rosa has lost the
ability to maintain her ancestral home and land. And, consider this equally likely postscript: newcomer Kristin had purchased her ten acres from
Rosa's sister for $1,000 an acre, enabling the sister to move to California.
Kristin in turn sold five acres of her new land for $35,000 per acre to defray
the expenses of building a better home than the one she sold in order to
move to New Mexico (Ludvigson 2001).

These are the everyday realities foreshadowed by the Santa Fe County
planners in the 1970s; within the last five years the city of Santa Fe has
taken some measures to protect its cultural and social resources by shield-
ing lifelong residents from the worst of these tax increases, but the pace
of growth in the county continues. Growth advocates center their arguments on the need for growth and economic development, jobs, a widening tax base, and a philosophy that communities either grow or die. Usually
couched in terms of "growth is inevitable," boosters accuse detractors of
being "anti's and NIMBY's (Not In My Back Yard), that development must
take place in a free market and that there is no real sentiment in America
for preserving the environment at the expense of individual jobs" (Fodor
1999). In terms reminiscent of the early Anglo-Hispanic interface in which
Americans thought the Mexicans lazy for not producing a profit from their
lands, growth advocates do not see the value in undeveloped land. Similarly, developers' appeals to free-market capitalism mask an underlying
dependency on government agendas that have largely supported unfettered
growth at the expense of the common good. The common good must come
to mean more than the profits of the few if true sustainability is to be found
in the contemporary West.

The role of the federal government to hold the lands of the intermountain West in public trust while simultaneously allowing and encouraging
their expropriation was predated by the subsistence pastoralists and agri-
culturalists who overused the fragile resources of the land. America's industrial strength was built upon extraction of the mineral wealth of the West;

today's real estate industry is simply following in some very well-worn footsteps. The one institution to which all competing groups have turned for remedies is one that is inadequate, in many ways, to mediate for the public interest. As DeBuys writes, "In its contemporary context, the idea of wilderness is a sociological, not an ecological concept, and the Pecos and other modern wildernesses owe their preservation to legislation rather than environment. Essentially, wilderness is whatever people say it is ... " (1985, 289). As "wilderness" shrinks to become "open space" and "green-belts," the role of legislators and the legal system that backs them up become more acute, yet their resources and ideological underpinnings remain rooted in Enlightenment relationships of private property.

The Legal Fix

> There is one arena in the American political order where deeper conceptions of the nature of our life in common are debated. That is the courts, under the rule of law. ... Some of the most significant institutional and cultural efforts to deal with the social changes of the contemporary period have come from the courts. Many of them have tried to take account of increased social interdependence. (Bellah et al. 1992, 124)

A recognition of the common good, Robert Bellah and his coauthors argue, is what is lacking in the American psyche and her institutions. In their book *The Good Society* (1992), they argue that the American legal system has dealt with the complex interdependence of modernity by extending individual rights, and specifically by protecting those individual rights from arbitrary infringements upon their autonomy. But the emphasis on rights, part of our Enlightenment inheritance, is "only of limited help in developing new conceptions of the common good." Furthermore, "The legal order sustains a moral commitment to righting particular injustices, but it does not encourage consideration of the common good or of justice in more general terms" (127). Bellah points out the American historical tradition of using government only to regulate either individual excesses or the tyrannical potential of the government itself; there has never been a clear agenda for the state to engage in positive public purposes (25). At the heart of the matter, again, are our founding ideologies, drawn from Lockian philosophy:

... the right to life, liberty, and the pursuit of happiness is exem-
plified by the solitary individual's appropriation of property from
the state of nature. Government is then instituted for the protection of that property. Once men agree to accept money as the
medium of exchange, the accumulation of property is in principle
without any moral limit. All limits on the freedom and autonomy
of the individual, other than those he freely consents to in entering
the (quite limited) social contract, are rejected. (67)

No anthem for the American West could better state the relationships
between government, property, individualism, and resource expropriation.

The often repeated "tragedy of the commons" (Hardin 1968) acknowledges these relationships and the damage done when the common good is
appropriated for private gain. Our legal system at both the highest and the
local level has, with rare exception, sided with individual property rights
when deciding who would benefit—the entire community or the individual.
Planners such as those in Santa Fe County who have striven to find rational resource-based solutions to the real estate and development networks that
support sprawl have little recourse to the power of the law; in most juris-
dictions, as in New Mexico, general plans, master plans, and other attempts
at controlling growth are advisory only. Nor has the U.S. Supreme Court
been forthcoming with precedent-setting cases that establish guidelines
based on common interests instead of individualized rights.

The Supreme Court's first land use case was heard in 1922, when Justice
Holmes ruled, in a case involving the Pennsylvania Coal Company, that
"while property may be regulated [by government] to a certain extent, if regulation goes too far it will be recognized as a taking," meaning governments
would have to compensate property owners for any loss caused by undue regulations over the use and disposal of private property—including expected
profits from such property (260 U.S. 393, 43 S.Ct.). Three precedents emerged
from this ruling: (1) the court expressed its reluctance to use the police powers of the state for the general good unless the harm is widespread; (2) that situations must continue to be decided locally as there were no implicit rights
that were not part of contracts; and (3) that Fifth and Fourteenth Amendment
rights protecting private property from seizure or diminution of value must
be compensated for even when the proposed use is in the public interest. In
the above case, it was the continuance of subsurface mining rights that was

considered in danger of being "taken," as any attempt by local governments to protect property from subsidence went "too far" and compensation would be due the coal company (Hill 1993, xv). This meant that industrial and commercial property owners gained the right to be compensated for government "takings," but it also meant that the precedent was set for the lack of equal protection of any communal good because such goods are not part of private contract law.

In keeping with its precedence of local issues being the purview of local authority, the Supreme Court in 1926 established the right of municipalities to use their police powers to write zoning ordinances. While the wording of *Euclid v. Ambler* (272 U.S. 365, 47 S.Ct.) emphasized the clear responsibility of municipal governments to protect the public health, safety, morals, or general welfare of their communities, very early in its historical use zoning became the tool of developers who were concerned more with maintaining neighborhood property values and thus their expectations of profits than with the overall community's health or general welfare. Thus exclusionary zoning became the rule in the United States, forming homogeneous neighborhoods and subdivisions based on ability to pay, literally zoning diversity out of existence.

The Supreme Court did not hear another property rights case until 1978, when the city of New York placed restrictions on Pennsylvania Central's development rights of a historical landmark—Grand Central Station. Justice Brennan wrote that "'[H]istoric conservation is but one aspect of the much larger problem, basically an environmental one, of enhancing—or perhaps developing for the first time—the quality of life for people'" (Callies, Freilich, and Roberts 1994, 269). Reflecting the more liberal court of the time, there was a short burst of environmental rulings by the court, but overall the highest court has not produced a consistent body of rulings that make a strong statement for the primacy of the public interest over the rights of the individual, nor has the court backed away from its commitment to free-market-based expectations for profit (termed "reasonable, investment-backed expectations") in deciding whether a regulation is a "taking" or not.

By 1992, when the court ruled in *Lucas v. South Carolina Coastal Council* (505 U.S. 1003, 112 S.Ct.), the sentiment had shifted once more, and Justice Scalia, writing for the majority, held that "regulations that leave the owner of land without economically beneficial or productive options for its use carry with them a heightened risk that private property is being pressed into some form of public service under the guise of mitigating serious public harm" (Hill

1993, vii). The Coastal Council had been attempting to limit residential development along environmentally fragile sand dunes; in ruling that such government regulation meant that private property was being "pressed into service" to protect a common good, Scalia reopened the requirement that such regulation required monetary compensation to the developer. Declaring that this case cast a shadow on the rights of the states to enforce the public good, Justice Blackmun wrote a scathing dissent, reasoning that if developers must be compensated for every instance of loss due to protecting the public good, communities will quickly go bankrupt (Hill 1993, x).

Few cases other than *Lucas* have been taken on by the high court that dealt with an inherent value of undeveloped land. Two important but not precedent-setting cases are the *West Michigan Environmental Action Council, Inc. v. Natural Resources Commission*, in which the court upheld the use of state and federal lands for the public trust (405 Mich. 741, 275 N.W. 2d 538, 1979), and *Just v. Marinette County*, in which the court ruled that wetlands regulations protect water quality and that a property owner has no property right premised on a future alteration of the natural state (201 N.W. 2d 761, Wis. 1972).

The Supreme Court has been nearly silent on environmental causes since *Lucas*, but in April 2002 they ruled that interim development restrictions do not constitute a taking—and thereby do not require financial compensation. In a case involving Lake Tahoe, the court upheld the right of the regional planning authority to institute a temporary moratorium on development in order to complete an environmental impact report. This is not the same as saying that permanent restrictions can be placed on growth without its being a taking, but it is a start. The local homebuilders associations found the ruling "draconian." The depth of reaction on the part of builders and developers is typical; any constraint on the right to earn a maximum profit from investments is viewed as a threat to the very basis of American life and liberty.

In short, the small legal and judicial gains made over the past century reflecting concerns for the public or common good have been small, fragile, and easily reinterpreted. As I write this, environmental gains for air and water quality and the preservation of wilderness areas have been greatly compromised by presidential rulings, and it is unknown at the present moment how much support will be found to reinvigorate the environmental agendas of the past thirty years. Furthermore, local, state, and even national governments face far greater challenges in the wake of globalization, as the full effect of Chapter 11 in the NAFTA agreement allows multinational corporations to sue national governments when their "rights" to expected profits are threatened by local environment regulations.

Meanwhile, Back at the Ranch . . .

In New Mexico, the state legislature did not pass enabling legislation for cities to enact zoning and planning powers until 1947, compared to New York City in 1916. Counties in New Mexico with over 25,000 population were given zoning powers in 1959, and it was not until 1965 that all New Mexico counties were given zoning authority, although Santa Fe County had been included in the 1947 law. The 1959 New Mexico legislature adopted the State Planning Office under the auspices of the State Planning Act. This entity was to assist the governor's staff in making recommendations about the state's natural, economic, and human resources, and was mandated to prepare an annual report. In 1960, the State Planning Office issued a long list of proposals aimed at unifying and clarifying efforts and planning land development. The most extensive of these would have required enabling legislation for regional planning commissions, county planning commissions, master plan development, historic preservation, clarifying the rights of neighbors to enforce zoning regulations, and the development of official maps for reserving land for public acquisition. But the State Planning Office had a short life, as the office was disbanded by the following governor, Jerry Apodaca.

With the loss of the State Planning Office, information at a statewide level was not available to planners or the public. While many of the suggestions made by this office have been enacted, they have been enacted piecemeal, uncoordinated with any state or regional authority and not always interpreted in the manner intended. The main difficulty with regional planning initiatives in New Mexico is written into the legislation: paragraph 8 states that "Cooperation is recommended and plans shall be submitted to the regional planning commission, but the sole power to adopt proposals, plans, ordinances, regulations or projects remain[s] with the legal governing body or special district proposing them." In other words, such regional bodies would have no independent sanctions for nonconformance, and, even if a master plan had been implemented, participation in regional planning was left to the self-interest of local communities.

Cities in New Mexico have a clear mandate from the state legislature to enforce planning, platting and zoning, and other powers incidental and necessary to carrying out this purpose (3 New Mexico State Statutes Amended, 1978). Both cities and counties are to provide planning in order to coordinate harmonious development and to promote the health, safety, moral order, convenience, prosperity, and general welfare, but only municipal planning commissions are required to prepare and adopt a master plan; there is no such requirement for counties (NMSA 14–18–1 CB. Repl. 1968). Municipal master plans therefore carry considerable weight of law, even though individual cases can be overruled by a two-thirds majority of their governing bodies, but counties are not expressly granted these powers (NMSA 15–58–1 through 3, Repl. 1968). Even here, though, developers have a loophole under municipal master plans, because paragraph 4 of the planning statute states that the powers of such a planning authority are only to make reports and recommendations (NM Stat. Ann., 1978, 3–19–1). This weakness was seized upon in a recent suit brought in the city of Santa Fe, in which the appellate court ruled that any master plan is advisory only, that it is to be treated as a resolution and not an ordinance, and that it is therefore not binding (*Dugger v. City of Santa Fe*, 114 NM 47, 1992).

As a long-time observer of and participant in city and county land use and planning meetings, I have seen firsthand the power of developers to plead their right to expect profits from their investments, and to treat any regulations that get in the way of these expectations as unconstitutional infringements of their basic rights. The local government's mandate to protect the common good is always interpreted to mean the good of the developer, regardless of long-term consequences for others. The long-standing tradition in the West of disavowing any limitations to individual freedom continues to undermine attempts at maintaining the common good for the benefit of more than the privileged few.

Only a few states have taken steps to curtail the power of the growth sectors. Mandatory statewide planning exists in Hawaii (1961), Vermont (1970), Florida (1972), and Oregon (1973); other states have some form of statewide controls. These states acted and are acting in response to the same issues facing New Mexico: the unwillingness and inability of local governments to act beyond their parochial self-interests, the threat that historic features or resources will be destroyed by large-scale developments, and (in classic states' rights language) the threat of federal land use controls. These state initiatives have largely called on the execution of the police powers of the state to protect the general welfare, and challenges to date have been largely unsuccessful (Callies, Freilich, and Roberts 1994, 610).

Such regulations are not on the horizon in most Western states, including New Mexico. For instance, New Mexico's subdivision laws allow a two-and-a-half-acre minimum lot size everywhere in the state in unincorporated areas—one house, one well, one septic system—whether the land will sustain that kind of development or not. In some parts of Santa Fe County this law has resulted in an evenly spaced carpet of single-family ranchettes spread out as far as the eye can see. Another provision, unique to New Mexico as far as I know, is known as the four-lot split. Enacted to ensure the continuity of historic Hispanic land inheritance rights, through which each child inherits an equal portion of the estate, it allows a single parcel to be split into four units once every three years between people as distantly related as first cousins without the original owner's having to file a subdivision plat. There are a lot of first cousins among unscrupulous developers, and this has resulted in what are known as *colonias*, communities of shacks and improvised dwellings with unclear or nonexistent titles where the infrastructure improvements are a shared hose for running water and raw effluent running down the street for sewer. While more prevalent in the southern part of New Mexico, there is one on Albuquerque's west side and at least one in the northwestern part of the state.

At present there are no *colonias* in Santa Fe County, but the weak nature of land use and subdivision laws in New Mexico give even those local governments that are inclined to tackle growth issues little support in the battle for more equitable approaches to development. With little oversight by the county and little ability to address development in a coordinated, legally enforceable manner, high-end residential developments such as those proposed by Campbell Farming continue to consume land, water, and air without regard to the needs and rights of others. In the West, as elsewhere, having large concentrations of residential communities separated by ten miles and more from work and shopping requires dependency on nonrenewable energy sources because private automobiles are the only way to commute. This is equally true even for the tiny community of Madrid, whose residents may be somewhat less dependent upon polluting forms of energy than most, but who face the same type of isolation from urban services, as we shall see later.

Thus the legal fix was not much of a fix after all: neither federal nor state laws nor local political options offer much solution to the dilemma of uncoordinated growth. This is what Mark Gottdiener (1987) describes as the crisis of the local state. Since even the Supreme Court remains reluctant to expand the police powers of the state to protect the general welfare in land use issues (compare to its equal reticence to curb such powers regarding loss of civil liberties in other areas), state and local governments have no precedents for proactive planning and even fewer legal, political, and economic means of enforcing such planning. While local populations still look toward their elected officials to protect or improve the quality of community life, their local governments are increasingly unable to do so. Instead of fostering meaningful political input, local governments are absorbed in attempts to fiscally balance the costs of uncoordinated growth. "Capital flight, industrial restructuring, fiscal crises, the powers of higher levels of government, and the autonomy of bureaucrats all combine to hem in options for political adjustments. The local State is ascribed a role by citizen interests that it cannot perform" (Gottdiener 1987, 21). Thus growth (if you are an advocate) or sprawl (if you are not) continues with little ability for local governments—including regional planning bodies—to control what happens within their own borders or for local governments to provide equitable services in their increasingly fragmented communities.

The Emergent Community of Conflict

> Among the many reasons why the people of northern New Mexico must work diligently to gain greater control over their own lives is one that is often overlooked: the Anglo invasion of 1846 is still going on. . . . These new New Mexicans include the restless young and the restless old, and many of them openly claim to be temperamentally ill suited for service in the family business "back east." Recognizing this, one pundit has argued that much of what is peculiar about Santa Fe can be explained by the fact that its affairs are so frequently controlled by "The Sons and Daughters Who Didn't Fit In." (DeBuys 1985, 317–18)

The restlessness and hyper-individualism so treasured by Madrid's counter-culture settlers were long a part of the reality and the myth of the American West, and are, in fact, supported by most of our institutions, including the legal system's emphasis on settling claims through individual rights. The question of who speaks for the common interests of the larger social and ecological community has never been resolved, and Bellah and his colleagues' hopes for reinvigorating our institutions to reflect an explicit discussion of the common good remain mostly unfulfilled. Yet there are places like Madrid and Santa Fe where dialogues about the nature of communal interests have a thirty-year history, and perhaps both places owe their attempts to define and protect the common good to these "sons and daughters who don't fit in." But as long as we depend on implicit reflections of Enlightenment philosophies and invisible hands to mollify market forces, we will continue to lose the ecological and sociological bases for the social collective. The globalization of markets and capital has only strengthened the monopolistic and oligarchic tendencies of unfettered capitalism; consumption will continue to erode our interpersonal energies and our environment. The common good will become a residential "theme park."

The next three chapters of this study will focus on the microcosm of Madrid's counterculture resettlers, some of whom hoped to create new institutions of social and ecological justice, some of whom wanted to be free of the fetters of institutions entirely, and some of whom merely found themselves caught up in the place. Their successes and their failures can still educate us as to the difficulties of redrawing boundaries, of entering new frontiers, and, as Bellah and his colleagues remind us, of allowing "the moral thinness of individualism" to be the leitmotif of life (1992, 228).

What happened to the energy of resistance in the generation that reached maturity in the early 1960s is not a trivial question: as the earth runs out of resources to sustain modernity's cultural and economic materialism, the scenario of a few global elites surrounded by a groundswell of poverty looms ever more plausible. Were these counterculture experiments useful models of sustainability, or mere extensions of the individualism embodied in our myths and institutions? Will the inherent anarchistic tendencies of Madrid's cult of the individual be useful in maintaining its isolation and unique local culture, or will it prevent the kind of coherent and continual dialogue required to arrive at community consensus about the village's common interests? And where, if not places like Madrid, will we find pockets of resistance to the homogenizing tendencies of global capitalism?

CHAPTER THREE

Madrid's Resettlement
The Counterculture Migration

*During the period covered by this book, I was a member
of an anarchic West Coast community that had taken as its
collective task the rethinking and recreation of our national
culture. Such intentions were not unique; my generation was
struggling openly with problems of racism, grossly inequitable
distribution of goods and services, dishonorable foreign
policies, and the war in Vietnam. . . . This book attempts to
describe what the pursuit of absolute freedom felt like,
what it taught me, and what it cost.*

—Peter Coyote, *Sleeping Where I Fall*

The core group of people who make up this study are not easily defined;
I have used the term "counterculture" as liberally as other writers here
in speaking of the 1960s youth movements, but the word is neither
tremendously precise nor terribly useful—except as a sort of generic tag.
The people who moved to Madrid during this time frame were most certainly not original settlers, nor were they an organized group of people; they
were mostly small groups, "families," couples, and single people pursuing—
in their individual ways—what Peter Coyote describes above, ways of
resolving the dissatisfactions of the generation that had reached its maturity in the 1960s. But this was not just an ordinary youth rebellion; there
were extraordinary events leading up to this twentieth-century wanderlust.
The turmoil of multiple assassinations, the promise and then failure of social
policies under Johnson, the disaster that was Vietnam, and the repressive
institutions and drug enforcement policies initiated during the sixties led
many of us who were part of this generation to doubt the legitimacy of any
and all authority. Wandering from place to place and from group to group
was the norm for many of us during this time; wandering forged networks,

it created the illusion of freedom, it encouraged the open use of drugs as a symbol of that freedom, and it enabled a loose, albeit chaotic underground social system to function—a system difficult for outside authority to penetrate, for it never solidified in one place for very long.

A whole generation has been raised since these social movements surfaced; perhaps a short exploration of the era from an insider's point of view will clarify the hopes and delusions of those experiencing it. Coyote documents the philosophy of the groups he belonged to, the Diggers and the Free Family, how they tried to liberate themselves from the need to own private property and to "discover alternative modes of living and working together based on personal authenticity rather than on economics" (1998, 202). To outsiders—those concerned with the sacredness of property and the sanctity of propriety—hippies all looked alike. But there were vast internal differences among these aggregations. Some were associated with rock groups; some dedicated themselves to bioregionalism, to religious beliefs, or, like the Diggers, to liberating other people's wealth for the communal good. Some groups chose a relatively settled lifestyle and others a migratory gypsy life. There were groups whose wealth, such as it was, came from scamming the establishment and from arts, crafts, and trade items; others had trust accounts. Groups of hippies, flower children, and counterculture people were threatening to middle-class sensibilities and were often the butt of police reprisals, but the violence was by no means always from the outside. Drugs, jealousies, and unrestrained freedom took an internal toll on many groups.

Hippies roamed the West, looking for abandoned mining towns or areas previously laid waste by the industrial culture that they were seeking to replace. As Coyote observed, "The reason hippies are allowed to live on this land is precisely because it has been ruined. We are the second crop" (217). Living in the margins, yet maintaining communications with remote sites through their constant travel, these assortments of people surrounded themselves with ideologies of revolution and social regeneration that belied their true status. As Coyote observed of one set of people, "I could see that despite their poverty, the hippies were the aristocrats in the valley and deeply resented. Their real wealth, aside from access to cash [through drugs, connections with relatives and outsiders with money], consisted of their education, their social and political skills, and their mobility" (255–56), Instead of working cooperatively with local merchants, they pooled their internal resources and shopped in the bigger urban centers; instead of seeing themselves as part of the larger community, the hippies isolated themselves in their communes, and eventually tired of the struggle and moved on.

Madrid's hippies reflected this diversity of outlooks and experiences, but not all of them tired of their small valley with its minimal lifestyles, and today their village remains a viable community after thirty years of resistance to mainstream American culture—albeit, as we shall see, a community with significant ambiguities and internal tensions. As a community, they remain steeped in the rhetoric of the counterculture, determined to resist both internal and external forms of authority and committed to a life as close to absolute freedom as they can obtain.

A Note About Methods, Interviews, and Observations

My research in the community started in the summer of 1997 with casual observations at the coffee shop, the grocery store, and the tavern, and at events such as the Fourth of July Parade. I was commuting at the time between Albuquerque and Madrid. Entry into the community, described in more detail in the preface, happened in the fall of 1998, when I was able to move to the countryside in the mountains just east of the village in the capacity of a part-time caretaker. This caretaking arrangement was facilitated by a relationship with one of Madrid's later arrivees. For the next two years I was an active member of the community, and I continued to live in the mountains for another year even though the demands of work and family obligations required once again commuting between Madrid and Albuquerque. I reluctantly left the community in the winter of 2001 in order to analyze the data and commit the results of the research to the written page.

Of the approximately eighteen original resettlers who remain in the area— those who rented or bought from Huber directly—I have interviewed thirteen at length. All but two still consider the village their home. Of the later arrivees, I have interviewed fifteen and engaged in three years of participant observation and participant activism in the village, through which I gained deeper understandings of the dynamics of village life than through isolated interviews. It is impossible to know how many people constitute this group I have called the later arrivees, as the fluid and impermanent nature of the community made tracking individuals impossible. However, I did become acquainted with all of the current retirees during my years in the village.

I have asked people to recall things that happened up to thirty years ago, and for many interviewees these have been the most formative years of their lives. Many have recalled events with a great deal of obvious emotion. Different people have different memories, and I have made no attempt to reconcile exact dates or happenings; the variety of human remembering is part of the overall story, both for Madrid and for the West in general. Nor have I made any attempt to launder the language of the interviews to make it correct—they remain in vernacular speech. I have substituted pseudonyms for people's real names or nicknames, and have tried to find names that are not reflective of anyone in the village or the surrounding area, past or present.

Before looking at the narratives from the people who resettled Madrid, I want to add a few general comments drawn from my observations of the community. The fluidity with which people move in and out of the village, the tolerance toward drug use, sexual preferences, lifestyle choices, and the apparent freedom from formal governance structures are easily construed by outsiders to mean that the community is disorganized and chaotic; this opinion is only partly true. I will argue later that tolerance of lifestyle choices, defiant individualism, and a lack of cohesion do not equate to total disorganization, and that while this mode of community is not for everyone, it has perhaps no higher costs to individual creative energy and to overall community well-being than communities whose main streets are dominated by Starbucks. All forms of social organization and disorganization have costs—both to the individual and to the community; Madrid is no different.

Small parts of the hippie era survive today in such groups as the Rainbow Family, who travel through Madrid occasionally and who find a welcome among the older residents. Coyote and his friends stayed occasionally at a commune near Placitas, only a few miles south of Madrid, and one former commune member from that area is now a merchant and long-time resident of Madrid. Tawapa, one of the Placitas communes, persisted until about ten years ago, when it was finally pushed out of existence by upscale housing developments. For a long time a member of the Diggers lived in Golden, just to the south of Madrid, and maintained ties with the folks in Madrid. The strength of these weak ties, to draw on a metaphor from the sociology of formal organizations, is part of what allowed Madrid to succeed as a community.

It is important to remember that the original resettlers of Madrid were single people, couples, and families (regular and counterculture) that each

FIGURE 3.1. *Joe Huber's "fine industrial location."*

had their own agendas and needs. They were not part of any organized movement, did not represent anyone but themselves, and were not particularly involved with sustaining the mass movements that were occurring internationally at the time. In fact, in many ways they were looking for a way out of the chaos of the late 1960s and early 1970s.

Figure 3.1 shows an overview of the contemporary village of Madrid, resurrected through the efforts of these singular individuals. The photograph was taken in the fall of 2000 and looks southward along the long axis of the village from a vantage point above the Oscar Huber Memorial Ball Park. The Ortiz Mountains (where I lived for three years) are off to the left. The big building in the center of the picture is the Old Boarding House. The stone structure to the right in the foreground was the grade school during the mining days. State Highway 14, the only paved road in town (or into and out of town) is seen winding up the foothills to the south. The roadbed still visible on the slope to the left overlooking the village is the remnants of the narrow-gauge rail that served the mines located within these mountains. This photo encompasses about 90 percent of the contemporary village of Madrid.

When the original resettlers first drove through town to find Joe Huber and Frank Ochoa standing outside the Mine Shaft Tavern, there were only empty shops, derelict houses, some electricity, and the rudiments of a water system. Had Huber cared less about his town, had he not still hoped to make a profit from his real estate investment, and had he let the town become a true ghost town, there might not be a contemporary Madrid.

Discovering Madrid
Three Series of New Migrations

RESETTLERS

Historians commonly refer to DeVargas's 1692 military campaign into New Mexico as the *re*conquest of the territory for New Spain. I think the term *resettler* seems appropriate for the counterculture people who discovered Madrid in the early 1970s. Early resettlers rented from Huber and later bought their properties directly from him during the "land rush," as it is still known. These first migrants experienced the town as a ghost town of derelict houses and shops being refurbished and reinhabited. The discovery and resettlement of this space by communards, free thinkers, outlaws, drug subculture practitioners, and Vietnam veterans have imprinted the village with these founding ideologies, and once the initial rebuilding had taken place this core group of individuals brought many other resettlers to the village through the informal networks discussed above. The ambience of tolerance, free-thinking, and still-cheap real estate made the village attractive to a wide variety of artists, craftspeople, and those looking "to live in a free space" (interview). Today, a small cohort of this group who are left in the village hold on to what amounts to positions of power in the community, as I will explore in chapter 6.

LATER ARRIVEES

In this fluid and mobile community, it is hard to pick calendar dates when changes occurred in the village, but every one of the resettlers interviewed felt that the town changed sometime during the mid-1980s, when the tourist industry began influencing the character and economics of the village. As a group those coming after about 1985 were more mercantile oriented, less violent, and *somewhat less* committed to defiant individualism; I have called these folks *later arrivees* to distinguish them from resettlers.

Today these two groups form the bulk of the community, and while some long-time residents feel that the later arrivees are parasites living off the hard work that the original resettlers put into the village, for the most part the fissures over arrival status are relatively superficial. The village is still a difficult and somewhat isolated place in which to live, and the hardships are endured by both groups with some degree of equanimity.

RETIREES
To date, the third migration to Madrid is a small but growing group of retirees who find the village and its real estate prices attractive. They have comfortable transfer payment incomes, do not depend on the local economy for sustenance, and often participate in local village affairs more than even most long-time residents. Their small numbers, four individuals that I know of, have prevented any formal schisms around their presence in the community, especially since none of these folks is bothered by the expressive lifestyles of the villagers. In all but one case, these individuals are from the same generational cohort as the original counterculture population— one is somewhat younger. These folks have been in Madrid for around five years; two are from Chicago, one from the East Coast, and one from Albuquerque. If their numbers grow significantly, however, retirees could bring some realignments to the village's social arrangements.

Pioneering on the Frontier of the Great Society

The resettlers had a variety of reasons for choosing Madrid as a settlement space; some made conscious choices in order to pursue lives of greater freedom and hedonism than was possible in mainstream America; for some the myth of independence and self-sufficiency on the edge of civilization in the Wild West was compelling, while serendipity and economic necessity played a role for other folks. No single reason for settling in Madrid emerged from the interviews—beyond the wanderlust and unrootedness of the era. For most of the resettlers interviewed, the combination of wanderlust and the desire to remove themselves from the dominant political hegemony of the 1960s was enough to justify the work of living on the margins. Their stories follow.

Creation Myths of the Resettlers
He had a habit of being from somewhere else. (interview 1998)

Everyone who moved to Madrid in the 1970s remembers a counterculture family called the Madrid Ducks. They were the first people to repopulate the village on a permanent basis, and they were some of the most radical communards to strike a deal with Joe Huber. So it is appropriate to start with Sam, the only member of the Ducks (at this writing) who granted an interview:

> We were living in the Height-Ashbury district of San Francisco. . . . We [four men and one woman] were living communally in a flat close to Panhandle Park right across from where the Jefferson Airplane had their home and where Patricia Hearst had her hideout. . . . We were growing marijuana in our living room—everyone was—it was no big deal. . . . We ended up with twelve people in that apartment. They decided they were going to start a band in the desert. . . . We just said we've got to go. We left everything, all of our things. David and I got on the road and hitchhiked and followed them. (interview 1998)

With no more thought than a Midwest farmer leaving his plow in the fields to follow the gold rush, this family drove east into the desert in search of transcendence and a place to have a band. They tried Rhyolite, Nevada, and Jerome, Arizona, other places where counterculture people had settled. But they decided to come to Madrid to find Deirdre and her partner, who were either gypsies or hippies. Lawrence, who was looking for Deirdre, "had a Ph.D. in anthropology and lost his job when he gave his whole class LSD." Parts of this family lived in Madrid from 1972 until 1982, where they were known alternatively as the Adobe Ducks or the Madrid Ducks. Sam Duck documented their arrival into town (they all used Duck as a last nickname):

> We were in Will's truck—now this is a car—a '59 Chevy that he cut the back seat out of and made a truck out of the back. We had a little canopy for the rain. We pulled into Madrid and you come over the top of the mountain there from Albuquerque and you're driving down—and there it is nestled away down and when we pulled into town we drove through and came back . . .

The Ducks felt this was not the nicest place they had seen, but they were not even twenty-three years old and did not care:

There was no one there. We rambled around through homes that
didn't have doors or windows, we just walked around in and out.
And then we pulled around, we turned the curve again there, at
where the museum is now, there was Frank Ochoa, an elderly
Hispanic man, and Joe Huber. And they were sitting around talking the way they did every day. Every day Joe was there every
afternoon and sat with Frank for twelve years.

Even though it appeared to the Ducks that there were no people outside of
Frank and Joe in the entire village, Joe was not forthcoming with information about what might be available for occupancy, and Sam describes in further detail the Ducks' decision to settle in Madrid:

> I said, "We are driving through from San Francisco and is there
> anything for rent?" [Huber] looked over at me and said, "Frank,
> don't we have one or two?".... "Yup, it's the sixteenth house on
> the left."
>   I said, "What do you mean, only one is available [when
> nobody's here]?"
>   [Huber said,] "Tell you what I'll do. I'll let you stay in the
> company stores; they need to be cleaned up.... You can live there
> six months for free, and you can clean it up. (interview 1998)

The final decision was up to the Ducks' charismatic leader, David Lucero.
All the Ducks, according to Sam, depended on David's skills for survival
in Madrid's isolated setting:

> David said the star people could exist there, and I was sold. His
> name was Lucero, which meant morning star, and then there's the
> evening star and all those stars and maybe we do come from the
> stars, who knows, but David was very magical and had a whole
> history of being from somewhere else. (interview 1998)[1]

[1.]Sadly, David Lucero died at the beginning of the summer my research in
the village began, and I did not have the opportunity to meet him. It was
widely felt by those who knew him that he died because of his exposure to
Agent Orange during his service in Vietnam.

Not all the original resettlers came with such ethereal desires, but there is still a strong belief in magic, the supernatural, and the paranormal in the village. Everyone was definitely from somewhere else, however, often multiple somewhere elses. The Ducks had come from places as disparate as New Orleans and St. Louis before clustering in San Francisco. The search for a place to be took many forms, but most had to do with amenity and lifestyle choices. Deadeye Don, after serving in Vietnam and some time spent in Haight-Ashbury, came through Cerrillos, found a woman with a smile and a bottle of wine standing in her doorstep, and thought the area had promise. He later rented from Huber for $20 a month and then took the first house at the north end of town for $35 a month. The Smiths, originally from Chicago, and their two young children came from the neighboring settlement of San Pedro after the failure of a communal venture: "We came here broke after that. We could rent from Joe for $40 a month, the north end of this building" (interviews 1999).

Willie, originally from New England, had been moving around from Arizona to Kansas and back before settling for a time at Tawapa. Then he maintained a house in Bernalillo. In 1975 "[w]e heard about music happening at the ballpark, Madrid jazz.... And I came up and it wasn't at all appealing to me. The town. First of all it was very desolate. There was nobody there, there were only about five or about twelve people living here." But the next summer, after the town was for sale, "[s]o then I wanted to buy a house.... And I felt that the Madrid houses were affordable and that there was stuff happening now" (interview 1998). Jessie and her husband wanted to go to Guatemala but there was a problem with his passport, so they came to Madrid because he knew some people there. As Jessie described it:

> I was really young when we bought our house. I was only eighteen
> years old. When we came through in 1977—when we couldn't get
> into Guatemala—we just came back here and we had all this
> money in our pocket and we thought, maybe we'll just buy land
> out here. We came and we were living and it was as simple as that.
> There really wasn't a whole lot of deep thought." (interview 2000)

Jessie's present husband, Tullie, ended up in Madrid when the rebuilding of Route 66 through Tijeras Canyon for Interstate 25 dislocated his household. He and his first wife sought land south around Tajique, but Hispanic land grant activists had made the area impossible for Anglos to buy in there—even though his wife at the time was Hispanic. Her father had grown up in Madrid and was still well thought of by Huber, as evidenced by the following:

> So at the last minute I had to rent a place here [Madrid]. But Joe [Huber] didn't want to rent a place. He kept saying, "No, there's nothing livable." We would come up Sundays and find him in the bar. . . . I just mentioned Joe R. [my father-in-law]. "Joe R., you know him?" "Oh, yeah, that's her dad." "Oh, yeah, it is. Come here, follow me." So he walked right over to the door and unlocked it and gave me the key. "Here. Sixty bucks a month. 1973." (interviews 2000)

Rhonda came in 1974 with her partner at the time and set up a vintage clothing and accessory shop with another young woman. She had left a job out east working for corporate America because she felt (and still feels) that no one should have to work at an establishment job when they are young. She told her mother "that she [her mother] had worked so hard that she never had any fun. And I always thought we should play hard and have a good time when we are young and healthy and then when we are old we can go to work." She remembers her friends, who were only in their twenties and already tied down to mortgages, not being able to fathom her decision to leave the security of a real job—"But if it's not fun, I don't do it!" She remembers there being only about twenty people in town "and there was a cohesion to the place. People worked together, helped each other out, shared community resources" (interview 1999).

Ishmael (originally from the Rust Belt) remembers a similar sense of camaraderie among the original resettlers:

> What brought me here—it was the steel mills closing and it was time to get out of town. There was no work, thousands of people looking for work. A high school friend of mine asked me to go to Albuquerque. Where the hell is Albuquerque, I never heard of it. We hitched out here, took us about 3-1/2 days. That was when Yale Park was still going. Where all the hippies were, it was like

a commune, Alice's Restaurant. That's what it was. I came here [to Madrid] because it was peaceful and there was nobody here. I bought my house here from the first sales. It was a very busy time, there was always the sound of saws and hammers. We used what we could from abandoned houses, just taking whatever we could, window frames, doors, that kind of thing. (interview 1998)

Another original resettler, August, and his wife, Ellie, had been living in Mexico in an abandoned hacienda with no electricity or running water. Ellie had lived under similar conditions while in the Peace Corps. Ellie was from the East Coast and August from Australia. When they came north to New Mexico they were looking for "some place that certainly did not have a whole lot of people." They had been told by acquaintances about Madrid, and that if Joe Huber took a shine to you, you might get a place to rent. Selling paintings and pottery at the Santa Fe flea market provided a bit of income:

We were greatly enamored of the fact that it [Madrid] was a ghost town, there was really nobody here, virtually. There were maybe about six of the buildings in town that had people living in them at the time. But the real criterion was that we could rent the place with this other couple, and Joe was going to charge us forty dollars a month. We had another friend who came here because we were here, and, the couple who we used to be in the import business with in Mexico came here, also. (interview 1999)

The quotes above are representative of the feelings of the original resettlers who could be located and who agreed to be interviewed. It is hard to say how complete the data is as the population is unknown; however, the serendipitous nature of community formation is clear in these conversations. Only one of the interviewees lives elsewhere; the others continue to make Madrid and its vicinity home. There is a smaller group of original resettlers who have been in the community for as long as these folks, but who have never owned property. This is not due to economic circumstance but rather to lifestyle choice. And they also have interesting stories; two of these stories follow.

Alf had been living in New York City after living overseas when a letter arrived from a friend who had just moved to Madrid:

So I came out in the spring of 1975, and in no time flat, I went
back to New York, got all my stuff, and moved here. It's the actual
physical space, not the people. It was a change to begin all over
again, and it was a bit like Morocco or the Greek mountains. And
the stars are so sparkling, so clear that you can see the colors spin-
ning in the clear crisp nights. But always—never in the core, in the
middle of it, always pulled away. I am somewhat of a loner, very
content with my own energy. (interview 1999)

But owning property or being settled in a specific site—to the exclusion
of other possible sites—was not what Alf wanted. During the time that the
village properties were being sold by Huber, he had no interest in obtaining one: "And these houses were being sold for $3,000 on almost an acre.
And I didn't jump at the chance, nor did I ever give it consideration. . . .
That's why I never bought land, so I could be free."

Alf was in a short segment that *60 Minutes* shot of Madrid in 1982, pre-
senting Madrid "as the last chance of the new frontier. It was resurrection,
frontiering, pioneering, which the West represents anyways." As Alf commented, the new pioneers moving to Madrid were "from a whole bunch
of other places, mostly city life. And we were all having attitudes about city
crazy stuff and the establishment" (interview 1999).

Even those earning a fair amount of money don't always choose to own
property. Norma has done caretaking and painting for over twenty years in
the area, sometimes staying for nearly ten years in one location, but never
settling down and buying anything. As she expressed it, she's "always been
leery of owning land because if you have a mortgage or payments and you
lose your job or your health then you lose everything." When she and her
husband had good years, they could earn $30,000 a year (field notes 2000).
I am personally acquainted with a dozen people of both genders who live
similar lives.

Living with minimal possessions and depending solely upon your own
ability to barter, trade, or find a series of temporary jobs seem strange ways
to ensure one's independence from those of the dominant culture in
America, yet that is precisely what these resettlers were counting on for survival. This immediacy of experience fostered the sense of self-sufficiency and
independence from external demands that has so characterized ideologies
about the West from the time of the first Anglo conquests. As the realities

of life in the nearly abandoned mining town are examined in greater detail, we can see how much of the resettlers' survival was due to their own initiatives and how much due to dependence on outside resources.

Survival in the Early Years of Resettlement

When these young people came to Madrid, there was little in the way of infrastructure or amenities. There was no church, no school, no stores, one telephone line, one marginal gas pump, one part-time tavern, minimal water and sewer systems, and, as we have seen, very few people. Yet these were the very things that attracted these people to the site. How did these early resettlers get by? A combination of subsistence survival skills, trade and barter, sharing the proceeds from wage work in Santa Fe, and government assistance sufficed in these early years.

The Ducks built their own composting toilets and outhouses. "We had solar outhouses and church outhouses and different kinds. . . . After a year we would plant a tree where the outhouse had been. Beautiful trees grew up where the outhouses had been." As Sam Duck recalled, "The first year the garden was really horrible because . . . of all the coal. We worked it and worked it. But we took all the coal out. After eight to nine years we had lush gardens that would grow anything [including marijuana]. With a minimum of water. It was great." While the Ducks were living communally in a free-love environment, they were not atypical of other less radically organized families who shared living quarters in order to save money. It was not uncommon for at least one member in each cluster of people to have marketable skills, similar to the Ducks' experience:

I went to Santa Fe to work in restaurants, the opera, landscaping; Bob was a nurse; so we were able to make things happen because we had the wherewithal. We had ways of making money. We had food stamps—everyone was getting them. We were getting like $400 worth of food stamps per month in the '70s." (interview 1998)

Jessie worked as a seamstress in Santa Fe at a "funky job." It was always seasonal, the women were always getting laid off over the winter. "When we got laid off, we just all go on unemployment . . . then we would just all take off doing whatever, come back in June or July or whatever. . . . I was with them for about . . . nine years . . . until they folded."

Others worked out of their homes, relying on pottery, painting, hand-crafts, or cooking to get by. "All anybody wanted to do was to be able to have enough of a business going on that you could support yourself. We never thought of becoming wealthy off it or anything like that." Attracted by the cheap rents, "we thought, well, we can open up a store in the front of the house. And we did that for a few years." Even after the town sold, the covenants required business signs to be no larger than two square feet, placed on the front of the house, and businesses would be allowed only on the main street. "What people were conceiving of when those numbers were chosen, was that in front of your house you would have a discrete sign that said perhaps, 'Potter,' . . . And people would come by word of mouth, because of the quality of what was being produced. Not pitch" (interview 1999). Some typical ways of surviving were:

We had baked goods, [the tourists] they'll buy all of them and then we have our money. So I guess that was easy to handle, we could make money off the tourists coming in . . . tourism I always thought was a good thing in that people were coming to spend money as long as they left. (interview 1998)

There were these two women on the side of the road with a table and they were selling taquitos, ok. . . . They were trying to paint this sign up, it was called "Not Just Another Roadside Attraction." So I helped them out . . . I painted a sign for them in exchange for a couple of taquitos. (interview 1999)

I got started selling vintage clothing with Suzanne. I was making clothes to sell but didn't like having to do custom clothing or alterations, so selling old clothes was fine. Then it was not so good after a while and I started selling Western Kitch. . . . I could buy stuff for a nickel and sell it for five dollars. (interviews 1998; 1999)

Not everyone tried during this time period to get by in these minimal ways. One young woman worked in Santa Fe as a nurse but could not find affordable housing closer in, and Madrid filled her needs. At least two other women in the village worked as nurses and commuted to Santa Fe. For these

families, it was the men who stayed in town watching the children and
rebuilding the houses or running the marginal local businesses.

These rented properties required a great deal of work, with plumbing,
foundations, and roofs taking precedence over aesthetics. As one person
described the experience:

> Even when the town was up for sale, we didn't want to buy.
> We never bought property. . . . I had a roof over my head and,
> you know, as funky as it was then, at least we had running water.
> We repaired the pipes, we had a bathroom, toilets. There was a
> kitchen. We literally took shovels and shoveled pigeon shit and
> dog shit out the windows . . . the four of us worked for about six
> weeks before we moved into it. But we were only renting, too.
> (interview 1999)

The Ducks also put a great deal of sweat equity into their lifestyle, even
before Huber sold the town. In a passage that sums up many interviewees'
remembrances of these early days, Sam Duck recalled the impetuous nature
of the decision to settle in Madrid, for they had never even looked in the
back of the company stores they were to be living in. By the time the Ducks
had returned from selling all their belongings in San Francisco, they realized
what they were into:

> We never even looked at it. Then we walked in the store in the
> back and we see these piles of dog shit that were in the basement
> stacked up a foot and a half deep . . . bat shit, and oh, God, it
> was rats, dead rats. [And] twenty-four TVs that some repairman
> had left.

I should explain that pack rats have a delightful fascination with dog
droppings and will collect them from far and wide, arranging them in neat
piles in their nests—handy for cleaning up your yard, but not so wonderful if their nests happen to be somewhere humans also want to inhabit. Sam
borrowed money from his sister and they took about a month to clean up
the stores. Then,

> It was fabulous. . . . It was just great to have this huge space.

We could sleep on the roof. We had mattresses on the roof; we'd
sleep under the stars every night. It was just natural. . . . It was
new, we considered San Francisco Act One of our family and
Madrid was Act Two. (interview 1998)

Two themes emerge from these narratives. First, while the resettlers
were often characterized as "lazy hippies," or castoffs from the world of
those who went to work every day, life in a derelict mining town was not
easy. There is an unfinished quality to these life experiences, an ability to
take the leftovers that Madrid had to offer and make do with things as they
were found. They were young, all from the same generational cohort, and
not tied down to comforts of the materialistic culture that they had grown
up in, but they were not totally self-sufficient either. The second theme, then,
is that they had the collective ability and the means, as Coyote discusses,
to obtain and exploit resources beyond the local environment. Sam borrowed money from his sister, he and others in the community worked in
Santa Fe when economic necessity dictated, and many obtained food stamps
or other forms of government transfer payments to make their seemingly
carefree life a reality. The kind of self-imposed poverty of contemporary
Madrid is a far cry from the lack of choices characteristic of the mining town
era. However, that does not take away from the dedication and hard work
the resettlers had to put into their new homes in order to make them and
their village livable again.

The Land Rush Days

Until 1975, everyone rented from Huber, who still owned the town. By the
time Huber decided to sell the town as individual lots, the word had spread
about the counterculture village with low rents and easy lifestyle, and Huber
found himself landlord to quite a few people. Sam Duck recalled that Huber
was not totally comfortable with the flower children, and Jim Mocho,
Huber's real estate agent, remarked that Joe tolerated the hippies but was
not overly keen on their lifestyles. As Sam described the situation and Joe's
decision to sell the town:

So he had a problem on his hands after about a year and a half of
this because he had about fifty to seventy-five people living here
and he didn't want to be a landlord, and so he put the whole town

up for sale. So we called our friends. . . . But he got three and a
half times what he could have made the other way. . . . So at some
point there were forty-five dogs and nineteen people. And then
there were forty-five dogs and forty-five people. Then there were
seventy-five people and forty-five dogs. (interview 1998)

The story about the dogs is one of the local founding mythologies, as are
other stories of the "land rush" or "the sell off," as August describes it:

When we all went—at the time of the land rush when we were
given the opportunity to put down payments on the property.
I don't know if you have heard the story that we were all in the
bar and they [Huber and Mocho] said, "the town is for sale and
we can have any lot. If you have ten dollars in your pocket, that
holds the lot for you." Then there was a certain amount of time
that you had to come up with a 10 percent deposit and that
would really hold that.

People started coming into town and people started living in all sorts of different places. When the prices were $500 for a miner's shack—there were
a lot of people who came to town and figured, that's a pretty good deal.
(interview 1999)

These miner's shacks sold to the resettlers were in pretty bad shape;
some had been hauled in by rail from another site by sawing the houses in
three pieces to get them on the rail cars. When they were reassembled in
Madrid, the saw lines remained clearly visible through the rough wood sid-
ing. Moving houses around in the mining camps was facilitated by the lack
of permanent foundations and plumbing, which meant that the first thing
most resettlers had to do, whether renting or buying, was to stabilize the
foundations and do something about indoor plumbing, although outhouses remained for many years the facility of choice for many residents, as Sam
Duck described above. Much of the housing stock and most of the stores
constructed of wood were not in much better shape than the shack pictured
in figure 3.2 when the counterculture migrants discovered Madrid, and had
the hippies and flower children been more wedded to materialistic values,
or as lazy as they were accused of being by many, Huber would not have
made a profit selling the town.

FIGURE 3.2. *An unrestored miner's shack. The sag in the roof*
corresponds to one of the saw marks, both of which
can be seen extending from the top of the windows
to the roof.

Huber is remembered for taking care of those whom he liked in the village. August and two others had bought adjoining properties and then discovered that they didn't have enough area for a septic system. So they went to Joe
and said, "'Look, Joe, you are selling us these properties and the state won't
even let us put a septic system in.' So Joe gave us a lot between the three owners and we built a two-thousand-gallon septic tank and hooked three houses
up." Similarly, the Smiths were out of town when the sale happened, but Joe
saved them a building. "We [were renting] from Joe for $40 a month, the north
end of this building. We were in California when the town sold out but Huber
saved us the whole building. Fred wanted the solar access. Joe had offered us
the general store, but Fred wanted the dealership" (interviews 1999, 1998).

For a long time the ethic in the village was to fix up only the inside of
the houses; the exteriors were left as original as structural concerns allowed.
Today, all but one of the houses along the former Silk Stocking Row are
painted and repaired, reflecting both the greater wealth in the village and

FIGURE 3.3. *A residence that maintains the tradition of unrestored exteriors.*

the accommodations to the tourist industry. While no one interviewed would admit to it, other reasons for keeping a low exterior profile were to keep tax assessors and other county officials from snooping around gardens and greenhouses containing suspicious crops.

The owner of the house in the figure 3.3 remarked that he put a new metal roof on the house only in order to get fire insurance. The porch floor had disintegrated in front of the door, making entry into the home resemble an obstacle course, and in fact, our interview was not conducted in his home. Even though he is one of the original resettlers, many of his cohort as well as new residents have mentioned to me that "he could at least do a little to fix up the outside of his place."

While today there is more concern for appearance, even among the original resettlers, in the 1970s such things were luxuries few could afford. The formation of social cohesion in this counterculture community was not an easy task, nor have communal sentiments ever completely gelled. The reasons for this will be explored in later chapters, but here I want to continue the story of Madrid as seen by its resettlers and residents.

‑p Madrid's Resettlement ‑p   85

The Difficulties of Creating Cohesion on the Social Frontier

Coping with primitive conditions and marginal amenities left most resettlers with a feeling that these were the best of times, the most cooperative of
times, and the only time when the community worked together with a relatively common sense of purpose. "We were a culture in some way, shape,
or form. And we had sort of a common—somewhat of a common vision.
The general sense I think was that we really did want to have a community with the sense of community and to have everybody else leave us alone.
We didn't want any sort of outside input" (interview 1999). The feeling that
the resettlers could isolate themselves from the larger society was one of the
attractions, of course, to the nearly abandoned town. And for a while, people did work together, as represented by this typical memoir:

> That first spurt, living in one of these houses with a cook stove,
> kerosene lamps . . . we all needed each other; no one had any extra
> bucks. Come over, we're having a potluck. I need to rebuild this
> chimney, that kind of trade and that kind of thing was really, really
> wonderful, wonderful. Those days are gone. (interview 1999)

In Madrid, this early sense of frontier communalism through hard work was
tempered by the desire to maximize individual freedom, and the desire to
simply have fun.

Jessie expressed this sentiment while speaking of the water in the village, which then, as now, is fouled by the underlying coal seams through
which it is pumped. Remarking that you can't even drink the water, she went
on to say, "Everybody in town was drunk and having fun, that was kind
of the unique thing about the town. It's probably one of the only towns in
New Mexico where you don't have a police department and a church. Or
a stop sign" (interview 1999). Not having a stop sign is an interesting
metaphor for Madrid, as the need for individual freedom usually wins out
over the desire (or need) for cooperative action, and attempts at building
internal cohesion have generally foundered on the egos of individual residents intent on preserving their autonomy.

This autonomy, after all, was a hard-fought battle in the early days of
resettlement, given the minimal survival skills of most of the formerly urban
young who moved there. Witness this moment of discovery for the Ducks,
as recounted by Sam:

So we're all sitting there, the kids and everyone huddled with us, and then someone . . . profoundly said, "What's that in the middle of the floor? . . . We lived in a house like that [in Brighton] and I could swear it's a furnace." He crawled under there and he said, "Yup, there's a furnace!" So we started taking the windows that were all broken up and throwing them in there and we got warm! . . . Then someone said, "Why are you burning all these things and burning all this wood; it's a coal furnace!" And we thought, where are we going to get coal? This is a coal mining town! . . . So we found out and we started using it—tons of it. And then, lo and behold, two winters later we learned how to bank it and it was amazing we learned all this stuff there! (interview 1998)

As an extended counterculture family, the Ducks could pool resources in ways other families could not, as witnessed by another resettler.

Jessie and her husband paid $1,000 down for their house, with payments of $35 a month for ten years. "The first summer we were here it was just all we could do to just try and get the foundation on the house done, a roof on, and some windows in, and boarded ourselves up into the two front rooms of the house for the winter." And she remarked about something else:

We never had enough money to get out. We thought we needed to—well, we can't move until we fix the house. We didn't have the money to fix the house. There was no real estate market here. If we fixed the house, if we sold the house, we really couldn't get anything for it. We never had any money. It goes into the house. We used to travel a lot, so we did trips. So, yeah, for a lot of years the house really looked like hell, but we traveled a lot. (interview 2000)

Even with minimal monthly payments, Madrid presented a hardscrabble existence for most of its early residents, and their success in rebuilding the village is no small accomplishment. Yet the work on their house, as for many resettlers, never preempted the importance of traveling and having fun.

While the individuals and families were busy taking the mass-produced housing from the industrial era and turning the village into a place of personal self-expression, they were creating a different type of model town than Oscar Huber and his son Joe had envisioned; the openness and tolerance attracted a wide range of settlers, as expressed in this quote:

> I was going to say, at the tail end of the hippie era, and I would say that most of the people here were hippies, well, hippies and outlaws. The outlaws and the drug dealers were kind of hippies. The rednecks in some ways are hippies. There is such a mix. . . . It's pretty "live and let live." (interview 1999)

Another early resettler expressed this tolerance and let-live attitude another way, while still privileging these early years as the best years in Madrid: "In 1974 there were probably only twenty people in town. There was a cohesion to the place. People worked together, helped each other out, shared community resources" (interview 1999). She also feels that her generation "was the last one to have a sense of morality. . . . The younger people—no sense of right or wrong." She didn't care if her friends did drugs; her house was always open, always safe. She feels that "there was more loyalty, to each other, to your group" (interview 1999).

The mix of people coming into Madrid widened during the mid-1980s to include some who took advantage of the counterculture's tolerance and the lack of any institutional forms of social control. The fragile cohesion of community members was based on the deeply felt belief that differences between people were artificial constructs of the classist and racist economic and cultural practices of the dominant culture. Madrid's counterculture resettlers embraced this imperative to break down these differences and treat everyone equally. From this imperative stemmed the reluctance to judge people or to limit the freedom of others to live in their community. This tolerance was a problem for many alternative communities during the late 1960s and 1970s, as I will discuss in chapter 5.

As the town prospered, real estate began to change hands among early residents, and the village's continued success attracted more people who shared the overall permissive attitudes of the original resettlers. Not all were outlaws. More typical was Ed, who trained in art in the eastern United States and who had been looking for a place to set up a studio after graduating from college. He had fallen in love with New Mexico in 1974, while still in school. He needed a place in the country to set up a wood-fired kiln, because they are smoky and can't be built in urban areas. While visiting a friend in Santa Fe, he saw an ad in the local paper, "$90 a month, Madrid." His friend said, "Oh, yeah, you should check it out. It's an old ghost town twenty miles south of here. Just a bunch of hippies and artists." So,

> I called him [the person in the ad] up and it was still available
> for rent. I came out—hitchhiked out here and saw this little town,
> ramshackle. It was starting to come to life. I thought: this is
> perfect. So I rented a shack on the back road. Tourists started
> coming up the back road to buy my work and [other residents
> complained about my having a business on the back road, which
> was in violation of the covenants]. So I pulled my Checker station
> wagon up to the highway, put the tailgate down and a sign,
> "Pottery for Sale" and started stopping traffic and selling
> pottery off the tailgate. This is 1979. (interview 1999)

Among the resettlers, Ed is considered to be the best example of an artisan who kept to the original ethic among the "new old-timers" in the village. He makes and sells his own high-quality art from a studio in the front part of his residence; he does not own other property in town; he does not exploit anyone else's labor, and he leaves other folks alone unless directly threatened himself.

Some pictorial views of contemporary Madrid will express the results of the villagers' hard work better than words. Figure 3.4 is a photograph of the Ducks' old residence as it looked in 2000. They sold it to the present owner for $50,000 in the 1980s; it was on the market for over $400,000 in the summer of 2000 but did not sell. During our interview, Sam showed me many photos of the interior work the Ducks did to this house, but while they owned it, the exterior remained untouched, similar to the residence in figure 3.3. Included in his photos are pictures of the French doors the Ducks constructed from the screens salvaged from the twenty-four televisions left by the repairman in the company stores. The Ducks were able to acquire several properties in the village, using their skills and their ability to exploit outside resources, and were, at one time, probably not only some of the most radical people in Madrid but also the wealthiest and most independent.

Figure 3.5 is a view off the main street in town and shows the renovations to some of the miners' shacks. The shacks were a mixture of the story-and-a-half style shown and a full two-story style. Gaps between

FIGURE 3.4. *The Ducks' former residence.*

FIGURE 3.5. *Restored miners' shacks along Opera House Road.*

houses resulted from fires and the recycling of less-complete houses to make whole residences.

The reconstruction of Madrid by folks using minimal resources and, in these early years, depending heavily on each other for help did help to create a sense of community that many remember as being part of the good times in the village. This frontier, pioneering era only lasted a few years, but is worth exploring further before moving on to the problems that success brought to the village.

A Fragile Sense of Community Emerges

The early resettlers had, or thought they had, a common vision of a community of anarchists that everyone else would leave alone, as August described above. Even in a community of individualists like Madrid, normalizing routines emerged, giving residents a common meeting ground. One of these was the village grocery store operated by a succession of local owners—the townsfolk would take advantage of each one and run up too much credit, putting each one in turn out of business—but while it was owned by any of the series of local people it was the place outside of the tavern where people met and socialized. Willie's memory of the store was:

> You'd run down to the store to get, right, to get eggs or a candy bar and maybe some bacon. And there'd be six people sitting there at four tables. And, "Hi," and you'd start talking to somebody, right. And then you'd grab a cup of coffee and before you know it, it's an hour later, you're back home with this bacon. And the wife says, "I'll go for the bacon next time." (interview 1999)

When the store was sold to people from outside the community, who "sanitized" it and stocked it with what they wanted—rather than what the town wanted—people drove to Santa Fe instead of using the local store. But in keeping with the contrary nature of Madrid, Willie remembers that even when owned by a popular local couple who had to start cutting people off from too much credit, "When they started cutting off credit, people started stealing and stuff." Willie also told of the time he discovered his son was stealing from the store. When he asked the owners why they never said anything about it or disciplined the boy, the owners replied, "We knew you'd make good on it" (interview 1999).

This reluctance to interfere or to set rules even when your own liveli-hood was at stake was a normative stance; unfortunately it usually meant that eventually individuals sought personal revenge, as we will see below. However, there were a few times when the townspeople took a more proac-tive approach to problem solving in order to protect their new communi-ty. Sam Duck recalled that twice during the early years of building the town the tavern became a trouble spot. Joe Huber kept the liquor license and the tavern property for many years after selling the town, and it had a series of managers who were mainly concerned with profits. Sam described the owners of the tavern as encouraging violence and drunkenness through their business practices. The Ducks took action:

> We [the Ducks] walked to the bar and we told the people running the bar that we want this bar closed. This is our town and we have families and kids, and we don't want it. And they were like, well—they didn't live there. So we petitioned and everybody [who] lived in town quit going to the bar and that was the end of their business. . . . Everyone participated, not just the Ducks.

In many ways, the bar remains both a major agent of socialization and source of irritation to many Madrid residents.

Figure 3.6 is a photograph of the bar today. The property and the liquor license were bought in the early to mid-1980s by folks who settled in Madrid; the husband moved on but his wife and her second husband own the tavern, the museum, and the Melodrama Theater.

I remember the bar from these years as a "biker" bar, a dangerous place to go unless you were looking for trouble. People would get drunk at the bar and then "go slumming" through Madrid, destroying property and taunting the hippies.

Such concerted action as the Ducks pulled off with the tavern was not easily repeated during these years, as when a series of fires consumed most of a row of still empty miners' shacks on a back road, and once again it took the leadership of one of the town's most charismatic characters to bring forth what sense of community existed. The town matriarch, a former pro-fessional lady who chose to raise her three children in Madrid, often played the role of the village's conscience, even when the villagers did not realize they had a common stake in what was taking place. The fires, a series of

FIGURE 3.6. *The Mine Shaft Tavern today. Note the*
       "Frontier" logo in the sign.

arsons combined with the stupidity of vagrants building fires on old wood
floors, were quickly eroding whatever sense of community existed at the
time in the village; everyone blamed his neighbor, fearing that his own house
would be next. Tia, the matriarch, went around to everybody in the village
and said, "This has got to stop! Be at the ballpark tonight at sunset."

> Tia was there and she says, "Everybody's got to hold hands,
> because you know what we are all thinking is that it's one of us."
> And everybody did hold hands. About twenty-five people, practi-
> cally the whole village. And they all held hands. . . . It was one of
> those moments which defined the community and in which they
> realized they had a community. (interview 1999)

The fires did stop shortly after Tia called this meeting. Yet this sense of con-
nectedness never went very far, even during these hard times of rebuilding
a town from scratch when nearly everyone was in the same situation.
Witness this response about community from Willie:

I [see the need] to not go too far with a relationship in the community, as a form of protection. In a larger community, you have
space enough to get away from people you don't want to associate
with, but in a small pool, you need this distance. . . . [Yet] At
some level, you need to have contact with the people you know
are thieves, so that you can develop a sense of trust. As surreal
as that sounds. So maybe you give them some food or something,
you never know what it is that puts you in a valued position.
Otherwise they will come back and retaliate. It's complicated by
those who don't know the rules, so to speak. (interview 1999)

Others have expressed to me much the same sentiment; for example, to protect themselves from the thievery of the drug addicts in the village one family provided them with free needles—a member of this family was a nurse
in Santa Fe (interview 1999). This is reminiscent of the shop owner's not disciplining the young shoplifter; rather than take action to eliminate a problem, or the people perpetrating the problem, the villagers tried instead to
limit the impact of such behavior on their own and their family's lives.

Another peculiar thing about Madrid in these early days of resettlement
was the number of people who never entertained inside their homes; people
maintained outdoor areas for parties, but seldom let others into their house
(interview 1999). Only the Ducks' house was open for everyone in the village. Was this caution due to fear of retaliation or fear that your neighbors
would see what you had and covet your possessions—or your drugs? These
questions foreshadow a series of themes to be discussed below concerning
the difficulties of curbing individual excesses in a counterculture community founded on, if not absolute freedom, then on the maximum individual freedom attainable.

Even outsiders from much more radical communes felt a peculiarity
about Madrid. The communards from Tawapa, one of the nearby communes, warned its members, "don't go into that town. Just for groceries
or something. It's a strange place" (interview 1999). This opinion was
expressed to me by a former member of the Tawapan commune, who did
settle in Madrid. The sense of community forged on the social frontier of
individual freedom was a very tenuous and fragile one, easily eroded by suspicion and fear of neighbors. Ironically, this situation did create what
August had expressed earlier, a community unto itself, that others—even

other counterculture people—would leave alone. But isolation could not shield the community from change.

Within a few short years, Madrid was no longer a ramshackle town of derelict shops and houses, and the relative population explosion had strained the minimal infrastructure left over from the coal camp days as well as the delicate and emerging social structure of the village. The way the resettlers resolved—or did not resolve—these needs has left a legacy for the contemporary management of the village. It is clear that the anarchistic, individualistically oriented ethic of the counterculture days has been a mixed blessing. I will discuss these issues as separate problems that came up as the village population grew, but in reality they overlapped and were often confounded with each other. Solutions had to be found for physical problems relating to water and sewer limitations, but underlying these issues was the ambivalence the community experienced every time it was faced with the consequences of upholding individual freedom and watching that freedom being abused. Drugs, violence, and when and how to draw the line on individual behavior were—and are—the most contentious internal issues for the villagers.

Growing Pains: Madrid's Wild West

The minimal social cohesion formed during the early years of reconstruction was put to serious tests as the village prospered. Water and fire were constant problems inherited from the coal camp days, but the new immigrants brought with them the cult of the individual, drug use and abuse, and a seeming paralysis when it came to the need to develop consensus and act communally. These latter issues will be discussed at length later; here I want to continue the historical accounts by the resettlers about what had to be done and how they approached tentative solutions.

Water, Sewer, and Fire

It is unusual to talk about the history of sewage in a sociology work, but the realities and the reactions of Madrid's new inhabitants to effluent are quite revealing of their individualistic approach to problem solving and their resentment of outside solutions to village needs.

When the mines were working, water had been brought in by rail car from Waldo. After the rails were finally pulled up, Huber's resident

manager would go to Cerrillos and "fill up a truck with water and he would
come here and he would back it up to the reservoir and dump it off the back
and he would drop a gallon of Clorox in it. That was the water system"
(interview 1999). Learning to cope with the lack of water (still a problem in
the village) was another adjustment for some. "In the winter we had a big
cast iron tub which we filled with water and put on top of the stove." By the
time dinner was done, the water would be hot. "It would be eight of us, taking turns. So if I was one, two, three, or four, I would use the water, but otherwise no" (interview 1998). In the early years of resettlement villagers
coped with the remnants of the coal-mining-era water system, consisting of
a reservoir and pipes that in the 1970s only supplied some of the buildings
on the main street. Over the years the pipes from the reservoir had been
blocked off as they developed leaks, so there was no logic or order to the
remaining piping. "If we sprung a leak in this main line [off the reservoir],
then the water would just disappear and we didn't always know where it
was going. . . . We repaired it with hose clamps and inner tubes. You didn't
replace the pipe" (interview 1999).

People made do with this system or they hauled water for domestic use
and gardens. But water was not the only problem for the resettlers. As a coal
camp, Madrid probably had at most three thousand inhabitants, and there
were remnants of septic systems for the shops and houses on Silk Stocking
Row, although no one knew (or knows today) where they all emptied. This
state of affairs became a serious problem as the village repopulated, as evidenced by the Ducks:

All the bathrooms for our house and across the street, too,
and the company stores met in a joint in the middle of the
driveway. And every summer there would be this problem
because they would back up and it would back up into our
basement. . . . So we told everyone we've got to do something
about this . . . and no one was dealing with it. . . . One day we
just dug it up—we were always having to dig it up to see where
it was clogged—and it was just open sewage, all the pipes were
rusted. So we took a big bag of cement and we mixed it up
and we poured it in there and then we covered it up. So then
everyone's sewer backed up. So at that point everyone had to
do something. (interview 1998)

As no one wanted to deal with the sewage, eventually the lack of water and sewer infrastructure caused an epidemic of hepatitis. For those suffering from hepatitis, these were rough times:

> There was a hepatitis epidemic. And that was major, major. There was a backflow of water the way things were connected. Kerry [her young daughter] and I both had it. All that summer I leaned against the wall and sold dresses and hoped I could keep myself standing. (interview 1999)

The hepatitis outbreak was so severe that the county intervened and insisted that the village have a community water system. The well and system were installed in 1980, but this imposition of rules, regulations, metering, and payment systems caused one of the early rifts in the community, because a community water system required the organization of a water cooperative association to deal with maintenance and management, and the resultant squabbling over rules and dealing with divergent personalities caused some of the Madrid Ducks to consider leaving. Sam felt if he had to put up with arguments over rules and egos, that he might as well go back to living in a city; he felt that this was the end of the first era of their Madrid experience. Before the co-op, "it was just people." Sam had not minded getting the water; what he objected to was paying for it and having it run by a bureaucracy (interview 1998). Madrid still does not have a community waste water system, and residents rely on holding tanks that must be pumped out frequently; the town is too densely developed even for regular septic systems with drain fields.

Some of the Ducks stayed in Madrid for another year or so, but the village's most communal family had pretty well disbanded within a few months after the water came to Madrid. Today, water is almost a daily issue of contention in the village, as it is tied to larger problems of growth and threats to lifestyle choices that growth will bring to the area. There is currently a moratorium on new water hook-ups (as there is in neighboring Cerrillos), and most people in the village still buy bottled water to drink because the third of three wells the county drilled produces water fouled by the coal deposits that underlie the town. Unfortunately for those who want to eliminate further growth in the village, the moratorium is not very effective; any property owner living in an unincorporated village can go to the state engineer's office and get a five-dollar permit to drill a private well, taking their chances with finding water.

The fact that new residents are thrown back on themselves for finding water is typical of the villagers' legacy of individualism. Later, we will meet virtually the only water commissioner Madrid has ever had; he is also currently the head of the volunteer fire department. Water and fire control are inseparable problems for Madrid; there are (as of this writing) no fire hydrants in town because of the low flow of the community well. There have been plans to put in a high-pressure fire line, but the old reservoir that would be used to pressurize the line cannot be filled because of continued problems with its piping (and some say with the commissioner).

Fire is a real threat to a community of wood-framed buildings set close together with little available water; last summer the village lost part of its old adobe schoolhouse to fire, and nearly one whole row of miners' shacks was lost to fire in the mid-1980s due to stupidity and vandalism, triggering Tia's intervention. The threat of losing the whole village to fire has mobilized the village to maintain a volunteer fire department, one of the few long-standing organizations in the village that is actually proactive in village and inter-village affairs. Funded largely through state and federal monies, it now has its own building that doubles as a meeting hall for village gatherings.

While these may seem trivial issues, the very real lack of water and the use of that reality to forestall change in the village is a common thread to many communities in the West. The villagers are divided over the use of water as a deterrent to growth, as many residents would like better water for their own use in homes and shops; we will see later the conflict over related amenities such as port-a-potties for the tourist industry. In the case of water and sewage, today's Madrid has inherited the physical limitations from the industrial period and the organizational limitations of the counterculture era. In the next set of conflicts, Madrid has only the legacy of the counterculture settlement with which to deal.

Drugs, Violence, and the Defense of Individualism at any Cost

DRUGS

Tolerance for lifestyles and drugs has always been a characteristic of Madrid. As an original resettler put it, "It's been a mixed bag all the time."

Madrid for this person represented "a mix of what was going on in the country at the time—the whole milieu. Earth Day and all that, the spirit of conservation. On the other hand, it was also 'let me blow whatever I want into my body.'" Madrid above all was a place people moved to because "there are things people do here [that] in other circumstances people just wouldn't tolerate. We tolerate a lot more of that here. That's part of what the town is all about" (interview 1998).

One interviewee characterized the beginning as "this community derives from needing a place to have some of this freedom [to do drugs]. And almost everyone in town was involved with drugs . . . everybody had a monkey of some sort or another." If it wasn't drugs, it was draft dodging or some other need to be in a place where you could search for yourself. This person also characterized the town as "a merciless community, in one sense, and it still is." He was referring to the fact tolerance is extended so far that individuals have been punished for attempting to prevent people from hurting themselves, especially with drugs. To give another example:

Now Madrid has always been the kind of place where . . .
we never say anything to anybody about [their choices] . . .
there are three things missing in this community which make
it a unique situation. There is no church, there's no police,
and there's no peer pressure. Because we have many times—
I say we as the members of the community—watched people
come in here totally together and that same day they're crawling
on their belly like a reptile and nobody would ever say, "Oh,
you know, you should take care of yourself." You would never
[say that.] If they said, "Give me a joint, give me a beer," we
would give it to them. You know. And, they would go further
down. (interview 1999)

The freedom to do drugs was coupled with the need to remain nonjudgmental, at whatever cost, yet this lack of judgment created a social atmosphere of self-reliant individualism that rivals that of the first frontier settlements in the West. It is a tolerance bordering on mercilessness, as the resident above expressed, but for the folks coming to Madrid during these first years of resettlement, the risk of social isolation was less than the cost of remaining in what to them was an oppressive mainstream society. The space created by "living free" was a refuge not only to outlaws but also to some relatively dysfunctional people, people who nevertheless found a home in the community. As explained by one resident:

> By the close of '81, there was a lot happening in this town. A lot
> of people. A good majority of the newcomers had children. . . .
> It was very interesting because there were these very dysfunctional
> people, trying to have this sense of normalcy. And, it worked.
> That was the beautiful thing about it, was, though everybody
> had something that they were secretly holding on to, no one ever
> asked. No one, like, no one knew that so-and-so smoked pot or
> did amphetamines, if you didn't do it, you didn't need to know.
> But yet we all met, you know, at a number of public events.
> We daily dealt with each others' children, and we would meet
> at the company store. . . . And so there was this beautiful sense
> of community coming about. (interview 1999)

This "beautiful sense of community" still lingers today in the village; the ability of Madrid to integrate seemingly seriously dysfunctional individuals into the normal flow of life is one of its strongest points. Yet here again is evidence of the isolation experienced as a member of the community. Drug subcultures, as I explore in detail later, separate and isolate individuals into small groups of users and nonusers. Even in a village as small as Madrid, with perhaps under one hundred people during these early years, those "who had no need to know" about others' drug habits generally did not know, and made it a point not to know.

August, for example, asked his two now-grown daughters if they had ever been exposed to drugs while growing up in the village, to which they replied, "Well, Dad, it *was* Madrid." August had not thought much about that while his children were growing up: "I knew that there was some other stuff going on. But all I ever saw was people smoking grass. . . . And I know that there were people that were on harder stuff, but that was sort of on the fringes and [I] didn't have anything to do with these people" (interview 1999).

But most people interviewed emphasized that while drugs have always been a part of the community, it was the tolerance, and not the drugs themselves, that was the crucial difference about living in Madrid. Drugs were "part of the community but it wasn't really what made the community what it is. It was just a part of life, the way it is in America. People overplay the importance of drugs" (interview 1999).

It *is* easy to overplay the role of the drug culture in Madrid; nonetheless, drugs were part of the underground economies upon which many of the residents of Madrid depended for at least part of their living. Some of the rough frontier element to these early years derived from the intersection of an outlaw culture with the emergent American drug culture. Understanding the roots of Madrid's tolerance toward people's behaviors includes looking at the culture of violence that was almost guaranteed by the lack of social control mechanisms and the drug culture that the resettlers brought with them to Madrid.

VIOLENCE

The Wild West nature of the early resettlement years was explained by Ed: "[T]wenty years ago there were outlaws hiding out here, basically, I mean, really, outlaws. People on the land ...everybody had firearms." Even today, Ed is adamant in letting people know that anybody breaking into his studio will be facing a firearm, and that there will be no second chance. He does not share the tolerance toward drug abusers who are known to rip off other locals in order to feed their habits. Another resettler stated that "[t]here was a time in the early years that, you know, you came in [to town] with at least a knife. Because you never knew when somebody was going to jump you" (interviews 1999, 2000).

Others view the drugs and the violence as just part of the village, and avoidable as long as you stayed away from the bar. Jessie felt that "[t]here used to be just so many outlaws in this town, and usually the outlaws fought with other outlaws, outlaws ripped off outlaws, outlaws took care of outlaws. So, the rest of us just went about our lives. I never felt threatened. I knew all those people. [I'd] Say 'Hi!' or whatever [to them]. . . . The only difference now is that people call the police."

Violence has become part of the village legend, forming one basis for defining what living in Madrid meant to the "new old-timers." These stories add credence to the founding mythologies and serve to separate those who experienced these times from later arrivees who are perceived, by some, to be living off the hard work of the former group. Violent episodes occurred between Madrid and neighboring Cerrillos, but I want to concentrate on the stories of internal strife within Madrid, as these incidents illustrate the complex nature of life in the village, foreshadow the difficulties of maintaining order without passing judgment, and illuminate the beginnings of the rifts that today divide Madrid's population.

Among the interviewees who lived in Madrid during these early years, everyone remembers the trouble with a particular Vietnam vet, who drank continually and often drove through town too fast while shooting a gun at random. August described him as "a rough and ready character, I tell you." He lived in an old school bus or trailer right on the main street. He had two pre-teenage boys. The young mothers who lived on the main street worried about his crashing his truck into one of their houses or killing someone with a stray bullet. One night he and his lady got drunk and as usual he became abusive. She stabbed him to death, then set the trailer on fire while the boys huddled beneath the trailer. August thinks it is the first fire the volunteer fire department put out. Sam Duck remembers that afterward they took in one of the boys, giving him a pet chicken to care for as solace. Both boys finished growing up in town, but have been in and out of prison as adults. No one in the village blamed the woman for the killing; she returned to Madrid after some time in a mental hospital, and today is still a protected member of the community. Other folks have acted in their own defense but usually with less drastic consequences.

Most of the community's residents relied on themselves to take care of problems; calling on outside authorities such as the sheriff or state police was a rare event. This reliance on individualism could easily devolve into personal revenge and vendetta, and this, too, has left its mark on today's Madrid. Back in the early resettlement period, Rhonda recalled a time when she was collecting rents from some of the houses for out-of-town owners and had given one family an eviction notice for overdue rent:

> This pissed [him] off and he came and shot out my sign at
> the front of my shop. And he went up and down driving
> crazy—he was drunk or high or both—and he then tried
> to drive home when someone else shot out the tire on his truck.
> The next day I confronted him about the sign and I told him
> that I was only sorry they got only one tire. "You can't do
> that in town," I told him. "If you do, if you ever bother
> me again, I'll hunt you down." Well, he never bothered
> me again.

Rhonda's condoning the shooting is typical of the street justice meted out during this time period, and face-to-face stand-downs between antagonists were common when tolerance failed. Rhonda witnessed another piece of street justice involving the town matriarch, Tia.

Tia and her children were living in a teepee on one of the vacant lots on the main street at the time. As Rhonda recounted,

> [a]nyway, one day Johnny [a biker outlaw living in town
> at the time] asked Tia to watch his dog, Ruby Redhound.
> Tina was living in a teepee with her son, Morgan. . . . So this
> [other] kid comes over to the teepee looking for Morgan,
> who is not there and the dog comes out and scares him—
> he claims he's been bitten, attacked, etc. So somebody calls
> the pound and the sheriff and they all come. Then Tia shows
> up. The [parents of the child] are going on about how dare
> this dog attack this boy. So Tia gets down on her hands and
> knees and bites one of the [parents]. She gets up, confronts
> him, and says, "You thought you had trouble before, now
> you've really got trouble!" And they just kind of faded away
> and never mentioned anything again. (interview 1999)

Tia still has a reputation for unique solutions to the town's problems, such as the time she organized a group of women in town who were tired of being abused by the same man. They went to his house, gathered up all his belongs, stuffing them into a car. Then they found him, stuffed him in next to his few possessions, and drove over to the expressway, where they dumped him and his stuff along the road. He never came back (interview 1998).

Personal retaliation, generally, was the preferred method for dealing with non-normative behaviors in interpersonal relations. Willie put it this way, while describing another time when the authorities were called about someone's dogs:

> I just couldn't believe that they turned him in. It's really odd
> because even myself I've been a victim of crime. I have to drive
> by them [the thieves] every day but I don't ever go that far. . . .
> [But speaking of others] in some cases you take matters into

your own hands. Whether it's physical encounters, stabbings,
shootings—we've had them all here. And they are the result
of trying to retaliate for something that was happening. These
things are not random acts. I remember someone strapped to
a chair in the desert, dead as could be. (interview 1999)

The fact that most people "don't ever go that far" in dealing with theft and
intimidation is partly due to the fear that people still express toward speaking out or taking action against those few people who are violent. Petty theft
and property crimes were dealt with through maintaining relations with the
known perpetrators, by simply taking your own possessions back, or by
retaliating in kind. Serious retaliations involving murder or disappearance
usually revolved around drug deals gone sour, but revenge, bitter relations,
and feuds are as common today as they were twenty years ago. The experiences early resettlers had in dealing with each other and with the outside
world set a pattern for village politics and social relations that still adheres
in Madrid today. A society of anarchists, free thinkers, and illicit drug users
is a strange mix of individuals out of which to form a community.

Individualism at Any Cost

August expressed the dedication of the resettlers to individualism this way:

Even now, you still have a lot of the people—they may be bugged
by what their neighbors do, but they don't want to have to deal
with it—if I could just live my life the way I want to live my life, I
will be happy to let you do that. Except if you keep doing that, all
of a sudden you realize that the way you want to live your life is
no longer an option to you, because everyone else has done something else and it's impinged upon what you see as the ambiance of
your life. We all thought it was going to happen in, well, maybe
ten years. So in some senses it took a lot longer than anybody ever
thought. (interview 1999)

Nearly everyone from this era in Madrid's resettlement history felt similarly and grappled consciously with the inherent contradiction of too much
freedom. While there was ample recognition of the dilemmas of individualism, the villagers created neither institutional nor communal structures to

deal with conflicting egos, leaving individuals to ignore conflict until it boiled over into personal confrontation if not outright violence.

Even the Madrid Ducks experienced some excesses of individualism among their members. For the Ducks to consider something excessive it had to be indeed bizarre. Sam Duck recalled the behaviors of one of their group:

> DeDe was kind of pushy. She roller skated through town all the time and wore wedding dresses all the time. She walked around town naked, and this was after there were lots of people in town. And she lived next door to Frank Ochoa [Huber's resident manager]. . . . Then she'd wear these sheer things you could see through. Frank built these huge fences [around his place] and she was offended—[she said,] I'm going to tear this fence down. This was one of those things that kind of [hurt the community.] When we walked around naked, we built a fence around our house. Once there were that many people you couldn't. (interview 1998)

This quote shows why, in many ways, the Ducks represented the best and the worst of Madrid's early resettlers. The Ducks were able to realize that other people's sensitivities needed to be respected for the community to work, but could not bring themselves to truly discipline their own members. As a counterculture family, they carried out some of the most radical experiments in alternative living in the village, taking in many of the seriously walking wounded in the village, giving them a place to stay, food to eat, and, ironically, help in kicking various drug addictions if that were needed. Perhaps this was because, as a communal family, they had considerable resources to share with others, whereas so many other resettlers lived in more typical nuclear families or alone. The Ducks realized that the conflicts over individualism had threatened the harmony of their first years in the village, yet rather than find ways to ameliorate the conflict, one by one they left the community and resumed lives in the mainstream economy.

One last story from these days illustrates some of the difficulties faced by the folks who wanted to be tolerant of aberrant behavior and who were reluctant to intervene even when the need seemed clear. This incident involved a woman who had been living with her husband and young child "out on the land." Living off of a remote and difficult road south of Madrid, she had begun to display erratic and dangerous behaviors; she would take

the child and sleep along the side of the highway or break into people's houses in town to take showers. Yet her behavior was not ostracized until one
day when she chose the wrong house to break into; the owner of the house
did not abide by the rules of taking care of local problems personally;
instead she called the police. As Sam Duck recalled the incident,

> she had Pat arrested for breaking into her house to take a shower.
> That was the straw that broke the camel's back. It had never hap-
> pened before. She had called the police because Pat wouldn't leave
> her house. The police came out and that's when they found all our
> marijuana growing in the back yard over the fence. So they came
> to the door and asked us to look in the back yard. We said, "Do
> you have a warrant?" They said, "No, we don't." So we said they
> couldn't look in our back yard. So they drove to Santa Fe to get a
> warrant and we pulled all our pot plants up and they came back
> and there was nothing there. It was a little early but they were
> good healthy plants. (field notes 1999; interview 1998)

Pat was later killed in an auto accident and her husband was so traumatized
that the village took over raising the child. This incident also highlights another problem for this counterculture community; they were, for the most part,
required to solve their own problems through whatever means available
because few in town were innocent in the eyes of the law. As Willie had
observed, nearly everyone in Madrid had some kind of a monkey on their back.

    Cynics point out that this lack of innocence undermines the authentic-
ity of upholding individual liberty, that the hippie movement was an excuse
for unbridled drug use, hedonism, and living on the welfare rolls. I believe
that there were still some principled stands taken by these counterculture
groups, positions toward social and ecological relationships based on creative and sustainable lifestyles rather than the exploitative and destructive ones of the dominant society. The willingness to accommodate those
who were clearly deviant—whether outlaws or burned-out drug abusers—
is evidence of this tolerance, as is their collective concern with the village's
children. That this accommodation to deviance undermined the good
intentions of many counterculture groups, including those in Madrid, does
not detract from the value of natural experiments in alternative community structure.

The Frontier Legacy Continues

The commitment to alternative ways of living and working and the search for authenticity in relationships created a loosely tied community in which the defense of individual liberty usually outweighed the need for communal sanctions against excessive individualism. The founding experiences of these early years of reconstruction set the cultural norms for new immigrants down to the present day. The resettlers left behind the exploitation of competitive economics but also abandoned controls over the excesses of absolute individual freedom. The resultant dependence on individual persuasion, retribution, and occasional violence when tolerance failed has continued to be the norm for social relations in the community.

As the houses and shops were fixed up and the town came back to life, it became an attractive location for those who had more in mind than just living an alternative lifestyle. The outlaws moved on to less populated areas or died of natural or unnatural causes, and the village assumed a less overtly violent ambiance. Both legitimate and underground businesses flourished at a level beyond mere subsistence, encouraging even more entrepreneurs to try the village as a place for economic success. Money could now be invested in real estate with some expectation that reasonable returns would be achieved, and the community gradually inched toward less radical social relations. Yet it retained its tolerance and openness as well as the collective inability to resolve the inevitable conflicts arising from growth. Those moving to Madrid after the early phases of resettlement found they had to fit in with this culture of individualism and frontier-style self-reliance if they were to prosper, for those relationships had become the norm.

Later Arrivees and the
Normalization of Individualism

The Transition Period

In keeping with letting the residents of Madrid tell their own stories, I will introduce this transition period as seen through the experiences of some long-term residents of Madrid. Some date this transition from a hippie refuge to a commercial venture to around 1982, some as late as the mid-1980s. It was certainly gradual, whatever time period is chosen to represent this transition, and the changes involved the growing attraction of Madrid as a tourist destination. These changes were laid over the culture of individualism remaining from the founding years of the village.

One of the problems the resettlers encountered was having little to hold their youngsters in the town once they grew up; there were basically two choices, the underground drug subculture or tourism. Tully estimated that most of the thirty to forty kids who were born to the first generation of immigrants have left town. Even the adult population has decreased, in his perception, from about 320 to about 200. Part of the decrease is lack of economic opportunity. What legitimate opportunities existed came to revolve mostly around tourism, and this threatened the original free-spirited, unrestrained lifestyle choices of the earlier resettlers. Sam Duck recalled this change:

> There was really a sort of anti-tourism thing there for
> years. . . . And they would mock the residents. . . . It's perverse
> the way the tourists took over. They're there every day and
> night. . . . I always thought was a good thing in that people
> were coming to spend money as long as they left. I don't mind
> giving up my Saturdays in the afternoons. . . . But when it
> became a gross and capitalist economy, all those needs which
> had to happen everyday—to survive on a grand scale. I just
> thought it was time to move on.

But a more critical view is given by Tullie, who also witnessed all these changes; he still lives and works in the skilled building trades in the village:

> There is a little bit of economic opportunity here [now]. Tourism.
> I don't think [people in town are against it]. Even the ones who
> proclaim that they are against it hang out here all day so they
> can watch tourists. They don't hang out in the middle of Cerrillos,
> do they? So that is more of a matter of them being hypocrites
> than that they are against tourism.

The tourist industry brought a different kind of migrant to Madrid; this change was well-expressed by August, who also still lives in the village:

> People who are coming more recently, they do come with the

sense of, well, this may be a great place—now it's more it's a
great place to have a business, rather than it's a great place to
live. . . . the balance that has occurred over the last ten years
or so [is] where a majority of the businesses that are operating
in town, but people do not live in town.

Others express more opposition to this change from living place to
working place. Ishmael claims that the town is "too commercial. . . . That's
all anybody has ever done in this town is take, take, take and never give anything back." An original resettler, he works for one of the newer merchants
in town, and feels that "the main reason the people I work for here, they are
here just to make money. They don't do anything for the town."

Sam Duck, as documented earlier, rebelled against the bureaucratic
regulations the water co-op brought to the village, but also deeply resented this changing dynamic of property ownership. "The old people don't
like what's going on with . . . all those guys with all that real estate mumbo
jumbo. . . . " And it isn't just those who left the village who resent the intru-
sion of market forces in the real estate business. August summed up many
people's feelings this way, "One of the things that's happened, of course, is
that as properties have been sold . . . a lot of people came, had great expectations, weren't able to realize them, . . . and left. So they always made a little profit on their property." After a while, those individual decisions have
meant that "as those turnovers have gone on, now you have places on the
main street with asking prices of three hundred thousand dollars. It's totally absurd."

This inflation in the prices of properties resettlers bought for as little
as $500 translates into some houses in town selling for upwards of
$250,000 in the real estate market of 2000. August, typical of many I have
spoken with and interviewed, expressed his understanding of the market
this way:

> Harris [a broker who lives in a side valley next to Madrid]
> makes his living buying and selling real estate. His income
> derives from the movement of property from one owner to
> another. He doesn't care, and he doesn't even care if it is a
> successful change of owner, because if it turns over again,
> in a year or two, he does it again.

August, and many other long-time residents, resent Harris, who owns a real estate brokerage firm in the village, arranges many of the sales of local property to outside investors, and is perceived to be accelerating the pace of change in the town, since he personally benefits from such transactions.

This change in patterns of ownership and property relations is contrary, of course, to the original culture of Madrid's resettlers, and from this conflict stems the belief among the more adamant adherents of the counterculture ethic that the newcomers are exploiting the hard work and privations suffered by those who rebuilt the town, and, not only that, but the newer people don't give anything back to the community. This is an ironic stand, of course, because it could be argued that the lack of social structure in town was a result of the original resettlers "not giving back" enough also. Nor is this the only irony to development; some of the original resettlers have themselves profited immensely from the growth in real estate values and the tourist industry, as Willie put it:

> And as I later was quoted on a TV interview that I felt Madrid
> would even be a very nice residential community or an artsy type
> of artists colony. And that I thought my financial investment
> would be strong either way. [And] There's not too many places in
> the country that have had the jumps in real estate values [that
> Madrid has had.]

August also remembers that the resettlers had an "original concept of the town, after it was sold and we were all thinking: In another ten years this is going to be an artist colony. Somewhere along the lines of an early Taos." But he recognized the split that grew in the community when the artists and shopkeepers were successful, a fault line dividing the business interests in the community from some older residents. August put it this way: "And if you are coming into the community and you want to have a business in the community, then really you want to put your advertising out there." What this means, of course, is that "You want to draw the people to your store and the main interest of the business part of the community is that there be flocks and flocks of people." Resettlers like August feel that they established the village as an artist colony of sorts, making do with weekend tourism or flea market sales. They now perceive that their homes and studios are being taken over by newer arrivees who have taken that reputation and exploited it for personal profit, without becoming part of the village life. Now there are tourists clogging the road through town nearly every day of the year, with the seasonal surges of summer and Christmas making driving through town a chore. Resettlers like Willie, on the other hand, run highly profitable tourist-oriented businesses.

The business people that bring tourists to Madrid today are different in several ways from the first counterculture entrepreneurs. Newer arrivees are usually older than most of the resettlers were when they first migrated here; they have often had successful businesses or jobs elsewhere before relocating, and, importantly, they belong to more than one generational cohort and ascribe to more than one set of ideologies. Not all of the later arrivees come for the business opportunity; some come to live and raise families, as had the earlier groups. Yet to stay in the community and become part of it, they all find the founding culture of defiant and rebellious individualism remains a salient force in Madrid.

Madrid Today

I wanted to see what happens when I was in a free space.
(interview 1999)

The later arrivees exhibit a wide range of reasons for moving to Madrid, and the kind of energy and tolerance evident from just visiting the village as a tourist draws some newcomers to the town. Typical of these newer migrants is Rebecca, a young woman in her mid-thirties who had been a social worker in Chicago when she got the message to "Go to the sun" and decided the message must mean the West.

She found Madrid cute, but "kind of a hard place to get off the main street . . . and into the life that's going on here." Walking into one of the shops, she asked, "What's going on here?" and she was told that "if you want to get here you can, but not through me. But hopefully someone else will help you out with that." So seven years ago she came back to stay because "I think it [Madrid] has a certain energy about it and I think it has different energies so that a lot is available to you whatever you're looking for you can find it here." She and her husband (whom she met in Madrid) live in one of the outlying "suburbs" south of Madrid. He works in the building trades and she does healing, ministering (she is an ordained minister in an alternative free-form church), and occasionally working in the village when a shop owner needs help for a day. She is also active in the Little League and volunteers with the health clinic in Cerrillos.

Another couple in their mid-thirties, George and Melissa, live in the same residential area as Rebecca, and when their car isn't working (which is quite often) they ride their bicycles the three miles into Madrid, where they work for various shop owners. George describes where they live as "unique." It is an area where everyone is on solar power, and there are no utilities, underground or otherwise, and people are proud of their self-reliance. As George expressed it, "Everybody is solar, committed to solar. Self-reliant, there'll never be any poles or anything like that. If somebody ever did that there would be a chain saw party. We can't even—I mean there's been several county [street] signs . . . but the signs don't last two hours. They'll just pull them out of the ground. . . . Underground phone lines are OK." His wife, Melissa, says "We like that. . . . Being off the grid, not having to pay someone every month. Everything you need is basically free." George left his high-paying government job to "live off the land" on forty acres with no real structure, just a dugout in the hillside. When I interviewed them, they were excited about getting a floor in their house after five or six years of not having one. Melissa had kept her job in Albuquerque for the first few years after they moved out on the land, in order to finish paying for their lot.

These kinds of new migrants recall the earlier resettlers who came to Madrid to create a free space of authentic, nonexploitative relationships. These newer amenity seekers survive using a combination of paid work and manipulation of government programs, as had the resettlers. For these folks, the defiant individualism and the freedoms of the counterculture movement are what draw them to Madrid. The idea "that everything you need is free," and "that you can find what you're looking for" is a reflection of the material excesses that the original counterculture simultaneously used and abhorred.

Others move to Madrid hoping to do more than survive; they come to run successful businesses. The resettlers' impression that these newcomers have a different worldview is not without substance, as this gallery owner typifies. Jackson has run a successful gallery featuring local artisans for about ten years in Madrid after moving here from Pennsylvania, where he had been involved with grant writing and business ventures unrelated to art. He rents his shop because, as he explained, you can do well in town if you are lucky enough to be renting a place from someone who has been in

Madrid for a long time and the rents are inexpensive. His shop has no water or restroom, although there is a spigot in the front yard. Typical of many shops in the village, he and several other shopkeepers share the use and the cost of one of the port-a-potties that are available for the tourists. He felt that the folks who get in trouble financially either buy at too high a price or rent at too high a rate and then can't generate enough income to make a go of it. He has been very pleased with his business in the village, part of which comes from tourism, part from informal networks of friends and professionals with whom he maintains connections, and part through the Internet. Jackson, however, has never lived directly in town, preferring places like Golden, ten miles to the south. He participates in the Christmas lighting displays, but that is the extent of his communalism as he usually does not spend time or energy on community issues.

Another new shop owner represents an alternative position taken by some of the later arrivees to Madrid. Bernice would like to participate in village affairs but has been discouraged by the distance people keep from each other. Bernice's experiences with this are interesting because they reflect the intersection of the old uninhibited freedom with the new commercial success of the town.

Bernice retired three years ago after thirty-seven years in the computer industry in California and was looking for a place to live and open a small craft shop. As she said, "I looked in Nevada, Colorado Springs, Texas." Here in New Mexico "I looked in Old Town in Albuquerque. I looked in Corrales, I looked in Cerrillos, I looked in Santa Fe, and this was the only place I could afford to buy. It's off the road." She is concerned that, as a newcomer, established merchants did not warn her of the local troublemakers, so she had no warning of who to watch out for in town. Unfortunately, at the time she moved in, a small group of village residents were engaging in erratic drug-related behavior, intimidating everyone and even beating up one of the long-time merchants. When she confronted one of the established merchants about these people and why she wasn't warned, she was told, "All you had to do was ask." The "live-and-let-live" attitude was a real put-off for this new shopkeeper, whose reaction to this was, "Pretty soon I might get a gun and learn how to use it." Complaints that new merchants are unwilling to participate in the village need to be tempered by the understanding that the individualistic ethic of the town discourages both newer and older residents from participating in cooperative association with each other.

For old and new settlers, the village presents challenges, many of them stemming from the founding ideologies of maximum personal freedom. Individuality remains the hallmark of the village, in spite of all the material changes in the town. Echoing the ideals of the original resettlers, Bernice told me that "People come to Madrid because they can do whatever they want and they can be whoever they want to be. They can be individualists here." Furthermore, "But it doesn't matter to me [what other people do], just don't lay it on me. I don't do drugs, so don't lay your drugs on me. I don't care, you can do them, it doesn't matter, you know, if that's the way you want to run your life, that's fine." But later in the interview, she remarked, "If I had known what the town was like—as far as people—I probably never would have bought here." Her realtor and a girlfriend had led her to believe that Madrid was just "a lot of older people, old timers, it was just a funky town." She was not prepared for the reproduction of the hippies and their freedoms in the younger generation, the "baby hippies," who carry on the older generation's traditions of drugs and violence.

For this and other residents, the contradictions inherited from the first days of resettlement are not just annoyances, they threaten the ability of the village to keep new businesses in the town. Yet the shop owners provide what legitimate work can be found in town for the unskilled and those walking wounded to whom Madrid provides a home. Even with the influx of new shops, economic survival remains both variable and uncertain, with flexibility, resourcefulness, and self-reliance requisite traits for getting along. Jessie expressed the employment situation typical for many in the village: "I only work there [at one of the village shops], I think three days a week, two days a week. I might be going down to one day a week because Ralph needs a job . . . and I will probably just let Ralph have the hours until he doesn't want to do it. . . . I have other jobs, it's just one of them." Jessie can afford to give away some hours to those more in need, and, reflective of the earlier communal ethic, willingly helps someone temporarily in need of a small income. The ability of some residents to have such a laid-back attitude toward money is partly due to the increasing values of real estate and the success of the tourist industry; but it is also a result of most community members making do with less, and generally not sharing in the consumption patterns of the dominant culture.

This has been the other hallmark of the village since its resettlement: the ability to live lightly off the land and use a minimal amount of nonrenewable resources. Part of this simplicity is due to poverty, but a goodly part is due to

FIGURE 3.7. *A new house built for profit, behind and across the arroyo from one of the derelict miners' shacks. Although none of these speculative houses have sold, they are rented out.*

the ethic of conservation and dedication to create a more socially and ecologically just culture. In spite of all the contradictions inherent in Madrid's founding ideologies and the difficulties with uninhibited individualism, this is also part of what makes Madrid a different place to be in. This subsistence living and the individualism that both encourages and results from it are now being challenged by a new force of migration: the newly rich and retired or semi-retired who are rediscovering the Wild West as a place to call home. These folks have not descended into Madrid yet, but the incremental growth from their ranchettes, mostly in the hills to the north and east of Madrid, is bringing million-dollar mansions and private hotels, bed-and-breakfasts, and other resort destinations that threaten the isolation of the village with encroaching gentrification, as has happened in many places in the West. Even in Madrid some housing has been built for speculation on the real estate market; they violate the covenants for buildings in the village, and the structures violate the old ethic of "use what you need and leave the rest." Figure 3.7 is a photograph of one of these houses.

FIGURE 3.8. *The north elevation of the Old Boarding House.*

The appearance of new structures, not the rehabilitated leftovers from the mining town, is a sure sign that the distant location that made Madrid as a marginal space attractive to counterculture people is no longer a protective barrier to outsiders who do not share the resettlers' commitment to maximum personal freedom, minimal social constraint, and the responsible use of resources.

Other photographs describe the ambiance created over twenty-five years of hard work in the village and the creative attempts at maintaining the mining town history. The building in figure 3.8 is the Old Boarding House, at one time owned by the Madrid Ducks. It currently houses a supermarket for groceries and supplies, video rentals, and one of the two public telephones in town. The owner and his wife, who bought it when it looked more like the miner's shack in figure 3.5, restored it and now live upstairs.

The lower floor of the boarding house is occupied by the Madrid Super Mart. During the mining days, it housed unmarried miners, as only married men qualified for a single-family residence. Architectural critic and historian Vincent Scully considers this building to be the best example of the stick-and-shingle-style architecture in the western United States (Kaufmann

FIGURE 3.9. *"Woofy Bubbles," a successful artisan's shop*
since the mid-1980s.

1970). Other buildings in town maintain the historic character of the mining era but also show the individualism of their current owners. Figure 3.9
is a photograph is one of the successful shops in the village, whose owner-
craftsman has been in town since the mid-1980s.

The third photograph is of the coffee shop (figure 3.10), a popular
gathering place for the locals before the tourists inundate the village after
about ten in the morning. At the time of writing, there are only three public places where the locals still spend much time: the tavern, the coffee shop,
and the general store.

These three pictures show the variety of facades, shapes, and sizes of
the shops along Madrid's main street. What still photos cannot capture,
unfortunately, is the dynamic nature of the street facade. These pictures were
shot in the summer and fall of 2000; the streetscape has undergone several
changes between then and this writing in the spring of 2002, although no
new shops have been built; the artisans and merchants must recycle the
resources already available in the town.

FIGURE 3.10. *The coffee shop, a popular meeting place. State Highway 14 is in the foreground, showing how close the stores and residences are to the only road through town.*

The flavor of Madrid today is a mix of colorful shops and people who have preserved parts of America's industrial past as well as part of its revolt against that past. Threatened by growth from both the north and the south, its peculiarities, strengths, and weaknesses are largely those the resettlers brought with them when they rediscovered the old ghost town, and reflect the contradictions of the counterculture of which they were a part. Today, the physical survival of Madrid is no longer a question; it has long since become a stable place to live and a reasonable place to earn a living if one lives simply and can tolerate the lack of social institutions. But the village also reflects the changes occurring throughout the West, as population migrations continue to consume former ranch and open land, threatening the villagers' resistance to the dominant culture. Some of these problems are depicted in the 2000 U.S. Census, the first census to show Madrid as a community separate from rural census tracts of Santa Fe County.

The Demographics Tell Their Own Story of Madrid

The 2000 U.S. Census reveals just how deep a mark the counterculture resettlers have left on the contemporary community of Madrid. We must be highly critical, however, before accepting the validity of the census figures for three reasons: (1) this is a group of people as likely to show a census-taker the front end of a shotgun as to grant an interview; (2) many folks live in households without addresses; (3) the census is most representative of those living within the historic boundaries of the village (newly established, as recounted above), and probably does not represent accurately the number of younger people and their children who live "out on the land" while still being marginally part of Madrid (interviews 1998–2001). Nevertheless, the picture that emerges from the census is one of a community predominantly of older men who live in smaller than average households and who are slightly more likely to rent than to own their domiciles. This information closely matches my interview data and reflects the material in my field notes. Also interesting is the predominance of men, at an age in our generational cohort when women start beginning to outnumber men.

In the United States, those between the ages of forty-five and fifty-nine (the age groups inclusive of the counterculture movement population) represent 18.2 percent of the total population; in Santa Fe County this age group represents 23.1 percent of the population (representing its attraction for retirees); but for Madrid this group represents 34.9 percent of the village, nearly twice the national figure. The percentage of men in Madrid is 52.3 percent, while the county's male population is at 48.9 percent, and the United States's is at 49.1 percent.

Another difference is in household composition. The U.S. population has 68.1 percent of its members living in family households, the county of Santa Fe 62.5 percent, while Madrid manages only 34.1 percent, half of the national percentage. Married households in the overall American population represent 51.7 percent of all households, in Santa Fe County 45.5 percent, and in Madrid only 20.1 percent. Female-headed households represent a smaller percentage in Madrid than in the other areas: Madrid at 11 percent; the county at 11.7 percent; and the United States at 12.2 percent. The low level of household formation may well represent the number of men in the village and surrounding areas who are both older and who can barely support themselves, much less a family.

Household size is smaller than the national average at 2.0 for Madrid homeowners compared to 2.69 for Americans as a whole. For renters, Madrid's average household size is 1.5 compared to 2.4 for the rest of the country. Slightly fewer people own homes in Madrid than in the county of Santa Fe, Madrid's ownership rate being 63.4 percent while the county's rate is 68.6 percent. Americans as a whole have a 66.2 percent rate of home ownership. In Madrid, 20.4 percent of its housing stock is vacant, while the county has a vacancy rate of only 9 percent, matching the U.S. rate (U.S. Census 2000 Quick Facts).

These figures match the interview data fairly well; my concentration was on those of the counterculture generation who have hung on in Madrid and made the village their home. It is an aging population, with the younger shopkeepers living elsewhere and commuting to work or hiring others to keep their shops open. And even these part-time workers increasingly live outside the village and commute. Younger people starting families prefer the outlying areas for three reasons that appear in my field notes: (1) the cost of renting or buying in town is too high; (2) the old romance of the benefits of living "out on the land" and being self-sufficient and free of social fetters no longer exists in the town; (3) and the continuance of the drug culture that dictates the need for space to practice lifestyles too risky for congested areas.

So while the census figures may be skewed toward the older people, they are not totally unrepresentative of the social life of the village. In addition to the threat of inundation from development, Madrid may simply age out of existence as a counterculture community. In the next chapters I explore the social relations of today's Madrid and the concept of the cult of the individual that so informs this village. Part frontier ideology, part drug-culture imperative, and part New Age philosophy, individualism is the dominant leitmotif of Madrid, and any study of this village would be incomplete without a deeper exploration of its genesis, its meaning to the current inhabitants of Madrid, and its implications for the future of Madrid and other communities. This future is tied to the extra-local economic and political forces of multinational capitalism that, once again, have placed decision making beyond the control of local populations, whether those populations are organized to resist such change or not.

CHAPTER FOUR

Social Relations
The Intricate Social and Political Fabric of Madrid

*I really believe that if it wasn't for places like Madrid scattered
all over the country, every jail and every insane asylum
in the country would be full. If the country tried to close
all these small towns, then all these anarchists would
be running around looking for trouble.
Then the country would really be in a mess.*

—interview 2000

The quote above from a long-time resident of Madrid reflects the continued
legacy of the counterculture resettlers. The strands from which this community is woven reflect all the themes of this rebellious era. Individualism,
self-reliance, tolerance and acceptance, and egalitarianism were all part of the
subculture's beliefs. As Peter Coyote wrote in his memoir, it was not the failure of these beliefs that undermined the goals of the movement but rather
the lack of restraint in practicing these beliefs. Without any means of controlling excessive individual behaviors, the result was often anarchy. The nearly
total inability of many counterculture groups to create mechanisms of consensus that encompassed more than individual hedonism severely limited their
ability to act in concert for the common good. The counterculture's deep belief
that individuals freed from the constraints of exploitative capitalistic relationships would automatically create ecologically sustainable and socially just
communities proved to be an impossible ideal.

In small communities like Madrid, however, the experiments in alternative lifestyles continue in varying degrees. In spite of Madrid's anarchistic legacy and that legacy's continued importance as a cultural motif, the village has
grown, continues to attract new people—some radical, some not—and provides a viable place to live and work within some unique limitations. Lifestyles

revolve around making do with what is available, and material possessions are generally simple. Justice is still carried out largely by individual, not social, action; the town remains unincorporated and dependent on the government of the county rather than on locally elected leaders; and no one would ever mistake the village for a middle-class bedroom suburb of Santa Fe.

But the village is not entirely anarchistic; there are a minimum of status designations that layer the villagers into somewhat predictable patterns, and there are formal and informal organizations that provide outlets for those who do wish to have more steady forms of interaction with others in the community. Some of these organizations, such as the volunteer fire department, both link Madrid to the outside world and demand some conformity to it. Most of the influence of these organizations is diffuse, as few of the villagers belong to them, and, because Madrid is an unincorporated village, political power is not held locally. No original resettler from the village has ever run for public office that I know of, in keeping with the local culture's distaste for higher authority. This chapter will look at these forms of structure and organization, such as they are, and will examine how the Wild West and counterculture legacies interact with the needs of residents to protect the unique culture of Madrid.

The Diffuse Nature of Class, Status, and Power in Madrid

Social Class

Madrid is a most interesting place to look for social class distinctions because there appear not to be any at first glance. There are no wide differences in apparent lifestyle choices: clothing, vehicles, and housing are similar for most of the inhabitants—funky, utilitarian, and recycled would be apt descriptions. Merchants, gallery clerks, artists, and local residents all look similar, although they do not look anything like the tourists. The absence of business suites, new SUVs, and trophy homes is itself a social statement, and hints at the kinds of people who feel most comfortable here, but the deeper distinctions between villagers are not to be found by looking at income distribution. There are merchants and artisans, both resettlers and later arrivees, who have done very well, and there are some of both who only manage to "not get any deeper into debt," as one merchant, an original resettler, recounted. There are people with no visible means of income who are comfortable; and, as I have documented, there are people satisfied with their lives that hold a variety of odd jobs on a contingent basis. There is the real possibility, however, that some outward signs of income, clothing, cars, and housing may be chosen to represent their owners as slightly down-and-out in order not to draw attention to relative success at the various underground economies.

The village is too small for franchise business or brand-name big-box stores, so whatever the local people can generate is what people make do with for income, and when this fails they commute to Santa Fe. The kind of jobs available to support the population of Madrid and the surrounding area include housecleaning, working in the various shops and restaurants in the village (the owners of the tavern claim to have employed nearly everyone in the town at one time or another), carpentry and other construction jobs, landscaping, and maintenance work. The most typical full-time work in Santa Fe is nursing or teaching; other commuters hold similarly contingent-type positions as those working in Madrid. Several of the resettlers own one or more properties in town, having bought them when the prices were low, and use them as rental properties. This type of income is what allows folks like Jessie to give her hours at a local shop to someone more in need. Less obvious are the parts of the local economy related to the drug culture, which form networks of social and economic relationships maintained through a loose dialectic of trust and mistrust—part of the legacy of "the pursuit of absolute freedom."

There are perhaps 5 to 10 percent of the population who could not live outside the village because of their personal appearance and behaviors; in most other places they would be the homeless. In Madrid, they have an accepted place in the community (so far), find minimal work for everyday expenses, and are looked after by the village in general. Some of these folks qualify for Social Security disability benefits; most are long-time residents of the village. The culture of tolerance protects these people from being ostracized or forced out of the community, although there is a widespread recognition that the changing economics of Madrid may bring an end to this part of village life; the rise in real estate prices brings a different type of investor to the area, and the behaviors and appearances of some of the locals are becoming a concern to those in tourist-dependent industries.

Economic opportunity is one area in which arrival status in the village can make a difference. As I noted above, those who bought early and bought often have been able to weather the hard times in the village's history and now have comfortable rental incomes with which to retire, a fact that belies some of the hippie rhetoric about not being tied down by material positions and indicates that not all resettlers, in fact, were that far removed from the values of their middle-class backgrounds.

Social Status

Although social class distinctions may not be easily identifiable, that does not mean that the community has not evolved its own set of beliefs, values, and norms that govern how the villagers think of each other. I would like to introduce the folk categories used by Madroids to describe themselves—the term "Madroid" is taken from the last reincarnation of the local newspaper, the *Madroid Tabloid*, and seems a good term for describing the villagers. These folk categories can be useful descriptors because they illustrate status groups that may not be obvious to the observer, and because they hint at the fissures in the community. The following descriptions are taken from many conversations and observations during my three years of being in and around the village. They represent a composite view of Madrid, using the locals' own terms and definitions.

ELITE OUTLAWS

A small but important group of individuals who live their lives outside of the law. These are people usually deeply involved in various aspects of procuring and providing illicit drugs, and have been thus involved for a long time. Contrary to middle-class values and perceptions, the consensus in the community is that they are successful business people meeting a need in the community. They supply the local drug market but do not solicit business on the street corner. They are perceived to be trustworthy, dependable, and true to their word. They maintain extensive networks of friends, create low profiles, cause no trouble, and they pay their local debts and obligations. It is also possible to live in Madrid and have no idea who these people are or that they are part of the drug culture. Elite outlaws are to be distinguished from the outlaws in Madrid's past—the group of people Jessie referred to in her interview. This latter group included biker outlaws who called Madrid home from time to time and manufacturers of methamphetamines who have largely died or left town.

Interestingly, these people have not assumed positions of power in the community, in the past or now, nor do they exercise global power over village affairs in a Mafioso manner; bad drug deals are dealt with personally, and as we have seen, relationships remain personal and limited. The elite outlaws oil the machinery for those whose consumption patterns include drugs. They themselves do not speak out or take action on public issues; protests for the continuation of the old libertarian days of drug use are left to the consumers. I do not want, however, to imply that the users organize themselves for concerted public action; any protests vary from complaints aired at the coffee shop or the bar to personal reprisals. Given the overall tolerance and prevalence of drug use in the community—and the country in general—the elite outlaws are less dependent on their customers than their customers are on them.

REGULARS

The closest people to a middle-class bourgeoisie to be found in Madrid. These are the bulk of the shop owners, artisans, workers, and residents in the village and the surrounding area. They keep the daily business of the town going, feed the children, get them on the school bus, run the businesses, and produce and/or broker the arts and craft items sold in the village shops. They may or may not use recreational drugs.

POSERS, JOKERS, AND THIEVES

The folks who manipulate the high degree of tolerance in Madrid to run impression management games. They are perceived to be tricksters, unreliable but tolerated as part of the community. They are petty thieves, addicts, and showmen whose lapses are excused as being part of the landscape in Madrid. The transgressions of these folks are felt to be part of the price paid for "living freely." While sometimes perceived to be a negative influence on the community, attempts to remove them from town are nearly nonexistent. Two examples might clarify this ambivalence: one notorious "druggie," known to most of the shopkeepers (although not to Bernice, apparently), has finally qualified for Social Security disability. A typical comment about this was "At least maybe now I don't have to worry about Sorry any more since he got his disability" (interview 1999). Another younger individual passed away last year from doing too many drugs for too many years. He died while out of town and was buried out of state. In spite of the fact that he had stolen openly from local merchants—to the point of being banned from most of their stores—the town held a memorial service at the graveyard attended by over a dozen people to mark his passing and to show support for his former wife and their child, who still live in town. The overall feeling expressed was one of regret at a misspent life, even among some of the people from whom he had stolen. These are the folks for whom "the rules" of social interaction in Madrid traditionally dictated maintaining exchanges of small favors, in hopes that they would pick on somebody else when they needed the next fix. Below the posers, jokers, and thieves in the social hierarchy are a group referred to by the villagers as the scum of the earth.

The Scum of the Earth

The polar opposite of the elite outlaws. They are snitches; they are unreliable and untrustworthy. Their biggest flaw, as perceived by the villagers, is that they use other people's weaknesses (drug addiction, psychological needs of various sorts) for their own personal gain, while giving nothing positive back to the individual or the community. Note that this is different from not helping someone with an addiction—the latter being part of the accepted ethos in Madrid. Detachment and live-and-let-live also imply not exploiting others who are in trouble, and those who are perceived to step over this line are ostracized, at least in conversations. There may be individual reprisals and acts of revenge (and in fact there quite often are), but concerted public action is seldom taken. As the village passed its twenty-fifth anniversary of re-creation, a new category of folks has appeared—the baby hippies.

The Baby Hippies

Many of the younger hippies are the children of the resettlers who have grown up in Madrid; some are from neighboring communities and some drift in from other places, drawn by the same information networks that brought the original resettlers. While they are nicknamed "babies," many of them are in their mid-twenties to early thirties. At this writing a small part of this group has become embroiled in the divisiveness over development and growth in the community.

This small clustering of baby hippies deal drugs openly while hanging out in town with no visible means of support. To their own generation and to some in the older generation, they are the local heroes, continuing the good fight against unjust laws and repressive government institutions; to others they represent the failure of Madrid to outgrow its outlaw roots. I will look more closely at "the boys on the wall" later.

MISFITS AND DRIFTERS

This group of people drift in and out of town, usually thinking at first impression that Madrid is the answer to their problems. They are the seriously depressed, alcoholic, drug dependent, or nonfunctional people. Some stay because they can find a meager living among the shopkeepers who need occasional help or others who have short-term projects. With a few notable exceptions, they are generally perceived to be neither harmful nor helpful to the community, and most drift on to someplace else when Madrid fails to live up to its idealized image of perfect tolerance.

Two examples are illustrative of internal dynamics in the village. The first one took place three summers ago. An obviously distressed woman wandered into town and was asking for spare change from tourists and locals alike. Her behavior and appearance were beyond even Madrid's scruffy standards, she was perceived to be interfering with the tourist trade, and she was actually receiving some handouts. After two days on the main street, the merchants called the sheriff, who took her away. Thus, though similar behavior might have characterized some of the resettlers at one time, this is no longer an acceptable route into Madrid. Another young man who appeared during the winter several years ago finally left (on his own) after trying several avenues of acceptance. He was perceived to be looking for a handout, that the village would support him simply because he was there. His experience highlights an important aspect of Madrid that I will explore later— that it was not a commune nor a communal setting, neither in the beginning nor now. Although there was at least one group of communards who occasionally took in refugees, the village itself did not and does not simply take people in who need help. You either make it on your own or you don't. If you make it, the villagers do not begrudge you a place, but if you don't, don't go looking for sympathy (an interesting version of the all-American belief that "I made it on my own and so can you"). A third example of a drifter who ran into trouble in Madrid, Rachel and her baby Anna, will form part of chapter 5 exploring other issues that divide Madrid.

These categories form the basis for interpersonal relations in Madrid. The posers, jokers, and thieves are the folks to whom you offer free needles or a free meal in hopes that they will pick on someone else the next time they need a fix. The legacy of the counterculture's tolerance and inability to exert communal sanctions against drug-related behavior prohibit even those who are the regulars in town from taking measures against these individuals. Shunning and banning them from local businesses was the most extreme measure I observed. There were stories of retribution for drug deals that went bad, resulting in murder, but not in the recent history of the town. As in August's remembrance of the early days of resettlement, many who live in town have no idea of who the elite outlaws are—or that that is another of their roles; the norm of keeping to one's self and not interfering with another's business is still very strong. This ethic allows for a lot of contradictory and cognitively dissonant behavior to occur in the same space.

The misfits and drifters, on the other hand, represent a category in which the villagers are beginning to draw some lines as to who can be a member of the community and who cannot. This point was discussed above, but it is important to remember that younger folk, even though they may resemble the resettlers of twenty-five years ago, are not automatically granted a space in the village. The baby hippies, on the other hand, are much more of a divisive force in the town. The recreational drug subculture in the younger generation in Madrid brings the contradictions of personal freedom and communal good to the surface in ways even this tolerant community cannot avoid. As the tourist industry becomes increasingly important in village economic life, even old drug-using hippies who own businesses along the main street do not want visible evidence—such as the baby hippies—of the drug subculture to interfere with their profits.

Concerns or problems between these groups of people are still, with important exceptions to be discussed in chapter 6, handled individually. Seldom is organized, communal action taken to curb anyone else's behavior. Madrid is a space in which personal characteristics are more important than the position you hold. In a community with fluid social relations, little visible material wealth to divide the population, and an anarchistic heritage, it is not surprising that power is also fragmented in the village.

Power

I have spoken of the anarchistic heritage of Madrid's counterculture resettlers and its relation to the hyper-individualism characteristic of so much of the Anglo settlement of the West; in Madrid we can see how it operates in conjunction with the other strands from the 1970s alternative lifestyles. The same person quoted at the beginning of this chapter said during our interview: "The reason Madrid is a success is because no one has any power over anyone else; we're all anarchists here. Our anarchy is our strength." In some ironic ways, this may be true, but it also leaves the village vulnerable to the personal retributions so characteristic of justice in the town. It is the case that no one cabal of interest groups runs the town behind the scenes—not even the elite outlaws, who are the most invisible of people. But it is also the case that the village has no voice with which to represent its interests, should the villagers decide on a common interest, to the outside world.

By refusing to participate in power, outside of interpersonal relationships, the villagers have kept true to one of the counterculture movement's strongest ethics—to remove yourself from positions where you become ammunition for the uses of the dominant culture. But, similar to the refusal to set limits on tolerance and acceptance, this withdrawal also means that there is no conduit for positive energy to emerge—energy that might go for building needed institutions for the common good. So while it is hard to abuse power in Madrid—no one would listen or obey—it is also hard to accomplish much beyond the defense of individual liberties. We saw this demonstrated with the exchange of favors for freedom from victimization in dealing with drug addicts; people did what protected themselves, not what might have helped the addicts or the larger community.

The other way power and status could express themselves in a small community is through its institutions and organizations. Madrid has developed some formal and informal organizational structures over the years, and I will look at these next. As expected, not all of them function as fully integrated elements of the community, nor do they represent clear class or status distinctions among village residents.

Organizations and Associations: Efforts Beyond Individualism

Even the fragmented and tenuous nature of association in Madrid has supported some organized community life, and these organizations appear to function within the local environment at a minimal but necessary level for village survival. If we were to find any sites of power and influence in the village, it would certainly be here.

The Madrid Landowner's Association

The oldest formal organizations in the village are the Madrid Landowner's Association (the MLA), the Volunteer Fire Department, and the Water

Cooperative. Huber established the MLA for two reasons when he sold the town. All the village property owners, collectively through the MLA, own the Huber Memorial Ball Park and the waterworks. When you buy property within the historic boundaries of the village, you become a voting member of the MLA, one vote no matter how many properties you own. As described earlier, Huber had his real estate agent, Jim Mocho, write a set of covenants governing the use of property in the town to which every property owner becomes party. Huber wanted to preserve the mining town architecture of the village and prevent its being taken over by transients living in school buses and trailers. These covenants, never consistently nor rigidly enforced, were adopted last year by Santa Fe County as the official zoning ordinances for Madrid, which is now considered a Historic Village, giving the town certain privileges and subjecting it to some constraints under county governance.

It is too soon to tell how this set of rules, now enforceable by county officials, will intercept the villagers' desires to remain autonomous. County officials at one point urged holding village meetings to rewrite the original covenants, but a small group of original resettlers would not allow that, arguing that no accord could ever be reached and that such attempts would be a quagmire of personal recriminations and grudges about who had already violated such-and-such and who had already built so-and-so. Accordingly, the county adopted them intact, contradictions and all (field notes 1999, 2000).

An example of the inability of this local organization to effect change is provided by the seemingly unending controversies about the town's greatest publicly owned asset—the ballpark (shown in figure 4.1). Potentially at least, it could bring in good revenues to the village, revenues that could help build a community sewer system or at least better facilities for the tourists. The structure is very unsound, as the roof is in imminent danger of falling down, which could injure or kill people. The local Little Leagues use the facilities, as do the Jazz Festival and sometimes the Blue Grass Festival. The site hosts part of the Fourth of July activities that also bring some money to the town. A few years ago an engineer's estimate for structural repairs was $300,000, and the MLA seems paralyzed in its efforts to deal with the problem. They have not tried seriously to find outside funding, nor have they done much in the line of temporary safety measures. In the meantime, the ballpark continues to be used. Every time the subject comes up at an MLA or other meeting, much hand-wringing occurs, and that is about

FIGURE 4.1. *The Oscar Huber Memorial Ball Park, often a bone of contention in the village.*

all that happens. Part of the MLA active membership, about ten to twelve people, would like to at least fix it up, if not restore it; others seem content to let it continue on its predictable decline to self-destruction.

The photograph shows the grandstand at the ballpark, one of the communally owned infrastructures in the village. While volunteering to clean the park for one of the jazz festivals, I ran into an old ballplayer who was driving through town visiting relatives in the area. He had played baseball for a lumber company in Albuquerque and had often played against the Madrid Miners. He remarked that the structure and the grounds looked the same as they had in the 1930s.

This unwillingness or inability by the MLA to take decisive action toward the ballpark reflects the ambivalence of the villagers at large; many of the shop owners profit indirectly from the musical events held at the ballpark, such as the Jazz Festival. Yet when the time comes in the spring to clean up the grounds in preparation for the first festival every summer and to pitch in on needed repairs, hardly anyone from the village shows up to help. One of the local people who volunteers her own time at the park, doing things like cleaning up the outhouses, is also an organizer for the annual cleanup of the ballpark for the summer activities. Yet on the day the cleanup was held, she could only stay long enough to greet the vans from Albuquerque bringing up the Festival volunteers—she had to leave for some music lessons. The head of the Festival remarked to me that this is "so typical of Madrid." Even the few people who care for the facility seem stymied by lack of direction and personal priorities that take precedence over communal needs. The Blue Grass Festival has sought friendlier grounds the last year or two and has held its events elsewhere partly as a result of Madrid's intransigence about the ballpark. This is not an atypical pattern for the villagers, to take advantage of something put together and organized by others, but to be unwilling to participate in a proactive manner that could benefit both the event's organizers and the town.

Residents who expect action from the MLA board members are often disappointed. The back roads in town are unpaved and full of potholes big enough to lose a truck in, so this is a common complaint at meetings. Occasionally one of the locals will bring his equipment into town and do some temporary repairs, but the roads are in such bad shape that they need much more than one more Band-aid. Yet again, nothing much gets done. Claiming poverty, the board usually tries to delay taking any concrete action on village matters. It's no wonder that most of the villagers do not go to the meetings and consider the MLA "to be a joke."

The MLA does not officially represent Madrid at any county government affairs, and when it did arrange for a representative to deal with the new county zoning ordinances, there was much controversy over who was qualified to represent the interests of the town, as I write about in chapter 6. For the most part, the MLA does as little as possible about local affairs and removes itself from issues outside the village. So power in the usual sense we look for it in publicly vested bodies does not really exist in Madrid.

The Volunteer Fire Department

The Volunteer Fire Department grew out of the need to have local protection for the residences and businesses that were mostly frame construction, as I have documented earlier. Vandalism, retribution, carelessness, and stupidity have claimed many historic buildings in the village. The fire department is currently housed in a new building built for that purpose; in earlier years the fire department used the old Chrysler dealership and then for a while it was across the street from where it is now. There have been discussions of putting in a fire protection line (fire hydrants) for at least the last twenty years, but at this writing there are still no fire hydrants in town.

There is not much controversy about the fire department, perhaps because, like all rural fire departments, Madrid's must meet state and federal guidelines and the emergency medical technicians must pass exams in order to continue volunteering. Drills and coordination with the other local volunteer departments are mandated. This means that decision making is not local, and perhaps in the case of the fire department this is a good thing. There is little discretionary room if they are to continue to receive certification and funding. And, for once, the villagers themselves feel they have a stake in preventing fires, since nearly all the houses and most of the shops are of wood frame construction. This is one instance in which self-reliance has given way to the common good.

The Water Co-op

The Water Co-op, as we have seen, was brought to the village by a public health crisis in 1980. People had to sign on for water service when it was put in. The only other choices were to continue to haul water or to put in a private well. The present utility can serve a maximum of about 150 customers, but there has been a moratorium imposed on new connections in order to discourage growth, and it currently serves fewer than 100 customers. Some people have water to one part of their building but not another; some shops have no water at all. The water remains unpalatable because the wellhead is located in the coal seams, giving the water a distinctive sulfur flavor and odor; sometimes the whole town smells like the water. One man, an original resettler, has headed the water board nearly from its inception, and there is considerable controversy about the moratorium, the quality of water in the village, and the water commissioner himself. The commissioner's attempts at restricting growth by limiting the water are reflective of the entire issue of the inadequacy of local governments to control regional-level issues. As explained earlier, this means anyone in town with enough money to hire a well driller can put in their own well in the village.

But the commissioner's unilateral decision to use the availability of water hookups to maintain the village in a more primitive state has met with much local opposition, as many locals would like more water, better water, or any water at all in some cases. There are apparently real physical problems with the old system, but the lack of sympathetic leadership has created tensions about the commissioner and his policies. Oddly, absolutely no one has attempted to run against him or to publicly oppose his leadership. It is very likely that no one else is willing to sit in that spot and have to make those kinds of decisions. Once again in Madrid, the preferred solution is to complain but not take any proactive stands toward improving the water system.

The Amvets and the Lady Amvets

The only other formal organization in Madrid is the Amvets Post II, which serves the Vietnam veterans and their families, and its subsidiary, the Lady Amvets. They meet regularly wherever they can find facilities, as neither organization owns its own building. The Amvets have a regional representative based in Albuquerque through the Veterans Affairs Office, whose function is to help the vets access services at the state and national level; in spite of this assistance there are a few vets who refuse to get any kind of help from the government, even free medical help. Younger vets also sometimes join in activities sponsored by the Amvets, but for the most part it is comprised of men from the Vietnam conflict. The Amvets sponsor a picnic on the Fourth of July in conjunction with the annual parade held in Madrid, the proceeds of which support their other community projects such as the women's auxiliary's free Thanksgiving Day Dinner at the church in Cerrillos, open to anyone who wants to come. Both groups come together and have horseshoe-pitching tournaments several times a year, events that are open to anyone, although there are a group of about fifteen couples and a few singles that form the core participants. The Sons of Vets group was started by some people from both branches of the organization concerned with the youngsters of vets and has involved the kids in gardening and other similar activities.

There are at least two village resettlers (one current resident and one who has left the town) who refused to have anything to do with the Amvets; these men do not dwell on their experiences in Vietnam and would rather others did not as well. In part this is because of the reputation the Amvets have of being addicts and alcoholics—used-up by-products of the country's involvement in Southeast Asia. There is some validity to this perception, especially for the men. Ironically the Amvets and the Lady Amvets are the groups who sponsor the most public and communal events in the village and put that money back into the town in events like the Thanksgiving Day dinners.

Vietnam vets made up a high percentage of those original resettlers who first came to Madrid, and many came because it was isolated and away from sites of government power. Today they do form a large percentage of Madrid's population of dysfunctional folk—at least dysfunctional by middle-class standards. They are people who probably would not survive living in a more congested environment or around more judgmental people. Madrid is a refuge for these people and their families, and it is hard to imagine them coping anywhere else.

Some Consequences of Diffuse Organizational Power

All three organizations usually hold their meetings at the fire station, one following after the other, with only some change in attendees. As the village remains unincorporated, these organizations and their active memberships represent an as of yet unrealized site for power in the village; more importantly, these sites are places where the resettlers continue to have a presence in village affairs as their numbers dwindle. But to say that they have "power" is a bit misleading. No one in the village wanted to enforce the old covenants, for instance, and face a personal showdown with another villager. So the usual tactic was to call the health or zoning officials at the county—anonymously—and lodge a complaint. Sometimes this resulted in remedial action and sometimes it did not. Now that the county is directly responsible for enforcing the ordinances, there is concern that this responsibility will give outside authorities reason to exert their unwanted presence in the village.

While most Madroids dismiss the MLA as irrelevant, it was the MLA president (a later arrivee and real estate broker) along with the other active members (mostly resettlers) who coordinated the writing of Madrid's Master Plan with county officials. But it was the MLA president who got the county to accept a larger definition of the townsite's historic boundaries, allowing him to subdivide more parcels of land he owned as a broker into the smaller three-quarter-acre town lots, instead of the twenty-acre minimum lot size outside these limits. But this only gave him three or four more lots, not dozens, to develop. This gerrymandering of the historic town boundaries was strongly opposed by the core group of resettlers, but they were unsuccessful in stopping the president's maneuver (field notes 1999, 2000).

Legitimate forms of authority for governance have yet to emerge in Madrid, and the reason appears to be a combination of the counterculture's reluctance to acquiesce to anything beyond the individual and the ideology of the West, with its history of individualism, self-reliance, and abhorrence of government interference in local affairs. As with so many other legends about freedom on the frontier, Madrid was resurrected through individual efforts in collusion with the absence of government to dictate internal affairs, yet its present survival may depend on the very governmental authorities it so adamantly distrusts. This situation will be discussed in chapter 6 where I talk specifically about growth issues and local government structures, but I will give a brief summary here.

In reaction to the development impinging on Madrid from the north and east, there have been ad-hoc movements to preserve the village from too much growth, and while they were neither cohesive nor well coordinated, they did result in Santa Fe County's procuring land both in the village and just north of the ballpark as a buffer against both internal and external development. These groups coalesced only around this single issue of providing green space and open space, and their activities did not result in any permanent alignments in the village—as is typical of single-issue interest groups throughout American communities. This action, however, was made possible by initiatives at the county level, from which Madrid benefited but for which the villagers were not directly responsible. Again the villagers were more reactive than proactive in handling this opportunity.

Informal Associations

In addition to the formal organizations in Madrid, two newer associations have sprung up in the village within the last five years, mainly in response to a perceived need for more community-building activities. Both of these are struggling to become formal organizations but have not yet attracted enough people to carry on the work. These are the Madrid Historical Society and the Madrid Community Library. Both involve resettlers and newer arrivees, both consist mainly of the same six to eight people, and neither has been terribly successful in achieving its organizational goals. The library in particular has been a frustrating venture for those involved. I participated in this attempt for about a year; we found that everyone in town thought it was wonderful to have a library in the village but no one would help with the volunteer staffing and hardly anyone ever took advantage of its resources, even for their children.

The young woman who headed the initiative had gotten a small grant and provided computers and Internet access to the villagers, basically for free. The only people who used these resources were a couple of "drifters" who came to use the email functions but never reimbursed the librarian for her telephone expenses. In frustration, Cara, the librarian, posted signs all over the village venting her frustration over the "business as usual in Madrid," of "people taking from those willing to give something to the community but not willing to give anything back in turn." Needless to say, this was a very frustrating experience. One local sage volunteered that nobody in Madrid reads because they don't trust anything published by government-tainted sources—they would rather listen to the late-night talk radio shows about extraterrestrials and star children. It is unknown whether the failure of this first attempt at a community library was due to the small population and lack of interest or general decline in library use in the country as a whole.

Other Community Initiatives

There are other community endeavors that have met with some success, at least sporadically. For instance, from time to time people in the village publish a small newsletter. Started as the *Nickel News* by an original resettler and later called the *Madrid News*, it is now known as the *Madroid Tabloid*. Publication can be spotty, as it depends on the goodwill and volunteer effort of writers, the resources of an editor willing to collect the work, and the availability of a copy machine. The last issue in the current series was published about eighteen months ago.

Twice a year the villagers *dis*-organize two events; I describe them as dis-organized because the two events come off without a great deal of *coordinated* effort, albeit with a great deal of individual work. On the Fourth of July the village stages a parade, and for Christmas the town businesses make a more-or-less concerted effort to put up lighted displays. Both of these events were part of the mining town history under the Hubers, who used these activities for controlling the free time of the miners and their families (Melzer 1976). The contemporary community uses the Christmas displays to promote tourism, but the Fourth of July parade has more to do with community solidarity and fun.

In 1999, the lieutenant governor participated in the parade, a reminder of the mining days when the governor always was the grand marshal for Madrid on Independence Day. (We tried to get the governor to come, but pleading the press of business, he sent his second in command; because a representative of the state executive came, members of Frank Ochoa's family refused to attend, pleading disgruntlement over the governor's anti-union initiatives.) Diane Johnson (not to be confused with the former first lady of New Mexico, who shares the same name), who owns the gallery in the old Chrysler dealership, has spearheaded an effort for the last several years to invite anyone related to the coal mining days in Madrid to come for a reunion, held on the Fourth, called "Old-Timers Day." Two years ago, two families whose members were all in their eighties came from California, and contributed to the historical record of life in Madrid during the Depression. Other veterans of the mining days stop by from time to time, and some keep in touch through the Johnson Gallery, where Diane maintains letters, mementos, and memorabilia from Madrid's past. One or two others participate in this endeavor, and it is part of the work of the newly formed Historical Society, but it does not draw a large number of villagers willing to help with the work.

Some members of the community who operate businesses in Madrid are involved in regional associations related to tourism and business interests, but there is no strong thread of association here, either, although a few merchants are more proactive in tourist-related promotions than others. I heard rumors from several interviewees that there was a merchant's association, but while I was active in the community it did not appear to be operative. Merchants at one end of town often engage in heated debates with each other about which end of town gets the best advertising from the tourist associations, which end gets the most "police" protection from the ersatz "sheriff," paid by the MLA to maintain a "presence" on the main street, and which end of town is going to foot more of the bill for the Christmas displays.

An important informal association started by the resettlers was the Children's Workshop, a local school serving the children born in the village and surrounding rural areas. In the 1970s Santa Fe extended only as far as Siler Road, and children had to be bussed all the way into Santa Fe for public schooling, a round trip of over forty miles. There was also the difficulty of counterculture families sending their kids to mainstream schools. The Workshop was a communal effort of those folks who had school-aged children, with parents contributing their time as teachers. The Workshop has waxed and waned over the years, depending upon the number of parents. In 1990 Santa Fe County opened a new charter school, Turquoise Trail Elementary, about ten miles north of Madrid, and most parents have opted for public schooling over the local alternative. A few parents homeschool their children, for two main reasons: (1) rough roads can be impassable in bad weather, causing many absences, and (2) the continued disaffection with mainstream education by parents who remain committed to a life of radical freedom from social constraint.

The alternative school operated as long as there were folks interested in providing for their own children, a phenomenon not unique to Madrid. Those who had a problem with some aspect of life worked on that aspect as long as their own interests were being served; once the self-interest was gone, so was their involvement. This does not bother the resettler generation, who feel that this was what it meant to live freely, without constraint. The ethic was "do what you want as long as it is what you want to do." This works better as an individual ethic than as a basis for an ongoing community, and yet Madrid continues to attract people who have similar philosophies about life.

Not surprisingly, formal religion plays no real role in the social fabric of contemporary Madrid, although there are many alternative beliefs and practices available to anyone who is looking for spiritual or mystical association and companionship. However, these informal and fluid associations remain individualistic and are not organized along a social axis; they are strictly for self-help and self-healing—note the emphasis on "self." But on the plus side, the community is a friendly place for those with alternative gender or sexual preferences, and gay and lesbian folks have found in Madrid a comfortable and accepting set of social relations. Once a year the town hosts a "He-She Bang" at the Mine Shaft Tavern, and crowns a reigning king or queen cross-dresser; benefits go to local charities. (Contestants may or may not be cross-dressers normally.) If individuals choose, genderedness can be fluid and malleable, and transgendered people find little if any stigma attached to such role switching. Preference in the gender of partners is also fluid and changeable, and several men and women have switched from heterosexual partnerships to homosexual partnerships and vice versa more than once without any social stigma whatsoever.

In Conclusion

There is simply not a great deal of social cohesion in Madrid among any one identifiable group; the history of drugs, experiments in maximum freedom, and defiant individualism continue to work against the formation of social cohesion. Madrid is not entirely different from other communities, as the clearest distinctions in the community remain rooted in economic consider-ations, although you have to look beneath the surface to see the connections. Those who are oriented toward legitimate, formal markets (tourism, arts and crafts, amenity retirees) *and* who see that their own fate is tied to the increasing role of such markets in Madrid are more likely to involve them-selves in contentious development issues, while those who are content with Madrid the way it is (or was), or those who have only short-term gains at stake, are much less likely to become visible targets at town meetings and other public forums. There is considerable evidence, however, that this reluctance to assume leadership roles is not solely due to apathy and dis-enchantment with authority; the continued legacy of vengeance and retri-bution still underlies personal relationships in Madrid and prohibits the formation of cohesive publicly oriented networks.

It is less clear how this division over development impacts those involved in the drug culture in Madrid. Those individuals committed to maximum freedom of drug consumption are losing their legitimacy in the community, especially as a small cluster among this group is thought to be responsible for most of the acts of vengeance. But drug use and production is so pervasive in the community, and the live-and-let-live ethos is so strong, that moderate use of a wide range of currently illegal drugs is not likely to divide the community solely along this issue.

One person interviewed saw these changes and these categories a bit differently, and it is worth quoting from the letter she wrote in response to our telephone interview, as it sums up these issues from the perspective of an original resettler who now lives out of town to avoid "the traffic—auto-mobile and human":

> In the early years, many of us smoked pot and felt a little of the
> Anti-Establishment Spirit. For this reason, we were tolerant of a
> certain outlaw-ishness. This attitude seems to have continued over
> the years, our own drug use not withstanding. But, the element to
> be tolerated became increasingly ignorant and abusive. Pot gave
> way to heroin, recreational drugs gave way to serious abuse.
> Madrid's reputation as an "outlaw" town brought criminals and
> punks and general assholes. A new influx of business people may
> or may not be able to gentrify Madrid. (1999)

The gentrification of Madrid, and places like it, threatens to reduce the freedoms associated with alternative communities to real estate theme parks, where the aging hippie generation will once more be on display, this time exploited by the development factions looking for new themes and hypes to sell their products. Witness Harris's website ad for properties he has for sale in Madrid:

> ... the best thing about living in Madrid is that everyone is there because they want to be ... most of its residents are fairly new, are from someplace else, and chose to live in Madrid. They are for the most part artists and craftspeople who are independent but friendly. The art and gift of living in Madrid can be summed up in two words: Be yourself. (www.madridnewmexico.com/)

This "real estate mumbo jumbo," to which Sam Duck referred earlier, is partly responsible for moving Madrid from a loosely tied community of idiosyncratic defiant individualists living and being in a particular space to a commodified commercial opportunity, a space that can be exploited by outsiders for profit.

Treating the current residents of Madrid like animals in the zoo—untamed but harmless—turns the authentic experiences of life in a remote and marginal area into an image to be experienced secondhand, as if buying real estate in Madrid can cloak you with the semblance of authenticity and independence. This is indistinguishable from the hype about the restorative powers of the West used to sell ranchettes to urban escapees. As this chapter documents, Madrid today is a mix of individuals not easily categorized by social class alone, and while many resent this sanitized version of their village, there are others who clearly profit from participating in it. Time of arrival, space, water, growth, freedom, drugs, real estate and capitalism, and the excesses of individualism all play divisive roles in today's Madrid. "The art and gift of living in Madrid" is not as simple as the real estate theme park setting suggested in the advertisement.

To be yourself, as the ad implies, remains the community's reigning cultural motif. I believe that the ability to control one's own fate in Madrid has been closely tied to the amount of open, undeveloped space into which individuals could expand when existing relationships went sour—the quintessential frontier process. As this frontier recedes, social relations in the village

will change accordingly, and those who cannot change will move, as witnessed by one Vietnam vet and his son's family who left the village two years
ago, moving to an old lumbering camp high in a nearby mountain range,
seeking the solitude and freedom that, for him, no longer exist in Madrid.
The next chapter will explore the history of this cult of the individual and
its implications for the future of Madrid.

CHAPTER FIVE

The Cult of the Individual

Defiant Individualism as a Basis for a Loosely Tied Community

I have repeatedly referred to a concept of defiant individualism throughout the narrative of Madrid's resettlement. This idea is borrowed from Martin Sanchez Jankowski's 1991 study of inner city youth gangs, *Islands in the Streets*. Jankowski proposes that youth gang members are rational actors making contingent decisions that maximizes their opportunities given the limited institutional supports and economic advantages in their communities. They distrust authority in almost any form and take a defiant, manipulative stand toward agents of the state. They are highly competitive, oriented toward acquisitiveness and consumption, maintain relationships only so long as they are useful, and distrust the world both inside and outside the gang.

The Madrid resettlers share enough of Jankowski's analytical description of gang members to apply the term "defiant individualism" to the villagers. There are important differences, however, the foremost being that counterculture advocates consciously and rationally chose this world to live in. Madrid resettlers were defiant of *any* type of authority, distrustful and disenchanted with the actions of the state, and not willing to subjugate themselves to community norms that violated this sense of hyper-individualism and freedom. Beyond a certain level of acquaintanceship, they were distrustful of each other—maintaining social distances to create safe spaces for their own individuality. But they were not necessarily competitive in the same sense that Jankowski's analysis showed inner city gang members to be. In Madrid in the 1970s there was space to spread out, space to grow marijuana, to cook meth, to walk around naked. There was space to live in a free family communally sharing resources and sexual relations, and there was space to be alone. There was space to raise a family and there was space to overdose on drugs publicly. In these early years, one person's freedom could expand a fairly long way before it interfered with someone else's. The conflicts and competitions inherent in resource-scarce gang environments were never necessary in Madrid; in the absence of civil authority individual retribution sufficed. In that sense, the resettlers were able to engage in an even more extreme form of individualism than Jankowski's gang members, where intra-gang relations consumed a great deal of time.

Having the space in which to experiment with freedom from social norms is part, of course, of the romance of the West in the American consciousness, and the desire to live free of social constraints was not invented by the hippie generation of the 1960s. But it was a different kind of defiance that separates the resettlers' generation from other dissidents. This faction of my generation (and most, but not all, of Madrid's resettlers) was not looking to gain material advantage; we were looking for the freedom to live outside market forces in relationships centered on the minimal necessities of survival. Madrid's resettlers were not interested in acquisitiveness or maximizing consumption (except drugs for some), but in living self-sufficient and self-reliant lives while remaining beyond the reach of the perceived police state and its agents. Furthermore, we felt the emphasis on materialism was at the root of racism, inequality, warfare, and injustice. Most of the resettlers were from families who worked in the skilled trades or were lower-middle- to middle-class in orientation, and they had the economic and cultural freedom to escape from materialism rather than trying to obtain it through any means possible. It is most interesting, however, that the folks who were attracted to Madrid maintained the highly individualistic orientation of their middle-class roots, and did not attempt (except for the Ducks and one or two other smaller families) to live communally or to share resources on a continuing basis.

This defiance also meant experimenting with drugs, with alternative lifestyles of all kinds, and with tolerance toward those who were also experimenting with these aspects of life: this was the mix our culture offered us in the aftermath of the Vietnam War. This chapter will explore how many of these beliefs were ideologies justifying an underlying hedonistic selfishness and how much was genuine disaffection with American materialism. That these experiments were partly successful in Madrid suggests that it was a mix of both; the successes came, however, with price tags that I will explore as I look at this community founded on counterculture-style defiant individualism. A note about my approach to this material: I have tried to capture the flavor and usefulness of sociological analysis in this chapter without a heavy-handed use of theory and jargon specific to the field of sociology. Those familiar with Weber and Durkheim will find their ideas liberally represented; those who are not I think will still understand the dynamics of life in Madrid in a deeper manner than relayed in the previous chapters. Those readers like myself for whom theory is the stuff of life—I refer you to the final chapter.

Let me start by clarifying the variant of defiant individualism that informs the Madrid culture. Ideally, Madrid's defiant individualist was defiant of the authority of the state police apparatus *and* the state-supported economic system. She was highly distrustful of norms, values, and beliefs inherited from her bourgeois parents' generation, and she therefore sought new relationships outside of the market exchange in the dominant culture. She sought maximum satisfaction from self-made or bartered accomplishments in place of trading her time in a labor market for mass-produced goods and services. Or, in the words of Gilbert Zicklin, "it made no sense to labor at a task just for money or to work at a job that lacked potential for meaningful self-expression, if one could help it. One needed to remain free from the meaningless bondage [of work] . . . and to find or create opportunities to do things that enriched and validated the self" (Zicklin 1983, 8).

Competing for scarce and valued resources was not necessary because our society produced an abundance of goods and services that could be obtained easily through barter, working part-time, or utilizing government programs (Berger 1981, 113; Coyote 1998; Zicklin 1983). Once the bare essentials for maintaining life were met—food, shelter, warmth, minimal companionship among like-minded individuals, access and the freedom to use drugs for some—time was spent enjoying these particular lifestyle choices. In order to maintain a defiant stance toward the structure and dynamics of the capitalist state and its perceived repressive police agencies, a tolerance for all others who were likewise engaged in experimentations in living freely became essential lest the individual become part of yet another system of oppression; but that tolerance easily devolved into the tyranny of the individual, as I have described in earlier chapters. Each person perceived herself to be acting individually, as a free agent, toward personal goals irrespective of common communal issues, and only reluctantly and minimally accepted the authority of the community to impose any structure or obligations over her. This reluctance to participate in normative exchanges of mutual obligations for the common good creates a loosely tied community of defiant individualists interacting with each other on a contingent, fluid, and somewhat distant basis, in spite of shared experiences of relative poverty, material deprivation, and isolation from urban services.

But such ideologies and beliefs do not manifest themselves without historic precedent or cultural grounding. I propose that the individualism expressed by Madrid's resettlers was not as radical as our generation thought it was, that, in fact, we were the next step in carrying forward the secular ethical concepts begun during the Protestant Reformation and the growth of capitalism, as Max Weber argued in *The Protestant Ethic and the Spirit of Capitalism* (1958 [1904–5]). Because understanding the possibilities for and the constraints upon community in the postmodern era is one of my primary concerns in this research, I first want to explore what Weber saw as the antecedents to contemporary individualism and their implications for Madrid and, indeed, perhaps for contemporary communities in general.

Madrid, Defiant Individualism, and the Protestant Ethic

Weber argued that the beginnings of capitalism arose through complex interactions of ideas plus economic, legal, and political innovations that derived from unique historic events in Western cultures, the most unique of which were the early Puritan and Calvinist teachings encouraging worldly success while simultaneously demanding an ascetic way of life that rejected hedonistic indulgence in all its forms. This odd combination of values enabled nascent industrial capitalism since instead of building castles and accumulating kingdoms, early entrepreneurs reinvested their profits in their own businesses. Most importantly, this ascendant economic and social system freed men from tribal and family bounds, replacing traditional restraints with a single-minded allegiance to profits.

For Weber, the emphasis on the bottom line started here, with Calvin's doctrines of predestination that invited men to work hard and be successful—such success being taken as a sign of salvation in the afterlife. The worldly success made possible by this unremitting work ethic, of course, quickly undermined the asceticism of the original Puritan ethic, but not before it had given capitalism as a system of relationships primacy in human affairs. Cultural legitimacy passed from asceticism and simple living to materialism and the bourgeois concerns for class and status, and

Weber understood that once Calvinist "asceticism undertook to remodel the world . . . material goods gained an increasing and finally an inexorable power over the lives of men as at no previous period in history." As the new worldview took hold, Western European cultures moved from communities tied together by ritual, tradition, and mutual trust to communities of increasing individualism and mutual competition, as there was no longer any "repression of the economic impulse." Once economic gain was a legitimating force for community, it was an easy step for Protestantism to wipe out other traditional forms of authority—especially distant authority vested in traditional religious or sacred figures. Each person could communicate directly with his God, creating communities of equals. For Weber, this religious institutionalization of equality was the foundation upon which an autonomous bourgeoisie developed in the cities of western Europe, and in America these became special cases of "voluntary associations among persons who shared a common style of life and who wanted to exclude nonbelievers from the group" (Bendix 1962, 71, 181–82).

Thus the Reformation played the contradictory roles of creating sectarian communities of true believers while also providing impetus to the creation of a secular materialistic ethic based on *individualized*—and *depersonalized*—calculations of economic actions and their ideological justifications that replaced the earlier spiritual core of belief. Once individualism was out of the bag, so to speak, it has proven difficult to put back.

The more impersonal the bureaucratic decision-making apparatus becomes to suit the demands of capitalism, the more we remove ourselves from the ethical and moral fabric within which such decisions were formerly situated. Furthermore, the needs of family, community, and church—the keepers of the social fabric—are replaced by the calculated and rational requirements of business and government for productivity and efficiency. Soon the individual becomes isolated within her own interior space as the rationality of capitalism replaces the social and community foundations for decision making. Thus the heightened sense of self, placing the self at the center of all calculations, and the distancing of the self from traditional modes of legitimate authority have their roots in the dynamics of capitalism and the success of the middle classes in creating the secular ethic of individuality. Seen in this context, the counterculture revolutions of the late 1960s were not a total rejection of bourgeois culture; they were an extension of it. While we thought we were rejecting materialistic consumption patterns for peace and justice, we were carrying forward a goodly portion of the underlying cultural dynamic of capitalism in spite of ourselves.

Madroids were all from middle-class or nearly middle-class families, and virtually all came from urban environments, so it should not be too surprising that the hyper-individualism of defiance and the *self*-centered approaches to "living freely" that form the heart of Madrid's culture are not totally at odds with the society from which the majority of its members came. Nor is the highly calculated manner in which individuals approach the tenuous and tentative formation of social relations to be attributed solely to the paranoia of the drug trade; such suspicions are bred in the dominant culture's competitive consumption patterns and emphasis on individual accumulations of status markers. Where many in the counterculture differed from their parents' generation, however, was in the rejection of material acquisitiveness, and this is not an insignificant break.

Rejecting material acquisitions as overt status markers is not a return to the Puritan esthetic of hard work with no personal indulgences, and trading new Gap blue jeans for secondhand ones is merely swapping one set of status symbols for another—and just as surely tells the observer what lifestyle choices one is making. I wish to go beyond the fashion statement, however, as I believe these cultural choices are related to the depersonalization of human relations and the "disenchantment" of the world as society emancipated itself from the sacred and the magical. In a world where everything could be understood and counted rationally through the workings of science, business accounting practices, and bureaucratic regulations, the traditional relationship between man, nature, and God was profoundly altered. After the brief period of Puritan asceticism, worldly knowledge replaced the sacred element of enchantment and suspension of reason that had characterized most human societies. Out of this, the bourgeoisie created an empire of material goods and knowledge that set itself at odds with traditional forms of social and ecological relationships. The anti-materialism of many 1960s social movements was in part a reaction to this loss of magic. While not all of the counterculture movements taking place at the time Madrid was resettled partook in anti-materialist sentiments, most did, and whether groups were communistically or individualistically oriented the prevailing ideology was "to leave a lighter footprint" on the earth and to find "authentic" bases for relationships.

Authentic relationships and leaving a lighter footprint on the land imply an ideology centered on something other than materially mediated status markers and competitive consumption. While this belief system is not fully articulated among all the residents of Madrid, its central ideology is similar to social movements that have appeared in America and Europe in the last fifteen years. "Simple living," "voluntary downsizing," and "post-consumerism" are recognized phenomena encouraging individuals to partake less in the capitalist dynamic of competitive production and consumption in order to ratchet down the inequalities produced by mass commodification (Gordon 1996; Lasn 1999; Schor 1991, 1998). These quiet social movements may yet prove to be very damaging to capitalism in the long run, by undermining the critical dynamic of ever-increasing markets and profits required by the capitalist agenda.

Authentic relationships with other humans and with the environment are thought to result from this withdrawal from consumerism. It is not a wholesale return to magic or the supernatural (for most), but rather a highly calculated, individualistic set of beliefs that place the public good of environment and community resources ahead of the right to own increasing amounts of private goods. But I would argue that it is also an attempt to regain some of the enchantment with the world that was destroyed by the rationality and accountability of capitalism *by substituting another set of rational calculations* aimed at justifying these anti-consumer movements, just as materialism came to replace the early Puritan ascetic. For instance, Joe Dominguez and Vicki Robin's (1992) recipe for simple living, called *Your Money or Your Life*, comes with a nine-step program to help middle-class overconsumers cut back on their acquisitiveness while preserving their financial security. These are rational programs to use resources wisely; they do not advocate giving away all possessions and wandering through the world penniless or joining a nunnery. But joining a commune or rebuilding a ghost town could be easily substituted for our parents' materialism while simultaneously creating a shared sense of alternative spirituality.

The resettlers of Madrid were not interested in programs, nor were they interested in large-scale social change. But they were, as a group, pursuing goals far outside the mainstream society in terms of material possessions. As more people gain the ability to live in communities of choice, Madrid may be one example of what authentic, small-scale relationships might look like, stripped of commodified status markers and commercially mediated appearances.

There exists in Madrid today a deep sense that the villagers' interpretation of the counterculture values is far superior to the way the rest of us live, and furthermore that other people's choices are deviant and harmful. Historically, nearly all counterculture communities espoused some form of communalism and simple living, and their experiences are useful in appreciating Madrid as neither an intentional community nor a mere aggregate of individuals living in the same space, and through which Madrid's place in the history of such experiments can be better understood.

The Loosely Tied Community Seen in Comparison to Counterculture Communes

> The withdrawal of youth from conventional forms of social participation can best be described as a worldwide social movement. Communitarianism, of course, is only one of the many forms this has taken. But it is a form that very well reflects the movement's spirit: the quest for authenticity through reduction in scale. (Zablocki 1980, 21)

The values and hopes that emerge from the interviews with early resettlers clearly indicate a desire to break from the acquisitive, market-driven mainstream culture of late capitalism. Benjamin Zablocki's 1980 study of the American commune movement places these hopes in historical perspective, for while Madrid has never been a commune, many of its resettlers and current residents alike share much with the 1960s communal experiments, and indeed several long-term residents had experienced commune life before settling in Madrid. Madroids have more in common with this group than with any other subculture population, and I will draw on studies of these communards dating to the late 1960s and early 1970 as the closest parallel to the Madrid experience in order to better illuminate its social significance.

While communal experiments have never represented more than one in a thousand in the U.S. population, there has not been a single year in the previous 320 years of American history when there has not been a documented communitarian organization, with the earliest known dating to 1663. Whether historical or contemporary, communitarian communities "always functioned as a deviant, radical, or otherworldly fringe, drawing off idealists, social malcontents, and dreamers." In this context, Zablocki finds that

> during communitarian periods, meaninglessness and estrangement

from cultural values are the more salient dimensions [of alien-ation]. This can only happen in societies in which the problem of getting what one needs is overshadowed by the problem of getting what one wants which typically happens whenever the future seems to open a multiplicity of possible futures. Under such circumstances, a utopian vision, realized in the modest form of a small communal homestead, can easily seem a better bargain than a bloc of votes in the legislature or tactical control of the city streets. (Zablocki 1980, 11–31. Italics in original)

Believing that periods of communitarianism emerge at discontinuities in the monotonic progression of Western history, Zablocki delineates the last of these moments (in the 1960s) as the "crisis of internationalism and secular-ism" of the latter part of the twentieth century:

Each forced leap forward to greater plurality of values and fragmentation of roles brings with it a renewed longing for Gemeinschaft as well as the appearance of temporary cultural interstices in which significant numbers of people find themselves with the resources and the freedom to pursue this longing. (25)

Madrid's otherworldly fringe appearance is no accident: we no longer speak of "internationalism"; now the theme is globalization, and the en-croaching worldwide domination of secular, rational decision making by multinational capitalist systems has given groups with far less peaceful intentions than the hippies the ability to pursue reactionary dreams. If the villagers indeed represent one example of the search for small-scale, authen-tic, one-on-one relationships (*Gemeinschaft*), then its lessons are critical to understanding our future.

Hippies and counterculture folk from the 1960s and 1970s were not all communards, however, and the features that distinguish Madrid from com-munal experiments illuminate the strengths and the weaknesses of the vil-lage's grand experiment in anarchistic living.

Madrid's Relation to the Hippie Movement
Historically, such communal experiments have settled neither on the out-right frontier, where simply surviving created community, nor in growing

urban areas, but rather in favored areas that had been a frontier a generation earlier, where there were still opportunities without encompassing
social controls—at least controls from the dominant culture (Alderfer 1985;
Berger in Friedenberg 1971; Hayden 1976; Kagan 1975; Kanter 1972;
Spurlock 1988; Westhues 1972; Wooster 1924; Zablocki 1980). The communitarian movement in America between 1965 and 1975 encompassed
people who favored neither violent opposition nor accommodation to the
establishment, but who wished to find a third way of living.

   Zablocki defines the formation of communes as a continual social
movement in Western European cultures that waxes and wanes as social
conditions change. Madrid's generation had specific antecedents that triggered the 1960s–1970s experiments in alternative lifestyles. The Beatles, the
Black Panthers, the Tonkin Gulf Resolution, the Berkeley Free Speech movement all had emerged by 1964, and by 1965 the youth movement was a recognized phenomenon with its own music, charismatic leaders like Timothy
Leary, and charismatic events like Woodstock and Altamont (Miller 1991,
27, 82; Westhues 1972, 193; Zablocki 1980, 50–51). Other cultural symbol makers helped create the perception of a separate reality; in the words
of one participant, "'Many of the young thought of themselves as a distinct
social reality, a separate nation, or, in moments of high enthusiasm, a separate race'" (quoted in Cox 1993, 30). Janis Joplin, Jimi Hendrix, Bob
Dylan, Joan Baez, and many others gave us a concrete sense of this shared
reality, whether we were communards or not. Writers of the counterculture
such as William Burroughs, Allen Ginsberg, Ken Kesey and his group The
Merry Pranksters, and Norman Mailer, and outlaw journalists like Hunter
S. Thompson maintained informal networks reinforcing our worldviews
and our disenchantments with the establishment (Whitmer 1987). Others,
like the Diggers, the Free Family, the Mime Troupe, and eventually the
Rainbow Family, led by example.

   Our generation reached adulthood with the assassination of John F.
Kennedy and it was easy to think that the world beyond our own generation was out of control. The words of another generational cohort member echo Zablocki's understanding of the quest for alternative spaces:

   By the time of the Kent State murders and U.S. incursions into
   Cambodia [in May of 1970] many Movement [New Left] veterans
   wondered whether another mass demonstration really would be

worth the effort. Prospects for radical political reform had died
with Bobby Kennedy and had been further quashed by Mayor
Daley's police force at the 1968 Democratic National Convention.
If you couldn't change American society via the ballot box or
one more giant demonstration, then why not retreat and create
an alternative of your own? If the world was so out of control,
why not do everything possible to take control of your own life?
(Cox 1993, 3)

Timothy Leary had a parallel idea: turn on, tune in, and drop out: "Don't
struggle against society, just disconnect from it" (Zicklin 1983, 26). The
resettlers of Madrid chose to drop out by rebuilding a ghost town, while
others from their generation tried communal living.

Similarities and Differences

FAMILY COMMUNE VERSUS VILLAGE IDENTITY

The parallels between those who tried various forms of communal living
and the social structure and relationships in Madrid, even today, are as
important as the ways in which Madroids differed from the overall communitarian movement. The similarities include the sense of defiant individualism defined above (in all of its complexities), the desire to create a space
for authentic relationships, the overall communal nurturing of children, and
the belief that anarchists could create a community far superior to the ones
they were leaving behind: neither communard nor villager had any idea
what it would take to make that community a reality. On the other hand,
the experience of living in Madrid differed from the 1960s communard
experience in significant ways. With the exception of the Madrid Ducks,
property was privately held and developed along whatever lines the individuals wished. No one was compelled to work for the common good, since
individual self-interest, not the interests of the communal family, came first.
Similarly, work—both physical and ideological—was done for private gain
and usually remained in the private realm, with only the occasional crisis
(such as the summer of the fires or the drug problems in the winter of
1999–2000) drawing forth communal, public energies. Most significantly,
the amount of continual, daily ideological work required in most of the
communal experiments was and remains absent in Madrid. As Bennett M.

Berger (1981) documents, anarchistic communards had a major project that was the nexus of their communal lives—the creation and maintenance of "the family":

> [T]he family was their major enterprise; maintaining and develop-
> ing the communal idea (itself never entirely clear and still in the
> process of emerging) was their main business, rather than the pro-
> motion of a political or religious or psychotherapeutic doctrine . . .
> no one would even admit to the role [of leader] temporarily. . . .
> But few, if any of their ideas were compulsory, and virtually all of
> them were ideas already familiar around the counterculture by
> 1968: peace, freedom, love, spontaneity, spiritual questing
> (through drugs or otherwise), nature, survival, health, equality,
> intimacy, brotherhood-sisterhood . . . and the do-it-yourself thera-
> pies (. . . involving a great deal of talk about 'consciousness,'
> 'space,' and 'working through' hang-ups . . . (29)

Madroids realized, or tried to realize, their collective identity through the ethic of defiant individualism rather than of family; there was little sense, for most resettlers, that intentional ideological work was required for the village to be a valid space in which to live.

Yet in this quote from Berger, we also see some of the similarities between communards and Madroids, particularly the desire to neither con-front nor acquiesce to the hegemony of the dominant culture. Critics of the various counterculture expressions have considered this a form of retreatism, missing the serious critical social and cultural stances taken by many in the counterculture and, sadly, remaining ignorant of attempts at alternative forms for living. It is true that for some, "living in a free space" meant being beyond the reach of law enforcement agencies, but for many others it was a positive move toward less exploitative relations for working and living. Criticized by the center and the right for remaining irresponsi-ble and not growing up, criticized by the left for turning our collective backs on political action, the type of counterculture person who found themselves in places like Madrid sought a different set of imperatives, albeit perhaps not as revolutionary as many of us hoped in the 1960s. As Theodore Roszak (1968) described this situation, political activism had its moments, but for the majority this was not enough to sustain a life:

The activities [political actions] are noble enough. . . . Run them
together as one may, they have not the continuity and comprehen-
siveness demanded by a way of life. . . . Political action and organizing cannot even provide a fulltime career for more than a
handful of apparatchiks, let alone a pattern of life for an entire
generation. What, then, do the disaffected young have to grow
towards? What ideal of adulthood has the world to offer them that
will take the place of the middle class debauch they instinctively
reject? (201)

Put in this context, Madrid and other similar places became locations for
resistance that did not involve daily confrontations with authority yet yielded a life lived in opposition to mainstream values. I would argue, however,
with Roszak's view that the counterculture was any less debauched than the
middle class we rebelled against; the excesses of our generation were its
greatest failures.

Consensual versus Dyslexical Anarchy:
Focus on the Self Rather Than on the Community
An important parallel between the counterculture communes and Madrid
is the enduring ethic of eschewing leadership roles and the closely related
belief in the importance of spontaneity rather than reliance on social structures or institutions to resolve internal dissent. I have discussed the difficulties of leadership in Madrid at some length in the previous chapter, but here
I will add that it is difficult to separate the refusal to accept leadership roles
and the desire to be egalitarian and spontaneous from the other legacy of
the counterculture: violence and personal retribution.

There are other examples from Madrid that shed light on these dilemmas and illustrate the way in which sanctions can take a violent turn. During
a trying time in the community concerning the welfare of an infant who was
perceived by many to be at risk, an original resettler finally called upon the
state authorities to intervene in the matter; as a result he was beaten by
another of the long-time residents for violating the code of village self-
reliance. As Elizabeth summed up the issue of leadership and problem solving while speaking of another village trouble spot: "But people are afraid to
speak up," because although there may be many others in the village who
agree with you, "everybody knew they could put it on my shoulders"—in

other words no one in Madrid will back up the person who speaks up, even if they do agree (interview 1999). Problem solving in Madrid, with some notable exceptions that will be explored in more depth in chapter 6, does not generally entail public or civic action; rather, it involves a further turning inward to find solitary solutions to immediate problems. The dynamics behind this include fear, reluctance to become a spokesperson for others, and the continuance of defiant individualism. Thus, while Madroids share with their communard cohorts a common reluctance to assume strong leadership solutions, their reasons and methods differ somewhat. Research suggests that communards often approached these dilemmas between the collective good and the individual will by attempting a consensual anarchy (Berger 1981; Kanter 1972; Smith 1999; Spurlock 1988; Zablocki 1980; Zicklin 1983): in Madrid this process takes the shape of what I call "dyslexical anarchy" and results in a dispersive community form—dyslexical because everyone speaks for themselves and dispersive because such individualism is not a basis for an integrative community. This contrasts to the intense work communards engaged in using intense daily shared conversations about issues through which a consensus was attempted; in Madrid everyone was looking for their own definition of the situation and was "present" to the sense of community for what each individual could take away from it, rather than for what each person could add to the community.

From wanting to start a band in the desert, to doing only work that is fun, to being in the present without forms of association, Madroids share a sense of spontaneity and the primacy of the existential with 1960s communards. Yet here, too, the more individualistic nature of the village expresses itself. As Rebecca, a later arrivee, explained, "I try not to get too much into what people do because the number one thing is that they are free to do whatever they want to, and for me to learn how to accept that" (interview 1999). The search for spirituality through do-it-yourself therapies is prevalent in Madrid. Someone senses that a healing needs to take place and offers a drumming session out on the land, in much the same way as someone else might host a party. Or, again, through Rebecca's words:

> Every healer needs to be healed. People switching roles all the time. Without form. Going back and forth all the time. I know one person who was practically sainted around here who's really been vilified lately [the person who called the authorities about the per-

ceived child neglect]. It's like we all get to take turns at all these
roles we get to explore . . . (interview 1999)

It is worth taking a longer look at Rebecca's views, for her sentiments are
expressive of the way community is experienced and created in Madrid. She
feels that none of us can heal alone, that healing requires "the other." But
note that the emphasis here is that the "other" exists for the expansion of
self, not a true "communitas" of mutual growth.

Rebecca's explanation of community relationships illustrates the dilemmas faced by dispersive anarchists who want association but whose focus
is on the self rather than the community. She lets people know of her volunteer involvements because

> I try to put myself in public places so that we are already in
> relationship before we need to be talking about anything
> particular. . . . I try to let people know who I am and what I'm
> trying to do and where I come from. If that allows them to do
> any of that then I think we've built a little bit of community. . . .
> I feel free to build community. I think the main thing is to be
> present to what is going on. (interview 1999)

This is not necessarily a sense of putting the community ahead of the primacy of personal experience, however. As this longer quote from this same
interview reveals:

> We have community but it's not in the form where you'd know. . . .
> You have to be receptive to it. [Like] . . . Jonathan who lived among
> us and he was not particularly a person I would have sought out in
> Seattle to be my friend but here we were, we're familiar. . . I ran into
> him and he gave me a big hug and said, "You know, I'm so glad
> that you're having another baby. Thank you so much for being a
> mother.". . . it turned out he had died right after I'd seen him in the
> restaurant. So I thought he had really managed to give me a gift.
> I had managed to do that with him but there were still a lot of
> people that I saw myself as separate from or different from. And
> after that I thought, that's not true. And now I know, I work with
> that everywhere I go. And that has given me a lot of freedom.

Freedom to experience a sense of unity with others, however different they may be from you, is gained not through organized events or stable institutional forms, but through the flow of random meetings and unplanned, everyday events. Any sense of planning or permanence would impose an artificiality to the emotions, thereby interfering with the spontaneous eruption of this highly personal, existential, and fragmented creation of community. Rather than feeling the necessity to experience community among larger groups of people, a key strand in the cultural fabric of Madrid leads residents to seek a flow that can be tapped into by individuals interacting when the moment is right—not that community is something that has to be continually discussed, thought through, simultaneously questioned and verified daily with "family" members as in many of the consensual anarchistic communes of the 1960s.

Freedom from the Norm of Reciprocity

Thus the search for dispersive community forms a central strand of Madrid's culture. As a result, Madrid's defiant individualism is interwoven with its search for authentic relationships as each person's experiences of community become internally and individually interpreted instead of becoming a collective experience; there is little sense of Durkheimian collective consciousness, and therefore the dynamic of individualism can only support a dispersive rather than a cohesive community. Furthermore, authenticity is whatever works for each person, so meanings are seldom contained within a shared framework.

By pleading acceptance of others' shortcomings and abuses, Madroids removed themselves from the communal obligations to maintain a sense of social order. Being "receptive" to community wherever it is happening is not the same as proactively working to create and maintain a social collective, nor is using this dispersive sense of community to increase each person's individual freedom committing yourself to the communal good. And this is related to another strand from the counterculture era, the rejection of authority. By rejecting authority in all its forms and seeking authentic one-on-one relationships over institutional solutions to communal problems, the counterculture resettlers of Madrid also rejected the authority of the social collective to exert any control over individual behaviors. In the absence of communally felt obligations, individuals must rely on themselves, as I have observed many times in this study. Thus community in Madrid has become unhinged from the obligations of reciprocity. This reality is in contrast to the intense and nearly continual work of creating the communal "family" reported by most commune members from the period.

Madrid's residents do, however, share two other characteristics with most of the counterculture communes: the communal nurturing of the village's children, and the granting of dignity and a sense of belonging to individuals who could not survive in less protected environments. The downsides to these good intentions are not having a cohesive network of support for children and others in need and not being able to set clear boundaries for membership in the community. Both also illustrate the inner tensions of attempts at anarchistic community—whether consensual or dispersive. I turn to these two comparisons next.

Children: Wondering the Next Generation

Children, the Counterculture, and the Amature Community

Children in Madrid were and are generally treated as full members of the community, and are "safe and they could go anywhere in town once they were old enough to understand the highway." As several people responded, "To some extent, the village children are looked after by everyone—some people are very invested in that." Another added, "the town watches out for its own children, and there are things that are verboten with the kids" (interview 1999). August expresses it this way:

> I think it was a really good place to raise the kids. . . . The mothers
> stuck together and they did their [thing]—you call it a coffee
> klatch now—but people helped each other out. . . . That little play-
> ground there was built by a group of these people early on and
> there used to be a little doll's house there and some seesaws and
> stuff like that, and the energy was put into it when the people were
> around that needed it. (interview 1999)

Echoing August's sentiment that community emerges wherever it is needed, one young mother feels that Madrid is a "safe place to raise children and . . . I think that there's a real opportunity for families to interact on a real regular basis and again build community," because "We are all together at the school, we are all together in baseball, we're all together trying to put the greenbelt together."

We know from research that the role children assumed in many alternative communes was an elevated one in which the wonderment of the children was viewed as the proper way to relate to the universe (Berger 1981; Smith 1999; Zablocki 1980; Zicklin 1983). Zablocki, in fact, considers this a trait of communards in general, and calls it "amaturity, for this deliberate cultivation of unfinishedness." This refers to a sense of childlike plasticity, not to individual immaturity or stunted development. In one commune studied by Zablocki and his group, they found a sign reading "Find out What the Children are Wondering, and Wonder it" (335–48). This philosophy also underlies life in Madrid, and is part of the spontaneousness of relationships and the desire to always be tuned into the flow of events and feelings.

The Paradoxes of Counterculture Parenting

In a theme that repeats itself in different permutations throughout the social relationships of the counterculture movement, children also symbolize the constant tension between tolerance and authority. Zablocki shows how the tolerance parents felt toward raising their children created a paradox: "The communal parent often seems to combine a highly developed concern and regard for the happiness and welfare of his or her child with an unwillingness to act in behalf of that happiness or welfare" (350). Since the world is changing rapidly, parents did not see what role they could play in shaping their children to meet such uncertainty, and often believe the only thing to do is to stand out of the way as the universe unfolds around their children. As one parent Zablocki interviewed relayed, in considering what role models she had for her child:

> No [none]. Because there isn't any model. He's an Aquarian. He's in the year 2000; that's where he comes in. . . . When these kids are [29 or 30] it will be 2001. There is no mold that I have pictured for him because he is going to do something to blow my mind. I can't even picture it. (351)

The reluctance—perhaps inability—to provide role models for children is a consequence of the refusal to partake in authority structures in general. This refusal shows up in the attitude Madroids have toward their children and the drug culture.

The pervasive use of drugs in Madrid and other counterculture communities could hardly be hidden from their children, and indeed there was no attempt to do so. All the parents who had raised (or are raising) children in the Madrid area reiterated this attitude about drug use; the honesty of relationships was infinitely more important than the exposure to the people in town who use and abuse drugs. A typical response was:

> He's still exposed to all that but here it's real. He knows the guy who shot himself. He knows who got shot, he knows the guy who got run over, he knows the lady who lost the baby. It's very real. It's not abstract. He's able to deal with it right as it comes along. And because he's part of the community, things don't happen in a remote way. Going to the funeral or going to the birth or going to the wedding or going to the changes in our lives and participating. . . . I don't like the alternative; when we mandate how people should behave. That's more repugnant to me than the way people misuse their freedom. (interview 1999)

Once again the repugnance of mandating others' behaviors, even with regard to the effect of such tolerance on the children, is a dominant theme for counterculture participants. While the village's children were accepted as responsible members of the community from an early age and were not shielded from the realities of life in Madrid, the behavior of some parents has pushed the limits of tolerance in the village and hints at the limits of freedom even in Madrid.

The Tragedy of Rachel and Anna

Two or three summers ago a young woman who had visited Madrid for short periods of time returned with her infant and took up residence in the village wherever she could find shelter. Rachel and her infant daughter Anna were known to a number of people in town, many of whom attempted to help her and the baby, as the infant appeared neither well-nourished nor well-cared-for. Rachel did not stay in one place very long, and often refused offers of help with shelter, food, bathing, or infant care. The infant died of exposure one cold night when the mother and infant were sleeping in an unheated area. During the time that Rachel spent in the village before Anna's death, many people reached out to help her and the baby, but, as many people remarked at the time, Rachel only let others do what Rachel wanted done and no more. Rudolph (who has since left the valley for less populated environs) became so concerned that he called the county human services agency about the infant's well-being; as a result Rachel was temporarily confined for observation and the infant placed in foster care. Rudolph was beaten by someone from the village for interfering with the community's attempts at self-healing. Shortly thereafter, several people from Madrid convinced the county authorities that Rachel was competent and that there was plenty of help with the infant, and the county released Anna back to Rachel's care. The infant died within a few days of being reunited with her mother.

This death was a galvanizing, emotional time for most of Madrid's villagers, partly because in such a small place, many people had known the baby and most knew of the struggle Rudolph had faced during this incident. Angela expressed what many people felt at the time:

> A lot of people, like I said, were reaching out to her, because there
> was a lot of heartbreak there. But people weren't doing more.
> People were having her and Anna over, feeding her and bathing
> her and tending to her. And they would think of Anna as [theirs],
> but she wasn't really theirs. I had invited her to come and stay
> and—you know, while you get on your feet, again. That's a judg-
> ment—that she wasn't on her feet—you want to come and get it
> together a little bit. She said no thank you, and right as soon as she
> said no thank you I was frankly relieved. . . . A lot of people were
> like that—not knowing what the right action was and we didn't
> take enough. (interview 1999)

And Rebecca, who had also offered to help, expressed it similarly:

> I think all of our hearts got broken when Anna died. Everyone
> thought if I had only been more with it and more demanding
> that I spend more time with the child and demanding this or
> that for this child. I guess the freedom of the individual and
> the community really [were] up against each other during this
> incident and I am really curious to see how we are going to do
> it the next time. She is certainly not the first child [about which]

the community has said, "You know, excuse me, I'll be grabbing your kid." (interview 1999)

It is terribly easy to look at Rachel and Anna and see a total failure of the community to act, yet it is hardly that simple. Many tried to help and were rebuffed by Rachel herself. And the state is equally if not more culpable; the ease with which mother and child were reunited and returned to a community of minimal resources was a monumental bureaucratic error. The genuine desire on the part of so many in the village to make a difference for this infant must not be trivialized, especially in light of the failure of the state to provide a meaningful alternative. The community as a whole did feel responsible for this mother and child, and keenly felt their perceived failures in achieving a positive outcome, and it is not clear that any other community could have done much more without a more proactive involvement of state welfare officials.

After Anna's death, people in the community provided burial clothes, one man built a tiny coffin, and others arranged for the priest from neighboring Cerrillos to come and hold a ceremony at the Madrid graveyard, a ceremony attended by a great many people in town. Then, this tragedy was multiplied a hundredfold when Rachel went to the grave site, opened the coffin, and carried the dead infant around for a brief period until the community once again called on the state to act, this time without any reprisals. Today Rachel has become one of the fringe people granted a protected space in the community, for the most part staying out in the countryside. This desire to protect and nurture the disadvantaged is what Willie spoke of as "this beautiful sense of community" in Madrid—but Anna's death marks the terrible potential cost of unfettered tolerance when mere nurturance is insufficient to meet the immediate need.

While not as tragic as Rachel's case, another young girl in the village was being looked after by some members of the community while all of this was going on. Serena, whose mother is an alcoholic, was looked after by four village women who individually tried to see that she was clean, fed, and received some socialization, and that she was safe at night. With this child, too, we see the paradoxes created around the desires for freedom, acceptance, and community involvement.

Elizabeth could see the plight of this child as she waited for her mother to come out of the tavern at night, and she expressed yet another concern when speaking of Serena's situation. She felt that all the well-meaning intervention by individual Madroids was "attempting to protect Serena from being turned in to the state by giving her a false sense of being cared about. I know she is being cared for [here], but one of these days her mother—she's going to get kicked out of the bar or whatever, and she is going to move on and then the vicious cycle will start all over again for Serena." The desire to help but the inability to see how to help without passing judgment on the recipient (other than to call in the authority of the state—an institution most Madroids do not trust) is the conundrum that Madroids often feel about becoming overly involved with others' lives. Worse yet, Elizabeth fears that even the succor provided is going to be harmful in the long run when the child is no longer in Madrid. While anxieties and uncertainties over what to do about ill-treated children plague all communities, in anarchistic ones that value freedom as a means to ethical behavior and value children as exemplars of human-*beingness*, such events cut to the core of their ideological structure.

The Amature Community and the Future

The sense of childlike plasticity and amaturity Zablocki described among communal parents is often expressed by Madrid parents, whether speaking about their own children or the village children in general (field notes 1998–2000). This wonderment and sense of unfinishedness might also be said about the villagers' approach to their community's future, as much as to their children. When this uncertainty about future roles is combined with defiant individualism, fear of recrimination, and the ethos of acceptance, the reluctance of villagers to take direct action in approaching community issues is less surprising. The beating Rudolph suffered for interfering with Rachel's parenting is illustrative of the thinness of community consensus in Madrid, and it was particularly egregious because there were few people in Madrid who had more cultural capital in the village, as Rudolph had been a "tunnel rat" during his service in Vietnam, going into the Vietcong tunnels to clear them out armed only with a .45 automatic pistol. His Vietnam experiences had granted him a relatively privileged position until this incident. Rudolph's own refusal to take retaliatory steps toward his attacker—either through legal or extra-legal means, points to the strength of the tyranny of individualism, as does the fact that many people in town knew who had attacked him but refused to step forward.

The villagers are aware of these dilemmas. As Rebecca stated about the Children's Workshop that operates sporadically, "It's still a preschool. I've heard people talk about wanting it to be more, but I guess that's another vulnerable position because everybody has something to say about how to do it" (interview 1999). Taking a stand means becoming vulnerable, becoming visible, and risking becoming proactive instead of receptive to the flow of events, and risking losing the sense of amaturity so important to Madrid's villagers. In the case of some village children—and perhaps a few adults—who need more than self-reliance can offer, it is the lack both of community and state institutions that fail to provide a larger network of social support networks. The spontaneity and the unwillingness of Madroids to coalesce and take concerted public action are both a strength to the village and a weakness; they are a strength because they create these spaces in which the truly disadvantaged can find a home with dignity and a modicum of support. They are a weakness because some folks need more than just a tolerant space, and try as they might, the villagers seem incapable of taking meaningful action toward helping those people, in spite of wanting very sincerely to do so.

The villagers' need to remain present to whatever is happening at the moment makes it difficult to plan for the future of the village, in the same way that parents are reluctant to shape their children's futures. Caring and nurturing have not always been sufficient to protect individuals in the village; similarly, allowing the village to simply drift into gentrification guarantees the future exclusion of these special people—and that part of the community that makes Madrid a unique place to live. There is no guarantee that organized planning would protect the village from encroaching growth better than their present lack of action, but their inaction will most certainly end up threatening the very folks they are so proud of sheltering.

Communards also had problems with tolerance and the acceptance into their communities of problematic individuals. I will close this comparison between the communard experience and the village experience with this theme of how open, tolerant communities deal with setting boundaries.

Setting Community Boundaries

No community, no matter how accepting, can survive—as many of the "open" communes of the 1960s found—without limiting its membership in some way if it hopes to survive as an integral entity. Limiting membership for communes, of course, is a dynamic different from limiting the people who can live in an unincorporated village, yet the people who are allowed to stay in these two settings are often surprisingly similar. I have only partial evidence as to why certain people are eventually forced out of either set of communities, but what evidence there is points to people whose egos are both too fragile and too self-important to allow them to flow with the community's feelings and needs. In many communes, sexual relationships became so complex that bonding between individuals when done serially and/or simultaneously threatened the bonds to the overall family of the commune (Berger 1981; Kanter 1972; Smith 1999; Zablocki 1980). There is no evidence from any interviews or three years of observation in Madrid that this was the case here. Madroids, for the most part, practiced serial monogamy like most of the rest of America (with the exception of the Ducks, who had dispersed by the early 1980s). So intimate interpersonal relationships were not the threat to community solidarity that they often were in communes. But, as in communes, there are occasionally people who are asked to leave because they appear to threaten what solidarity exists. On the other hand, there are individuals who are fringe people (even in alternative communities that pride themselves on acceptance) who are allowed to remain on the margins of the community, and those individuals reveal as much about the dynamics of inclusion and exclusion as do the people who leave.

The ethos of acceptance common to Madroids and other alternative communities—even toward those whose conformity to the ideologies of the place are questionable—is expressed in this example from Zablocki's work. A fringe member of a rural commune was openly freeloading off of the community, did not share their ideologies or their educational backgrounds, and, was in fact, an alcoholic, a thief, and a bully.

> Everyone was a little afraid of him; he was always abusive and
> could get violent when drunk. But in his debilitated state he was
> no match in a fight with any of the other men, several of whom
> would beat him up from time to time. Neither was he treated
> much better than he treated others. He was often mocked,
> even by the children, and was frequently the victim of cruel
> practical jokes. He was often asked to leave, without much
> conviction. (1980, 139–40)

Zablocki suggests that this outsider provided needed definition for the commune members by being the resident scapegoat for releasing aggression and firming up communal norms. It is striking how many of the characteristics of this person match a variety of individuals we have already seen in our exploration of Madrid's social interactions: the abusive alcoholic who was stabbed to death and then his trailer burned to the ground; the petty thieves in town whom everyone knows, and whom most shopkeepers don't let in their stores, yet are never asked to leave nor turned in to the authorities; the village children who as adults deal drugs openly in the street and until very recently were excused for not growing up; the heroin-dealing families who are generally ostracized but still tolerated; and the dysfunctional mothers who refuse aid while remaining part of the village.

In addition to the above characters who compose the social landscape of Madrid, there are those who would be considered dysfunctional (some to the point of institutionalization) in less tolerant communities. As stated earlier, in Madrid they have valued places in the community, they have odd jobs that bring them a minimum of income (although many are able to collect Social Security disability in addition to these small earnings), and they are watched over by the villagers. The main group of such individuals is comprised of original or later resettlers; newcomers are not treated thusly so easily; as Elizabeth remarked, "I think we have what we can support." In this, Madrid parallels cities that send their homeless out of town on a one-way Greyhound bus ticket, conserving the community's resources for their own "deserving poor." Madrid's original poor are thus truly a privileged group, for the acceptance and tolerance shown these people are not easily extended to newer migrants.

One of those privileged folks in Madrid is town matriarch, and there are perhaps a dozen or so other men and women who fit this category, a large percentage of whom are long-time substance abusers. The villagers deal with the presence of so many seemingly distracted individuals ideologically by considering Madrid to be "the largest unfenced insane asylum in New Mexico" and by often remarking, "What homeless problem? We have them all right here." Many counterculture communities share Madrid's overt tolerance for dysfunction and the ability to find positive roles for individuals displaying such behaviors.

A not atypical example of this positive acceptance of idiosyncratic behavior outside of Madrid is found in Berger's 1981 study of communes.

Berger's book looks especially at the ideological work required to bring communal beliefs in line with people's actual behavior, and the many ways in which communards had to work daily at justifying their actions. He documents an interesting example of positive acceptance:

> In a rural commune in central California, we ran into a young man who was clearly hospitalizably insane. He conducted dialogues with plants and animals. He would occasionally drop his pants and shit on the floor of the communal house, or, if he could be induced to go to the toilet, would sit on the stool for hours. But he was a gifted gardener and very good with the farm animals. The group banished him from the house to a shed in the field he cultivated and close to the animals he looked after. The group took care of him, protecting him from the world he was incompetent to live in, in exchange for the useful services he performed for them. (129, footnote 29)

Madrid has several individuals who consider themselves in communication with the universe of plants, animals, and the cosmos in general, and who will explain their ideas at great length if you show the least interest. One gentleman, Barefoot Brian, never wore shoes, and talked often of the star children who it was our obligation to become, so the earth could take its proper place in the universe. He, like other fringe people, are tolerated and protected from overt harm—although not from harming themselves with destructive lifestyles involving drugs or alcohol. This protective quality is also evident among other relationships in Madrid between those capable of working and being self-supporting and those who need nurturance in a manner not dissimilar to that granted the villages' children.

   While communards and the villagers of Madrid share many counterculture elements, it is evident that Madroids both create and experience these characteristics differently than do communards. Communards were mainly concerned, as we have seen, with "the family," while Madroids were more concerned with their individual lives and allowed their community to be one that was there for those who were open and "present" to it; in fact, we have seen that many Madroids were surprised to find they had a sense of community. Therefore it is not surprising that the sense of defiant individualism became more pronounced in Madrid than in most commune situations. This is reflected in how far each type of community could go in setting limits to its membership.

When "family work" and the need to spend long hours debating consensual anarchy became too much, communards simply left of their own accord. In Madrid there was no such demand to participate in self-conscious, shared discoveries of community; individuals went their own way but could stay in the village, especially because property in Madrid was never held communally. Intense interpersonal interactions were limited to close friends or intimate family members, not the entire village, and the openness of the landscape during the resettlement phases included space for many lifestyle choices. Interaction networks were therefore far less dense than in most family-oriented communes. Communards and Madroids were most similar in the nurturance both of children and those adults incapable of functioning in the outside world; they were most different in the ways that people created and experienced community.

Community for the family-oriented communards meant constant ideological work, and the messiness of often shifting intimate sexual relations placed great strain on the ability of many communes to survive (Berger 1981; Kanter 1972; Zablocki 1980). Zablocki's conclusions, in fact, were "that communal systems, in their search for consensus, tend to generate intense networks of interpersonal interactions, which, in the absence of periodic charismatic renewal, tend to be associated with communal instability." Therefore he theorizes that the density of linkages among members is inversely related to the stability of a commune. He suggests, based on his research, as Etzioni (1975) and Granovetter (1972) also found, that "too much bondedness can be as harmful to an organization, even a commune, as is too little bondedness." Importantly, however, he found that for individuals the opposite was true; the more linkages among commune members, the greater the tendency for that individual to stay (356). This is a somewhat surprising finding, because it indicates that what was good for individuals was not the same as what was good for the commune.

In their search for a nonconsensual anarchistic community, Madroids may have found a viable middle ground between the two extremes of too much and too little bondedness; the tendency for Madrid to be a dispersive rather than a consensual anarchistic community may be a key to its survival. As one villager described this relationship, expressing a sentiment felt by the majority of interviewees and observed in many others, "The fact that we are so uninterested in organizing is our strength." Without the need for consensus to order daily living, individuals were free to pursue their own ends without the constant need for ideological work to layer priorities and structure decision making. The consensus that evolved in Madrid was more serendipity, constructed out of the shared counterculture capital that the resettlers brought with them, the hardships of rebuilding a worn-out, abandoned mining camp, and the relative isolation from outside social control mechanisms. Madroids avoided these particular conundrums by not involving themselves with consensus or with leadership—charismatic or otherwise—and by capitalizing on the strength of weak ties.

The Positive Role of Individualism

Lifestyle Freedoms

The discontinuity of personal relationships does not mean that people do not help each other, support the occasional community activity, or care about the future of the village. It is just that the tenuous nature of village interactions never completely overcomes the individualistic ethos. There are positive aspects to village life that are palpable, and these are the qualities that those who chose to stay in the area rely on as social glue, even if that glue is not overly sticky.

I wish to discuss some of these freedoms because they are central to understanding the dynamics of tolerance and spontaneity in Madrid. I have mentioned the gender and sexual liberty that individuals express openly. Even among newcomers like Bernice, drug use is only a worry if it impinges on your life or livelihood. Because many people are involved with arts, crafts, or just plain subsistence living, the dress is at best utilitarian. There is a freedom in this simple, direct living; the lack of pretense can be refreshing. In such an atmosphere, posturing is both obvious and entertaining. Thus the "posers, jokers, and thieves" play an almost positive role in community relations as they form a known group of court jesters who can be relied upon to provide amusing incidents for conversation at the coffee shop or the bar.

Madrid's own walking wounded, on the other hand, fit in by fulfilling the community's belief in its own tolerance. And, indeed, these people are treated with a high degree of dignity and are able to live relatively self-sufficient lives without stigmatization because of the underground and off-the-book economies in the village that they utilize to stretch their other sources of income, which include government assistance and transfer payments. As there is no stigma attached to using such sources for survival—this was part of how the original resettlers provisioned themselves—there is no need for secrecy or shame in appropriating whatever aid may be available. It is, however, among this group of people that we find those most likely to either leave on their own or to be pushed out by changing norms as the village gentrifies. We already saw this process when Rudolph left, and even the town matriarch is feeling the pressure as her public behavior becomes increasingly subject to the scrutiny of tourists. Tia remarked to me that she "feels there's a tree waiting for me in Mexico" because there is too much pressure now in Madrid toward conformity.

As those who live and work in Madrid become more dependent upon tourism for their livelihood, the old tolerance for drug users is beginning to fade. But even here, the wrath of the merchants is aimed only at those who publicly use and abuse, and who thereby create a negative impact on tourism. These conversations are carefully couched to prevent any impression that drug use itself, or those who supply the local drug economy, should be banned. As Rebecca indicated in speaking about her children, the abuse of power by the state is felt to be a far greater threat than those few who abuse their freedoms. There is one exception to this attitude that I have observed; there is at least one family of long-time heroin users and dealers. After the death of one of the long-time locals under somewhat suspicious circumstances involving using and dealing heroin, there was some talk about the need to "do something" about that family. But for as long as I remained in touch with the villagers, this "something" never materialized.

Agency and Self-Sufficiency

The "quaint" quality of Madrid to which the tourists often respond is not, at least to date, a themed environment. It is still a hard place to live; good water, food, heating fuel, and even gasoline are not available in town. The supermarket in The Old Boarding House by necessity has higher prices than in chain stores in Santa Fe. Laundry facilities, auto repair, or recreational facilities (other than the coffee shop and the bar) are nonexistent. The town remains much as it was in the early days of resettlement: a place where you do things for yourself, find a friend with whom you can barter, or do without. This element, as much as the emphasis on individualism, weeds out certain people who are not as self-sufficient as Madrid demands. In this case, it is not social pressure but rather physical necessity that encourages some to leave. This is particularly true for those who live off the back roads and not directly in town. The only paved road in the immediate area is Highway 14; the rest are dirt roads, most of them private. Snowmelt or rain renders many impassible or nearly so for days at a time. There are few areas with electricity outside of town, necessitating solar systems or even reliance on kerosene for light. For many individuals and families, what they have built themselves is what they possess, having invested in raw land without any improvements.

The solitude and beauty of such a harsh life is undeniable, but such a life requires continual reinvestment of personal energy, constant renewal of daily rituals involving water, heating, and providing the other necessities of life, all this while located miles from paved roads, and while depending on ancient vehicles kept running by skill and knowledge of whom in the community has spare parts for barter. Life in the village proper is not quite so immediate and demanding, but it is not far from this. It is the loss of this sense of self-sufficiency and independence that the resettlers feel: houses are now built by contractors hired for the job and using new materials instead of by the owners and a group of their friends using materials scrounged from vacant buildings; people drive to Santa Fe or even Albuquerque now to shop, as modern cars are more reliable than the vintage 1960s vehicles of the hippies; and newer settlers are not as dependent upon the local economy or each other for sustenance. As Santa Fe encroaches ever closer to Madrid from the north, stores make consumption easier than making your own commodities. This perceived loss of authenticity in everyday living is keenly felt among many of the resettlers, as they see the commodified and mediated world they sought to escape catching up with their community.

If the American myth of self-reliance needs a place to reinvigorate itself, places like Madrid still exist to exemplify the roots of this ideology. That some of its residents use redistributive justice in the form of food stamps, welfare payments, and Social Security disability checks to aid in survival does not mean the frontier mythos has failed; this is simply another form in which the state plays its historic role as underwriter of the legendary role of the American frontier. Inasmuch as the people who stay in Madrid choose to do so, the villagers represent a form of voluntary simplicity that has always been a hallmark of the frontier existence.

Sustainabilities

The necessities of frugal living and making do that come attached to this semi-rural life have also brought with them different awareness of ecological issues. Some original resettlers intentionally came to the area in order to build a more socially just and ecologically sustainable community, as mentioned above. Many families and individuals live "off the grid," the vernacular term for living off of the electrical power grid. For some this is by choice, as electricity could be brought to their land, but for the majority of those who live off the back roads around Madrid, being off the grid is simply one more element of the frontier self-reliant lifestyle. It is a badge of independence, a form of social protest against the establishment and its rules and payments. Passive and active solar systems provide heating and electricity respectively, and can run from simple systems costing under $1,000 for solar panels and batteries to upwards of $20,000 for completely self-monitoring active systems.

Life in Madrid does have a heightened sense of immediacy under such conditions: dishes must be washed while there is sunlight to run the pump for the well; repairs must be accomplished during the warm (or cool) part of the day; water must be rationed between gardens and kitchen chores. Finding enough gas money to get to the feed store and procure kerosene and propane can be an accomplishment for those living close to the edge of economic subsistence. When these elements come together and these survival rituals are successfully completed, it adds legitimacy to the feeling of individualism, self-reliance, and self-sufficiency.

The ability to "live lightly off the land" and to "leave a lighter footprint" as you go is deeply tied to the frontier, experimental, unfinished edginess to life in and around Madrid. There still exists, in the interviews I conducted among people of all arrival times, a sense that they are the model for the future. This "authenticity" of having an unmediated lifestyle in which you must participate or not thrive (or in some cases survive) is seen as being the way the rest of the world should live if we want to escape a global collapse. This sense of continuing the fight against abstract, unjust social and economic systems helps people cope with the roughness of life in this semi-rural place. And, importantly, it forms an ideological bridge between the generations.

This bridge between the original resettlers who were, directly or indirectly, part of the counterculture movements of the 1960s and the later arrivees is one of the cohesive forces of the community, even though the attendant ideologies of individualism and self-sufficiency keep people from forming deeply cohesive interactions. Peter Coyote wrote about the costs to individuals of pursuing absolute freedom; there are costs to communities as well. An intensive, living-lightly-off-the-land lifestyle is physically demanding and requires a great deal of time. Energy and time, which might be put toward communal activities, are instead used for daily living. These physical and individual constraints are added to the disinclination of many Madroids to partake in communal activities. The inability or unwillingness to submit to anyone else's authority works against organized social activities, and, in a vicious cycle, the lack of communal activities decreases the amount of authority individuals will grant to the village collective. As Durkheim wrote, each individual in a community must come to see the collective consciousness as coming from outside himself—as being representative of a communal moral force—even though it is each individual in a collective who creates that force. But this moral communal force cannot be created in the first place if people do not meet and develop common opinions.

This dyslexia is why individuals in Madrid are continually returned back to their own resources; a complex interweaving of physical necessity and ideological constraints usually prevents the communal "effervescence" that carries individuals outside of themselves. This cult of the individual has been deeply internalized by many members of this community, and the individual ethos always seems stronger than the ability of the community to come together long enough to establish social rituals in which interaction chains last long enough to become lasting institutions; in Madrid cultural capital is invested more heavily in the individual than in the community. However, if the tolerance toward drug users and dysfunctional people were removed, Madrid does not look all that different from other communities where political power and efficacy are fragmented and residents appear trapped in the tyranny of individual and communal poverty that makes involvement with community affairs tenuous. In fact, there are some communities to which Madrid can profitably be compared.

Comparisons to Other Communities

In what ways is Madrid different from any other poor, semi-rural locale in America—communities in which poverty, disillusionment, and alienation are major factors keeping their members from proactive participation in changing their life circumstance? What relation does Madrid's alienation have to the "amoral familism" Edward Banfield (1954) studied in Sicily? Why should we not view Madrid as a free-rider community? I turn next to reflect on these comparative questions.

Why is Madrid Not Just Another Potter Addition?

In his depiction of a semi-rural lower-working-class community on the fringes of a major urban area in the Midwest, David Harvey describes this "hillbilly slum" in terms not unlike my descriptions of Madrid. Most of the residents of the Potter Addition, if they worked, worked at alienating jobs and understood, at some basic level, that the greater portion of their lives' chances was decided by forces beyond their control. Existing at a level of poverty hardly changed since the Great Depression, they made do with bartering, sharing family resources from generation to generation, and subsisting at a variety of trade jobs rather than investing in learning higher paying skills. The butt of jokes from those more affluent, the community seemed rooted in ignorance and in backward, traditional means of coping with poverty that only seemed to doom each succeeding generation to the same fate (Harvey 1993).

Madrid has its "Potterville," a side valley behind the main village where one family has settled and expanded its homestead with an assortment of vernacular structures and old vehicles. The nearby village of Cerrillos has an area known as "Poverty Flats" back in the hill country. Madrid proper, as we have seen, has its share of people who survive on the bare minimum of skills and resources. As documented in the introduction, New Mexico is a poor state, with little manufacturing. Rural areas are even poorer and the economic opportunities even fewer. The caution here is that most people in New Mexico are poorer than the average American, and many have learned to cope in various ways with this structural inequality—the folks in Madrid are no exception. If there were more water in many parts of northern New Mexico, the region would look like Appalachia.

Just as Harvey documents for the Potter Addition, people in New Mexico and Madrid make do with what they have and invent ways to make sense out of their environment. The most relevant distinction in communities such as Madrid is the voluntary nature of the relative poverty. As we saw with Rebecca and George, even the newer arrivees leave lucrative, middle-class positions to live on the edge, and they have the skills to return to that life again should they decide to do so. By and large, their children will leave the village, having been given the same coping skills their parents brought to the village. Cross-generational voluntary poverty has not been a prominent feature in Madrid.

Another element of the relative poverty of Madrid comes from the drug culture. The elite outlaws who reside in the area do not exhibit their wealth in flamboyant or obvious ways, for reasons that should need no explaining. Conspicuous consumption or conspicuous construction of out-of-scale residences would draw unwanted attention—to themselves and to the town. There is a loss to the community from this pretense of poverty, because just as these folks do not make a point of advertising, neither can they be approached for charity or goodwill causes. During the time I was observing the village, none of these folks came forth into the public arena with donations to any local cause—keeping a low profile is this group's main attribute. So, once again, interactions that in less individualistically driven communities might provide pathways for more stable institutions never really surface in Madrid. Blending in, a sort of existential reversion to the mean, takes place in Madrid. Even though people compete to be more individualistic than the next person, that individualism is found in bracketed expressions of genteel or working-artist poverty at the top of the scale, on down to barefoot and barely covered at the bottom. My experiences in the town suggest that these presentations of self are not even at the level of a folkway; there are neither negative sanctions for dressing well nor positive ones for dressing down. I believe this behavior is shaped as a result of the lack of positive sanctions for dressing up. If one is going to be treated nearly the same no matter what the outer appearance, why go to the trouble of dressing up, especially if one is also coping with old cars, muddy roads, and assorted village animals who are always willing to lend a paw to a clean outfit.

What Does Madrid Have in Common with Banfield's Amoral Familism?

While there are many superficial resemblances between Madroids and Banfield's (1954) Sicilian peasants, I believe the differences are more important than the similarities. The Sicilian Montegranesi are rooted in their historical status as peasants, people who stay in their place, literally. Their geographic roots and their economic desperateness remain unchanged from one generation to another. Hopes for improvement in life do not stem from internal motivations but rather from outside good fortune. While there is a certain stoicism present in both communities, and a similar sense of fatalism among some Madroids, the latter were not born into an intergenerational counterculture community. The middle-class skills, the abundance of material goods available in the American economy, and the ready mobility of Madroids set them in stark contrast to the Montegranesi. Rather than investing their future in their children and families, the folks of Madrid prefer a more hands-off approach to child-rearing. I think Zablocki's (1980) term "amaturity" is better suited to the attitudes of the average Madroid. While people in each community are largely apolitical, the reasons are substantively different. The peasant of Montegrano has never held political or economic power, and the self-centeredness Banfield documented there was a survival technique related to the structural and historic poverty of a whole social class. The self-exile chosen by most Madroids was a conscious retreat from engagement, a turning inward toward the self as a means of becoming receptive to the universe, and a reflection of their disenchantments with the political insanity of the dominant society.

In addition to some sharing of stoicism, there are those in Madrid whose fatalism approaches that of the Montegranesi peasants. The majority of these folks are the fringe people in Madrid, those who have heavily engaged in drugs and who are not deeply involved in running shops or businesses. These people express deep feelings of powerlessness to change their personal lives for the better or to engage in political activities to attempt structural changes to the world in which they live. As television reception is not good in the area, many listen to late-night radio talk shows, some of which emphasis the paranormal and the extraterrestrial. Overhearing conversations among these folks at the coffee shop or the store gives a glimpse into a world of paranoia and bizarre relationships between causes and effects that bear little relation to what most of us recognize as normal. Placing responsibility for events on such uncontrollable forces adds to the distrust of power and authority that is a common theme in the village.

For these small number of individuals, remaining invisible is their form of defense against an unpredictable, if not hostile, universe. Banfield does not document any such beliefs in the paranormal or extraterrestrial among the Sicilian peasants, but the withdrawal of energy from public relations and the turning inward toward private concerns—for Madroids usually the self, rather than the family—in both communities result in a paucity of civically oriented activity. The outward similarity, however, is the result of vastly differing histories.

The Free-Rider Problem

Why should Madrid as a collective not be viewed as a community riding along on the shirttails of America's wealth and political hegemony? This argument is harder to counter. Dropping out in the 1960s and 1970s may have seemed like a viable option to rebellion or cooptation, but thirty years later that seems a thinly veiled excuse for hedonism. The resentment felt by the working poor and the bourgeoisie toward the free life of the hippies has been well documented (see Coyote's discussion of such responses earlier). The incredulity expressed by outsiders at choosing to live such a minimalist life, when one has the skills to compete and succeed at middle-class occupations, is still a fact of life for current residents of Madrid, as we will see in the next chapter. Only by understanding that these freedoms have their own costs can Madrid be seen as anything other than a community of free-riders, especially when one considers the ease with which individuals use government transfer payments as an entitlement from the very power structure they so distrust. If we contrast the suburban village in Viditch and Bensman's (1968 [1958]) study to Madrid, we can highlight these contrasts better.

Among suburban community members, Viditch and Bensman did not find much awareness of the reality of the forces the small town of self-employed shop owners and middle-class professionals faced regarding the encroachment of a global, mass society into their lives. Their typical reaction was to work longer hours to compete with stores and facilities in the larger cities, while the reality was that their once self-sufficient town was becoming a commuter bedroom community subservient to outside economic restructuring. While Madrid is also in danger of succumbing to such restructuring and the gentrification of its counterculture ambiance, the depth of defiant individualism and the self-conscious choice of minimalist lifestyles contrast with the former's attempt at accommodation. As I will discuss in the next chapter, it is not the Madroids' desire to compete with the encroaching mass society that forms a basis for conflict in the village, but rather its inability to organize on its own behalf in the face of such dangers.

Ultimately, whether Madrid is seen as yet another group of free-riders living on federal subsidies on the frontier depends on whether one feels that alternatives to a mass society, now on a global scale, are valuable places for individuals to live or whether they are anachronisms from the preindustrial past that stand in the way of modernity's homogenizing hegemony.

Conclusions

A loosely tied community held together by the late-twentieth-century inversions of the Protestant ethic would, on the surface, appear to be vulnerable to dissolution. Yet Madrid thrives for the moment in its own fashion, attracting a few retirees and a few younger people who appreciate the perceived freedoms of the village. The disenchantment of the world, in Madrid, implies not only disenchantment from traditional beliefs and authority but also a dislocation from the forms of economic and social production in the dominant world system of capitalism. Yet, the destruction by capitalism of traditional forms of social control—religious communities and extended family structures—made secular communities of inwardly oriented individuals possible. Substituting hyper-individualism for the sacred has created a dispersive form of community documented here. But this disenchantment has also unleashed a dyslexical anarchy, wherein each individual speaks her or his own language of the self, and each person interprets the community and its everyday events individually. But this same dyslexical community has woven a fabric of tolerance and acceptance in which even seriously dysfunctional people have valued and positive roles to play.

There is a great irony to communities like Madrid, for while the material abundance of late capitalism has enabled individuals to concentrate on what they *want* rather than on what they *need*, what we want has often been defined in such places as simple living without taking more than you need. Once the productive capacity of capitalism reached a certain point, people could willingly choose to turn their backs on that wealth. Those of us with counterculture leanings felt that the abundance of material wealth was out there for everyone to share—indeed some felt it was an obligation to liberate other people's property if they were not using it and you needed it. This meant that what you *wanted* suddenly became defined as the bare necessities of life, since you could always get what you really *needed* for survival. This set of beliefs made it very easy to move from middle-class consumption and work ethic patterns to living lightly off the land and simple living outside of mainstream jobs and obligations. Witness the exploitation of government transfer payments as an entitlement by Madrid's resettlers. This sense that abundance is there for the taking is very close to the ideologies behind the first Anglo settlement of the West: the wealth of the land and its resources were there for anyone willing to exploit them—especially with a little help from the government.

For many counterculture practitioners the disaffection felt by Madroids toward authority in all its forms forced a retreat from mainstream society to these semi-rural areas where law enforcement was thin or nonexistent. But it also necessitated a retreat from engagement in local community forms of collective consciousness and the formation of a collective moral sense. The emphasis on self-healing, self-sufficiency, and self-awareness is a reflection of the cult of the individual and the ability of this ideology to be as tyrannical over social relations as would be a total dedication of the self to the collective good.

The spontaneous, unfinished amaturity of the counterculture movement keeps this sense of an always-emerging self in the forefront of community relations, overpowering any desire to form tighter community structures. Being receptive to the world rather than proactive in it, when combined with the paranoia of the drug culture and the physical demands of life on this semi-frontier, has created an ideology that Madrid's "unfenced insane asylum" will continue to protect the community from encroachments from the outside world. But as both resettlers and increasing numbers of newer arrivees capitalize on the village's ambience, the village's very difference becomes a commodity to be traded on the real estate markets. No community anywhere is immune from the larger forces of globalization and commodification of the environment. The temporary reprieve that the counterculture generation found in places like Madrid is in danger of itself being commodified. But in this temporary space, Madrid's villagers have found a way to partly defy the dominant culture's materialist hegemony and the state apparatus of control that comes with it: they have done this without living a life of constant mass protests or by acquiescing to it, but by simply living.

In the next chapter, I will look at some natural experiments requiring community cohesion that took place during my tenure in the village. These will more strongly highlight the primary strands and tensions of life in Madrid, and the dispersive community and dyslexical anarchy underlying it.

CHAPTER SIX

Natural Experiments in Community

I have presented Madrid as a community of defiant individualists pursuing semi-anarchistic lives of self-fulfillment combined with a simple living ethos. While I was living in the community, events other than the tragic death of baby Anna occurred that tested the community's ability to pull together for the common good; these events can be seen as natural experiments in how the villagers responded to opportunities for building consensus and taking communal action. The precarious nature of Madrid's dyslexic, dispersive community form was (and continues to be) tested against the twin issues of growth vs. no-growth agendas and the legacy of drug use inherited from the counterculture generation.

Planning: Authority and Ambiguity

The Historical Context

As I have documented in chapter 2, Santa Fe County planning officials had taken a proactive stand toward addressing uncontrolled growth and development since the 1970s. This stance resulted in the mid-1990s in a county-wide referendum in which voters enabled planners to begin an active program of protecting historic or other unique communities, incorporated or not, by helping these communities write their own master plans and zoning ordinances based on the needs and wants of their residents. To this end the county assigned planners to coordinate meetings in each village and work with community representatives to enact these documents. Planners hoped that this initiative would provide some protection from the exurban sprawl engulfing the county; this was a case in which the interests of local government, grassroots activists, and the general public coalesced in the effort to protect lifestyles in existing settlements as well as to preserve some areas in the county from any kind of development.

Not surprisingly, this was not to be a simple process in Madrid as there were problems both with picking a leadership coalition and with reaching a consensus, and the county of Santa Fe had to assign three successive planners to work with the villagers. The highest profile issue in the village was the water, followed by speeding through town, public parking, youth projects, public restrooms, and parks.

Madrid shares its contradictory feelings about growth with most communities. The same people who want better jobs—jobs that would require growth of some kind—are opposed to any change to the existing quality of life. Most communities have not found a good compromise between the two, for while tourism is often touted as the solution to economic growth without degradation to the environment, such development is seldom without costs, as we saw earlier. In Madrid these issues are particularly evident in the debates about roads. The main road through town has become clogged with tourists' cars and even tour busses carrying international visitors; conducting local business becomes nearly impossible during heavy tourists days. Additionally, most of the parking areas consist of simply pulling off the main highway, making walking from store to store a challenge as the parked cars take up what little space exists along the side of the road. Yet the merchants and other folks who own vacant land along the main street will not allow these areas to be developed into parking areas, so the chaos just multiplies as the villagers resort to their accustomed manner of solving problems by doing very little. We will see shortly what Madrid's answer to public restroom facilities has been.

The Village Boundary Debate

I began observing these planning meetings after a volunteer university planning group had turned their findings over to the county (Design and Assistance Planning Center 1997), and a county liaison (the second of the three) was coordinating meetings held in the firehouse. The purpose of the meetings now was not to assess community feelings but to decide what territory would be considered within the historic boundaries of Madrid and what zoning rules would govern this defensible space. The meetings were open to the entire village, but again usually only a group of ten or fewer came. Harris, head of the Madrid Landowners Association (MLA) and a real estate broker with an office in town, had assumed leadership of the planning forum and was pushing for extending the traditional boundaries of the townsite to include his properties at the south end of town. These boundaries were financially and culturally important; Huber had gotten Madrid's land rush approved by the county as a small subdivision with three-quarter-acre lots for individual dwellings. Beyond the village limits, the county's regulations require twenty acres per dwelling—a sizable difference in development potential, yet those limits had never been legally established.

The water commissioner (virtually the only one Madrid has ever had) and one other original resettler were arguing for the boundaries to be smaller, while Harris held out for the more inclusive limits so he could subdivide his own holdings into townsite lots at three-quarters of an acre instead of one larger lot. Two successive meetings deadlocked over this boundary issue, after heated and emotional debates between the resettlers and Harris. But in the end, the MLA president wore everyone else down and won the day; the boundaries were set to Harris's advantage.

Similar to many communities, the majority of villagers approached this whole county planning process with apathy. A typical quote from resettlers about these planning meetings was, "Planning meeting? No, why should I go, the county never comes out here anyway. Besides, they've been holding these meetings for years and never get anywhere." One resettler told me that he had already done his share of community "stuff," and he was not going to get involved with this because it would end up the same way all the other meetings had—a lot of head banging and creation of bad feelings with nothing concrete being accomplished. Some later arrivees simply felt this was not anything they wanted to be involved with because the outcomes were irrelevant to their involvement in Madrid as gallery and shop owners. As communities everywhere face changes that often emanate from global realignments, the villagers' apathy and inability to organize will give the town little protection against becoming another themed bedroom suburb of Santa Fe.

Open Spaces and Greenbelts
Santa Fe County's initiative for protecting traditional villages was not just another paper exercise in creating wish lists for future sustainability. The county residents voted additional county sales taxes to fund open space purchases in part to provide protection for these sites. This greenbelt and open space initiative on the part of Santa Fe County government goes back to the studies I have cited in previous chapters, when the county first perceived growth might become a problem. The planners' suggested vision for many

parts of the county called for swaths of undeveloped land—open space—to surround residential communities, especially the historically significant communities identified in their surveys. The hope was that these large undeveloped land areas would do two things simultaneously: first, they would prevent small villages like Madrid and Cerrillos from being overrun by real estate development; and two, they would provide undisturbed areas where rainfall could percolate back into the aquifer and where airshed areas could be maintained without the pollutants from traffic. County planners were also anxious for communities to set their own boundaries and ordinances; this involvement ensured communities had something to defend, preventing developers from pleading a "taking" in any future land use disputes.

The first year this public money became available was 2000, and villages and interest groups were invited to a general meeting in Santa Fe to display their community's proposals. The county had about one million dollars to spend, but would not spend all of it the first year, so competition was keen. Interest groups from all over the county put together visual displays and were given a few minutes each for oral presentations.

Two separate groups in Madrid worked on individual proposals; one small group presented their ideas for a greenbelt through the center of town to prevent development in the interior of the village as well as to keep a potential biking, hiking, and horse trail path that could eventually tie Madrid to Cerrillos and the latter's new county park. The other group of three or four people put together a proposal for the county's purchase of around twenty acres at the north end of town to preserve that area as open space and protect the ballpark. There was some coordination between the two but not much; it was a very informal, ad hoc set of arrangements. At the county-wide meeting, only a few folks from Madrid showed up; the contingent from the village mainly comprised those who had worked on the two proposals. In spite of this showing, the county did make good on its mandate, and within a year both the "greenbelt" park through the center of town and the northern buffer zone were purchased by the county, with the understanding that Madrid remains responsible for their management. The term "greenbelt" in Madrid's case is a misnomer, for this area is actually black from coal and red from slag from the coal mines, a constant visual reminder of its industrial past.

The relative disorganization with which Madroids have approached these issues is not typical of the other traditional and contemporary villages engaged in this county planning process. I can compare Madrid's efforts with those of neighboring Cerrillos, which successfully negotiated with Santa Fe County for purchasing a portion of the historic mining area in Cerrillos Hills as the first Santa Fe County Park. This area was in imminent danger of residential development, and a very active and coordinated group of people worked long and hard on this proposal that effectively protects Cerrillos from losing its rural feel to suburban sprawl. Community activists in Cerrillos have worked together on other issues of importance to the village. Likewise with a community south of Madrid, San Pedro, where any issue that threatens the lifestyle and security of this bedroom suburb is taken seriously, and a high percentage of the community responds by working together in efforts to protect their neighborhoods.

Madroids almost had their greenbelt and open space handed to them, if one compares the sustained effort that villages like Cerrillos have put into their park. Additionally, the county authorities are not suddenly going to have a presence in the community just because they made these purchases possible; their maintenance remains a local responsibility. So for Madrid it looks like a win-win situation: protection from some growth with no real loss of autonomy and very little responsibility. Furthermore, the greenbelt area had already been set aside for this purpose by Joe Huber; it consists of some of the old railroad rights-of-way through the center of town, west of and parallel to the highway. The MLA was to purchase the land with a balloon payment due just about the time the county open space plan was put into effect. The MLA had never been able to obtain the necessary funds for this payment, so the county got them off the hook, so to speak, by completing the purchase for the village. But growth issues are inseparable from water in Madrid and in the West, as the following illustrates.

Madrid, Water, and the West

Conflict over whose image of Madrid should prevail—the self-centered hippie culture or the glitzy tourist version of the village—breaks out over things like sanitary facilities. Tourism plays an increasing role in the economy of the village, rivaling the drug trade to provide economic gain, yet even those who benefit from tourism are often unwilling to improve conditions for the tourists. I discussed the parking issue earlier, and now want to return to the issue of port-a-potties, a mundane issue to be sure, but one that is debated with great heat by Madrid's merchants.

The lack of water in the village means that there is only one set of publicly available restrooms in the village, and those are in the tavern, closely guarded by the management for use by patrons of the tavern only. This leaves a few port-a-potties set out on the main street as alternative facilities (see figure 6.1). These are not always a wonderful solution to the needs of tourists, as evidenced from this letter sent to the July 1999 issue of the *Madroid Tabloid*:

> It's 6:14 p.m. on a Saturday, and I've been five places to try to pee. One building isn't plumbed, but the owner is gracious. One is out of order. The porta-potty is out of T. P. and has excrement on the seat. One bathroom is locked and the owner isn't recalling the combo, and so on. So, where do you pee? I've come from Athens, Georgia. My husband and I made a special trip to come back to Madrid, but probably not again as you all seem to not be very tourist-friendly. More eager to empty our pockets, not our bladders, too. And we did spend a good amount of money.

Just the previous month, the owner of one of the oldest galleries in town and an original resettler (and one of the few residents to consistently attend tourist boosterism meetings) had put a notice in the paper pleading with the shopkeepers that "We are desperately in need of additional portable toilets in town on Main Street (at least one). The ones we have are being used by locals, too, and more frequently than not in such gross condition that the tourists cannot use them. . . . some of you are not willing to contribute $10 a month" (June).

The water commissioner's stand that controlling water will control growth has been partly successful; it has at least kept any new public toilets from becoming available to the tourists or the locals alike. There are two other shops with flush toilets, but knowledge of their whereabouts is carefully kept to the locals; even for locals, using the one in the coffee shop can bring the wrath of the owner upon your head if she finds out you have deposited anything but liquid waste in her toilet. There is even a wastepaper basket for your used toilet paper. There is, in fact, some reason for this disenchanting behavior; these facilities do clog up easily, being connected only to the remains of the ancient coal-mining infrastructure or holding tanks. Yet it is harder to understand why successful merchants on the main

FIGURE 6.1. *Contemporary Madrid's solution to growth.*

street would not be willing to pay such a minimal amount for portable facilities, especially when the cost can be spread out over approximately thirty
stores. It is even more confounding when one realizes that these are the only
facilities available for many of the merchants as well, since many shops have
no water at all, and the tavern is at the far south end of town.

At some of the tourist booster meetings, there have been discussions
of trying to get the state highway department to put in an official highway
rest stop north of the ballpark that could have parking and restroom facilities. As long as someone else will take responsibility for paying for and con-
structing such facilities, the townsfolk appear to have no problem with it.
But any talk of the villagers being a part of such a design or taking the initiative for getting this idea off the drawing boards has met with failure.

There may be excellent reasons for discouraging more tourists or more
tourist-dependent shops in town. The divide between older residents for
which Madrid was a great little place to live and younger shopkeepers for
whom the village is a great little place to do business surfaces over these
types of restrictions. The commodification of the village space is heightened
by the tourists, some of whom decide to come back and buy land in or near
the village in order to enjoy its ambience of freedom and tolerance. But

rather than raising this issue as something to be discussed in a public manner, it is allowed to simply flow along with the currents that lie largely outside the purview of Madrid's residents. Fears of raising old rivalries and threats of outright intimidations keep Madrid's villagers from coming to grips with issues like port-a-potties, symbols of the larger divides over the future of Madrid and the West.

As the West continues to be commodified as a tourist destination, the growth in population places increasing demands on local social and physical infrastructures; Madrid, like much of the West, is a high desert, with barely enough water for the people who were here before the Anglo invasion. We have seen that U.S. environmental protections may not be enough to protect scarce resources such as clean air and water from multinational corporations. Likewise, water is rapidly being commodified by other multinational firms that stand to make huge profits from sales of imported water to the thirsty West. If water is transported from Canada to areas like Madrid—areas that are already fighting to survive the onrush of exurban growth—the water commissioner's water moratorium will seem paltry indeed. The growth in industries of all kinds, for those who might afford such resources, will quickly swamp small communities like Madrid. While organizing at the community level to face these issues head-on is no guarantee of success, not organizing is sure to leave Madroids at the whim of powerful extra-local decision makers—people who will care little for Madrid's legacy of resistance and independence from mass consumption.

In another group of circumstances, the villagers were compelled to take a more direct stand on an issue that has long divided the community: how far can individuals go in openly using and abusing drugs before the community will say "This is too far"? In an extended, intertwined set of events, the town had to confront the legacy of its lenient outlaw past and the ability of the tyranny of the individual to still underwrite present relationships toward authority, leadership, and spontaneity.

The Baby Hippies and Old Wounds: Internal Strife

For several years there has been a group of young men who hang out at the corner of Highway 14 at the curve near the tavern at the south end of Madrid. There is a short limestone retaining wall at this point that provides seating and viewing areas up and down the town thoroughfare. These young

FIGURE 6.2. *The Wall—without the boys. The sign to the right of center is for a shop at the north end of town, not the no trespassing sign; that was posted after this picture was taken. The Ferris wheel in the background is from the Huber days.*

men—some children of original resettlers, some from Cerrillos, and some who are hangers-on and drifters—have been dubbed "the boys on the wall" by the locals (see figure 6.2). They play hacky sack with each other and games of chicken with the cars coming around the bend in the road. They deal drugs and use drugs openly when no state authorities are in sight—in other words, a great deal of the time. Some of these boys are nearing thirty years of age and outside of drug dealing have no visible means of support. "The boys" had been tolerated by the merchants and residents until a series of events in the fall of 2000 brought drug dealing and its effects on the tourist business into the limelight. The story of the boys on the wall is connected to three other long-time residents of Madrid: the two brothers whose father was murdered in the trailer years ago and a woman artisan/addict who often palled around with the brothers when they were in town.

The two brothers continued to be a part of the village life—at least when out of prison. During the fall of 2000, both brothers were in town—one while on parole—and they hooked up with Dizzy Doris, the woman addict/artist. This combination of personalities pushed the community beyond its tolerance for drugs and those who use them openly.

The synergy between Dizzy, the two brothers, and the boys on the wall led all to become increasingly annoying and abusive toward merchants, residents, and tourists alike; the brothers seemed to aggravate the drug dealing by the boys on the wall and raised the level of overt drug use to the breaking point. One evening as Christmas was approaching, both townsfolk and tourists saw one of the brothers in his car parked in front of a local store along the main street nodding off with a needle still in his arm. When the store owner—an original resettler and no stranger himself to drugs—complained about the effect of this situation on the tourist business, the other brother beat him up for having the audacity to question the right to use drugs, and, as usual in Madrid's relationship to authority, the victim refused to file charges. This same brother was later implicated in a vehicular homicide that killed another long-time resident of Madrid and, along with Dizzy, was investigated for the accidental death of another former Madrid resident who died playing Russian roulette with a loaded gun in Albuquerque. The trio sought hideouts in the surrounding countryside and began a campaign of threats and outright violence against several rural residents, leaving the villagers feeling their community had spun out of control.

As the height of the Christmas tourist season approached, the villagers communally drew together to attempt to cope with this situation. In a move never before documented in the thirty-year history of the community, the town called in the police. A contingent of merchants, merchant–shop owners, and residents arranged for a public meeting in late December with the townspeople, the district attorney for the tri-county area that includes Santa Fe, the Santa Fe County undersheriff, a state police sergeant whose district included Madrid, and a liaison official with the county commissioners. The meeting required pulling out one of the fire trucks at the volunteer fire department to accommodate the one hundred or so people in attendance. There were people at this meeting from a wide area around Madrid as well as from the town itself. The fear these brothers and Dizzy engendered even among the backcountry folks, who normally do not partake at all in village affairs, was evident as they gave their versions of the intimidations they had suffered.

Not surprisingly, the person who organized and arranged for this meeting was one of the newer merchants whose successful gallery is on the main street, although she and her husband do not live in town. She spoke openly of not being afraid of the "bullies who intimidated others into not turning them in." She was neither afraid of the druggies nor afraid to break the rules of disengagement. She generally took the lead in mediating the discussions from the audience, although people were speaking, for once, freely about their feelings in an open forum. These feelings ranged from agreeing that it was time to exercise some control over the overt use of drugs as it stood to ruin the tourist industry in the village, to discussions of how to protect the freedoms so important to Madrid's character.

Much of the three-hour meeting was taken up with discussions of Dizzy and the brothers, as they were perceived by both the community and the undersheriff to be a real threat. Eventually someone in the audience brought up the subject of the boys on the wall. The state police sergeant took out his notebook and asked for their parents' names. He looked dumbfounded when the audience gently laughed and someone else said that some of the boys were in their late twenties or early thirties. The suggestion was put forward by the county liaison representative that the property owners could solve part of this problem by posting no trespass and no loitering signs along the area where the boys hung out. At the end of the meeting, the one concrete action that developed was the decision to hold a neighborhood watch meeting at which a state police officer would explain how to set up this citizen-based association.

At that next meeting, about twenty people showed up; the woman who had spearheaded the first meeting was gone, and the couple who own the tavern were setting the agenda. The state police officer was polite, offered suggestions for keeping track of each other, exchanging phone numbers, knowing who your neighbors were, and who should be where when and who shouldn't, as in any neighborhood. We discussed what kind of neighborhood watch signs to put up and where they should be placed along the highway. Money was collected to buy the signs and two people offered materials for posts. And that was the last thing that happened on this issue. No signs ever appeared, no one ever asked for an accounting of the money: end of story.

But these measures did meet with some success. The brothers and Dizzy started keeping a very low profile; within a month or two the former convict was picked up and returned to prison out of state. Dizzy continues at this writing to stay out of sight, although her whereabouts were known and no one revealed that to the police. The other brother dropped out of sight for a while. So, while nothing concrete materialized in terms of greater community solidarity, the community did accomplish the diminution of threats and restored a less threatening face to the tourist-oriented main street.

Even the boys on the wall were chastened momentarily. The owners of the tavern, who had appeared so eager to lead the community against this crime wave, did post "no trespassing" signs on their portion of the wall. But a small section of the property belongs to a woman who lives on one of the back roads in the village and travels a great deal. She has so far shown no interest in disciplining the boys, and she has reported to me that she is, in fact, sympathetic toward them. So the boys on the wall remain, a thorn in the side of the shop owners in the immediate vicinity and a symbol of how hard the old ways die in Madrid.

During the summer after the community meeting, one of the boys (the son of a resettler) was selling marijuana from his van parked at their favorite spot along the wall when a Department of Transportation patrol (known as the gray shirts in local parlance) came through town and spotted the suspicious activity. The patrol managed to confiscate the dope and the van, but the young man was able to run away into the surrounding hills and got away. He was immediately elevated to hero status by those in the community who feel anyone who resists authority is privileged. Thus, an effort to curtail overt drug dealing in the name of protecting the safety and economic sustainability of the community eventually devolved into heightening the status of those in the drug trade—the rejection of authority ultimately outweighed the other factors. And once again, the community's perceived need for collective action was undermined by the cultural incapacity for solidarity.

The fractures about what to do about overt drug users and dealers are as deep if not deeper than the growth issues in Madrid, and the two are intertwined with each other. The boys on the wall are not considered part of the elite outlaw group, although they might age into that position. At the moment the boys on the wall are symbols of the original retreat from authority, surveillance, and social control that characterized the early days of resettlement in Madrid, the in-your-face flaunting of restrictions on personal freedom. The elite drug dealers fill an entirely different role—that of providing a service to those in the community who consume drugs, and this latter faction cuts across all arrival times and income groups. To come out publicly against the boys on the wall—as symbols of resistance to unjust police state tactics—would be admitting to the need for restraint over others' freedoms. Since that would implicate control over one's own lifestyle choices and the diminishing of an unknown amount of economic activity in the village, the issue of drug use and abuse remains divisive.

Drugs, Growth, and the Defense of Lifeworlds

As I have documented, many Madroids feel their town's strength is in its anarchy. I believe that the perception of anarchy provides a sense of security, because it means that no one can mobilize the villagers for some hidden agenda either from the inside or from the outside: dispersion protects against cooptation. That this may well be a false sense of security has not yet become a salient feeling among the villagers. But, I will argue here, this distrust and anarchy are in part due to the culture of drug use and abuse, so integrally a part of the 1960s and 1970s lifestyle of total excess. The use of drugs brings with it its own set of paranoid relationships, contributing to the villagers' inability to organize more effectively in defense of their lifeworlds. Drugs add to the dyslexical language the villagers have developed to deal with each other, as drug use is an intense, inward-turning, and isolating activity. Those who tolerate drugs but do not use any themselves are as isolated from those who do as the drug users are from each other. Thus drugs, hedonism, paranoia, and tolerance for deviant behavior have all combined to legitimate a dyslexical set of scripts that isolate individuals rather than allowing them to come together and form consensus or social solidarity. These dyslexical scripts, in turn, underwrite the dispersive form of community in Madrid.

When I started this study, I was not the least interested in the extent or nature of drug use, abuse, production, or dealing in the village, but the presence of drugs is an inescapable reality in Madrid. While it is easy to overstate the drug culture in the village, to not appreciate its importance in village relations would be to leave out a large part of the legacy that makes Madrid a unique place to live. Drug use cemented a common understanding among resettlers: don't tell and don't ask. The faction of resettlers who did not use drugs did not censure those who did; as we have seen in the interviews, this is still something that attracts people to the village—both those who use drugs and those who do not. But drug use also isolates these factions of the population into similar drug user groups and likewise isolates those who consume from those who do not.

We have seen that this tolerance is now part of selling Madrid on the real estate market, while simultaneously being the outgrowth of the reasons the counterculture resettlers moved to this remote location in the first place. The desire on the part of the villagers (evidenced in the planning study) to remain small with a minimum of outside capital development is not *just* a no-growth agenda; it is also part of the continued resistance to the dominant culture and a desire to continue the relative security of using drugs in a space where such activities are not condemned. Yet, in important ways, the tolerance is also but an outward symptom of the mistrust with which most Madroids approach deep personal relationships in the community.

This deep level of mistrust comes from both external and internal factors, most of which I have discussed at length in previous sections. The reason to delve deeper into the nature of the relationships inspired by the drug culture is that it has always been one of the reasons Madroids do not organize more effectively when their lifeworlds are threatened. The perceived police state tactics that the 1970s counterculture generation wished to escape developed into a distrust that easily devolved into paranoia toward all authority; drugs have only added to this distrust, as has the continuation of the government's anti-drug policies. Thus the maintenance of a pervasive sense of paranoia is not simply internal to the village: continued government surveillance and social control measures reinforce this need to be distanced from authority—the reason why the boys on the wall are tolerated to some degree is because they are a symbol of this ongoing rejection of authority.

While marijuana is the drug of choice for most Madroids who use drugs other than alcohol, and small amounts are traded daily in underground subsistence networks, larger amounts of marijuana and harder drugs are usually brokered through the elite outlaws. As in Arlo Guthrie's song "Alice's Restaurant," "you can get anything you want at Alice's Restaurant," and Madrid is undoubtedly no different from any other community in America in its availability of drugs. The distinguishing feature of Madrid's drug culture is its openness, not the fact that it exists. And I do not want to leave a misimpression: people are not lining up and down Highway 14 to get into Madrid, and it is doubtful that more drug abuse exists in the village than in middle-class communities. Brokering drugs is a local, private affair, carefully cloaked in routine activities and concealed behind facades of the same genteel poverty that overlays the entire village.

Local legend has it that several fortunes were made in the 1970s growing marijuana out in the countryside; with the residential boom of the 1990s that activity is much more difficult. Also, aerial surveillance techniques have limited growing to small isolated plots, even to individual plants, scattered around the countryside. Growers know other growers, but those outside of the loop of procurement and supply usually do not. Great care is exercised to prevent plants from being "harvested" prematurely by one's rivals. It is hard to know which causes the most paranoia, worry about rivals or worry about state authorities. And herein lies part of the reason for maintaining distance from and distrust of one's fellow villagers: you do not want your potential rivals or even customers knowing what you may have available as such knowledge could ruin your market position. The counterculture's escape from free market capitalism was thus financed, in large part, by creating a ruthlessly competitive underground drug economy.

Even ruling out psychotic mental reactions from years of drug abuse, the competitive and highly profitable drug trade thus creates its own paranoia and distances people in the village from each other. While there is much to be admired about the honesty with which folks in Madrid approach drugs, the costs for such tolerance are high, both in terms of lives lost to the excesses of drug use and to the community in terms of trust and solidarity.

But just how do the personal preferences for drug use and the economy it sustains interact with growth issues? Those who still engage in outright defiance of the current drug laws—such as the boys on the wall and Dizzy Dolly—are becoming the subject of some community sanctions, as we have seen. Many of the original resettlers, drug users or not, are now running successful galleries and shops—activities increasingly dependent upon a good tourist business. This dependence ties them in—sometimes in unexpected ways—to middle-class growth agendas, booster groups that promote tourism in New Mexico, and groups advocating for road improvements and amenities like better restroom facilities for tourists. These merchants seldom attend these monthly meetings; they are content to rely on one or two regulars from Madrid who attend all of them. Yet even here we have seen how taking a stand against the boys on the wall based on their impact on tourism resulted not in eliminating their activities but in some ways reinforced the boys' symbolic meaning to a certain segment of the village. And sanctions were not taken too far, either, in the boys' case; again, the sense is very pervasive that eliminating their "right" to be on the wall doing their thing is somehow tied to everyone else's right to go their own way. As long as they remain only an annoyance, the boys will probably continue to be tolerated.

The elite outlaws are in a much different relationship to growth issues in the village. They keep such low profiles that unless you yourself are involved with drugs you would never know who they are. And while they do not come forward in public issues confronting the village, as discussed earlier, they are in a position to profit from growth in the community. Drug use is so pervasive in America that new shopkeepers and new residents bring with them the possibility of new customers. Elite outlaws would only stand to lose from excessive growth; too much new development might overwhelm their ability to supply a burgeoning market, opening the way for more dealers and cutting into their established customer base. It is not likely, however, that they would take the lead in confronting any such growth firsthand.

There is little concerted effort, therefore, to eliminate any but the worst and most visible drug use in the village. Drug use and dealing are an integral part of the village, an integral part of the tolerance exhibited by those who do not do drugs—up to a point, at least—and an integral part of why certain people are still attracted to the village. Whether the villagers' attitudes toward drugs are a model for other communities is difficult to judge; the tolerance and honesty are refreshing—if a bit shocking for newcomers— and the relative lack of hypocrisy could be the basis for a proactive and positive stance toward community members who become the walking wounded of our postmodern global villages.

For those of us who remember the goals of the counterculture movement, with its hopes for relationships based on social justice and mutual trust and for communities not dependent upon exploitation and class differences, the realities of places like Madrid have been mixed. While social class differences are of less importance in Madrid, the legacy of the drug subculture has undermined much of the positive work that we accomplished in other areas. And it is the drug culture, I believe, that is largely responsible for heightening the defiant individualism to the point where Madroids can find few avenues for mutual trust and community solidarity. It is not the only reason, certainly, but drugs and the atmosphere of paranoia surrounding their use and procurement are palpable currents in village life, and contribute heavily to the lack of sustainable community institutions outside of the drug subculture.

Conclusions

The cultural incapacity for building social solidarity in Madrid, rooted in the town's history, projects multifaceted problems for its future: whether that pressure originates in population growth from the north and south of

the village or in realignments of basic resource bases through international growth agendas, the villagers will have to come to terms with the
encroachments that will threaten the counterculture's tenets of tolerance and
absolute freedom.

The structural weaknesses inherent in the counterculture's search for
authentic relationships based on personal character resulted in a tyranny of
individualism without any moral compass beyond individual self-interest.
Anarchic sets of relationships emerged that were, from time to time, usurped
by bullies and thugs who used threats and occasional aggression to intimi-
date those who dared to stand in their way. While outright random violence
has been rare, these threats have developed into a general aversion toward
collective action, quieting those in the village who might have worked for
cohesive solutions to problems.

Threats and intimidations were not part of the original counterculture
agenda of peace and social justice, but they were natural outgrowths of the
lack of avenues in Madrid for building social solidarity. This lack of institutional tendrils for communal action both encourages and is a result of the
deep valuation of the existential present among Madrid's residents. To "be
present" to whatever is happening at the moment is the preferred method
of interacting with each other and the world. This "presentness," in turn, is
enhanced by the drug subculture that exacerbates the inward-turning nature
of social action in the village.

The drug subculture also brought with it connections to underground
economies on a global scale, at least for the elite outlaws, and serves to
underwrite the intimidation and threats of violence still present in Madrid.
The drug subculture encourages the suspicion of others and the social distance folks maintain toward one another, while also encouraging a ruthlessly competitive local underground market economy in illicit drugs. These
underground economies fund an unknown amount of sustenance in
Madrid, as elsewhere, and while the excessive public users are being sanctioned, it is highly unlikely that any deep-level change to the drug markets,
either demand or supply, will be forthcoming.

It is my observation that maintaining these networks of procurement,
distribution, and consumption uses up vast amounts of time and energy,
even before the drugs themselves are consumed. Thus energy that might be
available for communal causes or for the benefit of more than the individual buyer and seller gets siphoned off by this underground network—this

loss is in addition to the effects of using drugs on the individual's ability to be positively present in the world. The continuance of the government's anti-drug policies adds yet another layer of paranoia to Madrid's social networks; internally it adds to the suspicion and distrust of others, and externally the state's policies play the dual role of continuing the rebellion against authority and legitimizing those who do.

In my view, the nonjudgmental and forthright manner in which Madroids have always treated those who abuse drugs is a refreshing and positive attribute of village life. This tolerance is extended to other "sons and daughters who don't fit in," as DeBuys wrote of Santa Fe, granting legitimate and meaningful positions to folks who might otherwise be homeless or institutionalized. Yet even here we see how simply "being present" to your community is not a sufficient response to the real needs of many of its residents. In the case of Anna and Rachel in particular, it was only individuals who reached out to help; there was no coordinated action among a cohesive group of people. The resulting ambivalent actions were wholly inadequate in meeting their needs. Recognizing this reality is not to condemn in any way those who tried to help, but merely to point out that the primacy of the individual once again determined how action was implemented. Similarly, in the dealings with the county over boundary and zoning issues and the setting aside of open spaces, instead of a concerted, representative contingent working on these issues (as in neighboring communities), these actions were left to a miniscule handful of individuals—and even they did not work together in a really coordinated manner. I believe that this reliance on others to do things is another legacy from the counterculture era.

Groups like the Diggers and the Free Family advocated taking what you needed, as the material excess of capitalism produced more than enough for everyone; there was no need to work for a living when the world would simply provide it. This rationale for expropriating other people's goods was not considered stealing, and in most instances involved manipulating government welfare programs, and scavenging used clothing, leftover food, and wide varieties of unclaimed cars, trucks, tools, and similar utilitarian material goods. From this belief in the cornucopian nature of the universe it is easy to see all things that flow toward you as gifts, material wealth that you were meant to have and that the universe will deliver to you. Being proactive in the world might interfere with this impersonal gifting; therefore it is best to simply wait and see what the world will deliver to your doorstep.

I see this passive disconnectedness as part of the reason why individuals who are otherwise rational and involved with their lives refuse to become more committed to proactive community-building projects.

In addition to the suspicious and rebellious stance taken toward state authorities, many counterculture folks truly felt that being involved in politics—local or otherwise—simply made no difference. Political protests, activism, grassroots organizing seemed to have come to no avail by the early 1970s; worse, the outcomes of decisions made by remote authorities appeared to be irrelevant to our daily lives, as long as we could get far enough away from centers of power and lead our own lives in places like Madrid. Staying out of sight and keeping a low profile became ways of coping with a power structure we felt was unjust, arbitrary, and irrelevant.

As effective decision making moves away from local state institutions and authorities to corporate multinational organizations and their agendas of exploitation and commodification, other communities may begin to resemble Madrid's fragmented, individuated, and self-centered form of social structure. Decisions remote from specific communities will increasingly have an impact on the quality of life experienced locally, yet there is real danger that we as a society have no form of countervailing power to resist such impacts. Turning inward and maximizing one's self-fulfillment and self-satisfaction may seem the only viable alternative under conditions of disenchantment and alienation. Therefore, there is the potential for more communities to develop dyslexic scripts where ever-smaller interest groups defend only their own narrowly-defined needs, lessening the ability of the communal interests to be understood and discussed. Thus Madrid's dispersive community formation, underwritten by its dyslexical language, may well model future communities' reactions to the globalization of power relations. While this formation may temporarily create a sense of local empowerment—as in Madrid—this virtual sense of power can never effectively counter the power brokers operating at a global level.

On the other hand, the ability of remote political and economic forces to sweep over the West, bringing unforeseeable change to its peoples, has a history at least five hundred years old. The successive peoples of the West have shown a remarkable ability to sustain themselves in this fragile environment. Madrid became the latest new frontier for the generation from the Great Society, and those involved with the counterculture agendas bought themselves a little time to experiment in living with a minimum of social control and a fair amount of personal freedom. Perhaps local government initiatives similar to the one in Santa Fe County will provide enough protection for small communities like Madrid to remain sites of resistance to commodification on a global scale. As capitalism moves from mass consumer marketing to exploiting and creating niche markets, perhaps Madroids' ability to self-consciously see themselves as an amusement park—as a ready-made themed environment for tourists—will in the end allow them to exploit the tourists while maintaining their independence.

But the natural experiments in community in Madrid pay witness to the difficulties inherent in the counterculture's agendas of drugs, freedom, tolerance, and hedonism. Without a socially constructed set of limits that offsets the extremes of all of these experiments, the community has occasionally been ruled by the most ruthless. Yet in spite of these weaknesses, for those who do not need a great deal of social network for support and who are relatively self-sufficient, Madrid can be an exhilarating and self-affirming place to live. Now that the village must become more connected to local political agencies such as the county zoning authorities, and now that it has some experience in obtaining much-desired commodities from the county's open space program, it remains to be seen if that individual self-affirmation can be translated into a community-wide sense of efficacy.

CHAPTER SEVEN

Madrid and the West
The Future of
Dispersive Community

*Why focus on the community? The quality of our
lives depends on the quality of several things besides the
community: our society, our jobs, our families, ourselves.
And while all of these factors are undeniably important,
there is some reason to believe that the community contributes
more to the quality of our lives than many of these other
areas. But more important to establishing the potential for
the community as a focus for improving life quality is
the potential for meaningful change and improvement
that exists at the community level. Compare, for example,
attempts to improve the quality of life at the community
level with the more micro attempts based on providing
psychological counseling or the more macro attempts
based on implementing societal change.*

—Larry Lyon, *The Community in Urban Society*

Reprise

I have documented why Madrid became the community it is today from the
perspective of its resettlers and present residents, but where does Madrid fit
into the idea of community as we conceptualize it? In his book *The Community in Urban Society* (1987), Larry Lyon suggests that the community
remains an important institution that mediates between the power of the
state and the quality of life of the individual. In this study I have treated
community as a site-specific place where economic, social, and cultural relationships emerge, endure, and are defended. This mediation between the

state and the individual is particularly interesting in Madrid, where so few community institutions emerged to protect people from the opposite—the tyranny of individualism—and where the state was assumed by its resettlers to be so far removed from the community as to be virtually irrelevant.

However fluid, contingent, and even temporary a place to live as Madrid seems to be, it is a community that has shown its ability to outlive the individuals who resettled the village. It retains much of the tolerance toward lifestyle choices and behaviors that was its signature attraction; because of its relative lack of internal institutions and organizations, people who prefer a dissociative community find Madrid a comfortable place to be. My research questions were framed through the experiences of those people in my generation who chose to leave the Great Society to pursue lives of absolute freedom, as Peter Coyote documented. The basic research question was how and why did the original resettlers come to Madrid and what did the community they built look like, given the counterculture's agenda of absolute freedom? From that simple question, the interrelated cultural motifs that have been the focus of the previous chapters emerged:

1. How much of the resettlers' rebellion against mainstream American culture was a genuine search for a socially and ecologically sustainable community and how much was merely an inversion of their parents' secular pursuit of material wealth? In other words, how much of their experiment was principled action and how much was narcissistic hedonism? If there were principled stands taken by the counterculture generation, were the resettlers of Madrid capable guardians of these stands?

2. In what ways were the original resettlers reenacting the myths of the old Wild West? And how did those myths of the West correspond with or contrast to the counterculture's ideologies?

3. In contrast to the myth of the West's containing unlimited resources, much of the region's ecology was fragile, and 150 years of mining, timbering, and overgrazing have damaged the land and water beyond recognition. Given this fragility, how will Madrid—a community with its own fragile resources for community solidarity—find a sustainable equation for survival in the face of ever-increasing exurban overspill?

4. How much does Madrid's counterculture heritage of distrusting both authority and leadership roles model other communities'

difficulties in dealing with distant and fragmented power in
a world increasingly dominated by multinational, global
decision-makers—a world in which local politics has become
mainly a struggle to protect unique local lifestyles and to
maintain social control over those left out of the mainstream
economies (Gottdiener 1987)?

Madrid was resettled through the same impetus that drove Euro-Americans
to settle the West: resources that appeared unlimited and free for the taking,
open space without apparent boundaries, and a place free of the fetters and
controls of civilization.

Throughout its post-conquest history, the West has served a dual purpose in the minds of the peoples who used its resources: first, the West was
conceived as a place of renewal and reinvigoration of the psyche, especially for American migrants; second, the West has served as a dumping ground
for our society's misfits and those who did not fit into more crowded, more
civilized spaces. In the aftermath of the industrialization of the region, areas
that were first exploited and then abandoned were sought out by counterculture hippies, disaffected Vietnam veterans, and other restless young who
combined the need for renewal with the stigma of being society's castoffs.

Resettling Madrid was edgework, to borrow a term from radical jour-
nalist Hunter Thompson; the community was on the margins of more civilized society, and the people reconstructing the village had no desire to be
anywhere but on the margins. Even as a mining town, it was only Huber's
dedication to creating a model company town that kept Madrid from being
peripheral compared to more productive locations. The physical work of
rebuilding the town contradicts the myth of counterculture hippies being
lazy dropouts who lived off the dole, yet all the privations and shared experiences of the resettlers did not create cohesiveness even among this group,
and the community today remains loosely bound together by a culture of
individualism. The cultural tapestry that makes Madrid an edgy, exciting,
slightly risky place in which to live has not created any protections from
extra-community forces of social change. In this, Madrid shares a long history with other peoples in the region who had little real control over international political and economic changes that dramatically altered their lives.

The cultural inadequacy of Madroids to act communally for the benefit
of the whole raises serious questions about the continued sustainability of

this edgework ethos: how will Madrid's fragile social structure respond to the increasing commodification of their space through the real estate and tourist industries—industries that continue to degrade the West's fragile resources; will their lives at the margins of mainstream American life become a commodity itself, an eco-tourist theme park for the benefit of outsiders? Will local governments retain their interest in protecting sites like Madrid from uncontrolled growth and, given this willingness, will the village and local governments prove capable of sustaining that protection?

These are complex, interwoven questions, and a great deal to expect a small semi-rural community to be able to explain. I believe that edge places like Madrid, that have tried to remain disengaged from political power, local and national, may not be all that different from most communities. Active participation in local decision-making and politics has declined throughout the United States (Gottdiener 1987). Americans on average are highly individualistic; Madrid's villagers only carried that trait to an extreme. Where Madroids differed was in their belief in simple living, in not taking more than you need, and in eschewing high levels of material consumption. While not perfectly carried out in Madrid, these accomplishments indicate that a comfortable and satisfying life does not have to involve mass consumption. I believe that these themes represent important cultural strands, for it is unlikely that the majority of Americans will give up their individualism and move back to medieval cooperative communities (Maryiansky and Turner 1992; Verenne 1972). Madrid can model future communities in its opposition to commodification while alerting us to the need to channel the increasing tendency toward individualism into positive channels to avoid the near-anarchy of the village. As technologies such as the Internet allow us to become more independent from each other—although increasingly dependent upon that technology—our future communities may take on aspects of the independence and fluidity so characteristic of Madrid, and the possibility exists that through this technology some may become sites of resistance to the leveling influence of a global mass society. Therefore it is important to understand the nature of association and dissociation as evidenced by the residents of Madrid, and equally important to understand the tensions within the community and the nature of conflict between the community and the twin forces of the state and late capitalism. As Lyon remarks at the close of his book, it is not the good community that we should be studying, but the potential for many good communities, offering individuals a plurality of opportunities for maximum overall liberty (280–81). Madrid offers one of many possible forms that community can take, and understanding the positive and negative aspects of Madrid's experiments is more than just an intellectual exercise, as more communities may begin to reflect dyslexic and dispersive characteristics in the face of globalization. This chapter will be both a micro and a macro look at explanatory theoretical perspectives relevant to these issues.

A note about this final chapter: those who dislike theoretical material do not need to indulge in this part of the text to have learned something about Madrid and its people. This chapter is for those who wish to see how Madrid's experiment relates to the postmodern experience of community from a theoretical standpoint. I have shortened and clarified (I hope) complex arguments expressed elsewhere more fully. In the next section, I have summarized various historical views of community in each paragraph; readers will find relevant sources listed in a separate reference bibliography indexed under the same topics as in the text.

Views about the Nature and Structure of Community

The Chicago School Era and Related Studies

Community studies were among the first intensive research endeavors undertaken by American social researchers. The classic studies produced at the University of Chicago at the beginning of the 1900s became part of how we think communities look in America. Urban centers were disordered, chaotic, and crime-prone, while rural areas retained the essential American values of independence and self-sufficiency. I have investigated the role this ideology of space and freedom has played in the settlement of the American West, where it underwrote the initial Euro-American settlements and continues to inform the exodus from inner city to suburb to exurban space. Yet the diffusion of the population into increasingly dispersive spatial arrangements has greatly altered these early distinctions between rural and urban, and later researchers found many flaws with such a simple dichotomy between urban (*gesellschaft*) and rural (*gemeinschaft*) communities.

The Ecological Views

Other twentieth-century urban sociologists—still heavily influenced by the Chicago School—saw the urban community as a site of inevitable conflict, with growth, density, and distance from the urban center determining the quality of life for inhabitants. These views borrowed heavily from the biological metaphors of early twentieth-century ecological ideas. Once again, the dense urban center was thought to be the focus of crime and disorder, with order and civility increasing the farther away one got from the center. While a bit more sophisticated than a mere dichotomy, the experience of real communities is much more complex. Consider Madrid: the deviant behaviors theorized to be associated with the densely populated and decaying urban center certainly did not diminish in intensity as the counterculture moved away from its urban base. In fact, some forms of contemporary deviance, such as "growing your own," are augmented by the distances and spatial arrangements in rural areas.

Power and Conflict Models of Community

Another genre of community and urban studies has looked at the community in terms of power and conflict. I expected to find something approaching this model in Madrid, thinking that most of the original resettlers would have forged tightly knit associations that would be nascent institutions governing the village. Madrid did not look anything like this, as it turned out, and there is so little cohesion to the village that cliques or associations have not formed with enough power to gain an advantage over the anarchic relations that typify the village. Both cooperative and coercive associations in Madrid remain undeveloped.

Other urban researchers focus on the community setting as a playing field for powerful and conflicting organizational actors, as opposed to structures. What power there is in the village is invested in a small group of people who run the water cooperative and come to the Madrid Landowners' Association meetings, but they are ignored by most of the townsfolk. Being "powerful" in Madrid does not look like power in most other communities; Madrid's powerful actors seem as incapable of being proactive toward important issues in the community as everyone else in town.

Neighbors and Networks

Another subset of urban studies concerns neighbors, neighborhoods, or networks within existing urban areas. This view emphasizes the dynamics of emergent social norms and the formation of social solidarity, and generally views the community as a mediator between the individual and the state, as suggested by Lyon. This view also is in contrast to most Madroids, for whom the community has been a moment-by-moment event only, with no permanent features—although, as discussed, the underground economies in Madrid do feed a type of association that endures as long as individuals live by the rules of secrecy, discretion, and reciprocity.

Ethnicity and/or Shared Lifeworlds

Yet another set of ideas about community looks at places where individuals shared some life and/or work experiences or ethnic heritage that formed the core of their communities (and whose members felt their communities stood in some contrast to middle America). These ideas are an interesting contrast to Madrid, illustrating how shared experiences and common lifestyles do not necessarily result in a deeper sense of shared fate and community solidarity.

Socially Constructed Meanings through Community

Through this paradigm of community, people develop their definitions of self and their surrounding reality through their social interactions with others— especially those in their communities. I have used various forms of these ideas throughout my earlier discussion and hardly need to repeat them here.

The Conflictual Community

Most of the above viewpoints are represented in both theoretic frameworks and empirical studies of real communities. A small set of three studies forms a nucleus of evidence in support of the view that I take in this chapter—that conflict is an everyday event and that it is part of what gives meaning to life. Two of these studies I have already discussed in terms of their relation to Madrid: Banfield's 1954 study of a small Italian village and Viditch's and Bensman's 1958 work in a village in New York state. The third is William A. Gamson's 1966 study of eighteen New England villages. Gamson's stands in some contrast to the other two studies, having found that communities of conflict were much more interesting places to live by some standards than homogenized places. Overall, these studies indicate that dispersive communities are not limited to the 1960s counterculture and that factors aside from defiance, political disaffection, and drug use may be explanatory in other settings. Gamson's work hints at the desirability of dissent to deepen the communal experience, and at the desirability of more complex theory to frame our understandings of contemporary communities.

The Postmodern Community

The postmodern conception of community recognizes space as a site of contested, commodified, and transitory meanings, of community as a theme park for the global tourist industry, and of personal meanings that are simultaneously local and global. This is the crisis Madrid is facing: having escaped parts of a commodified, mass-consumer culture, the tourist industry and e-commerce have brought mass consumption to Madrid. This is a dialectical phenomenon; the more the village resembles a theme park for aging hippies, the more tourists come for this quaint atmosphere; the more tourists come, the more parts of the town come to resemble tourist attractions everywhere as local merchants respond to the global travel industry and begin competing with each other for more than just subsistence-level profits. This phenomenon has also driven the expanding real estate market with its intricate relationship to drugs, money, and growth.

Madrid is neither urban nor rural, neither a cohesive community nor a morally oppressive space. It is a place that supports, encourages, and reinforces personal idiosyncrasies to the point of pathology; a place where choices over presentation of self, gender roles, and drug consumption are less sanctioned (positively or negatively) than elsewhere in mainstream culture. It is also a place where experiments in "living lightly off the land" have been going on for thirty years. These reflections from previous community studies, plus the research questions driving the present study, lead to specific theoretical perspectives as explanations for Madrid's existence, its continuance, and its relevance to understanding the contemporary experience of community.

The Contradictory Community

> We were, I believe, first and foremost artists, and while we were
> addressing real fundamentals, we allowed our commitment to
> "authenticity" to blunt our sensitivity to the needs and aspirations
> of many who were not interested in being artists, or special, or
> anything other than out from under the heel of an oppressive
> system.... Neither we nor the people who supported us were
> fools. Many were successful hustlers in their own right, legitimate
> or otherwise, who believed or wanted to believe in higher ideals
> and a better future.... Those who saw altruism were no more

mistaken than those who saw cynicism and personal opportunism. Our contradictory behavior was like Penelope, holding her suitors at bay by unweaving at night what she constructed by day. The difference between her and us was that we were not aware of our own double-handedness. (Peter Coyote, retrospectively speaking about the Digger experience [1998, 350]).

Many Madroids firmly believe in the ideals of the counterculture—that they are escaping the exploitation of working for a corrupt system, that they are building a better community where social justice and sustainable lifestyles will flourish, and where tolerance and individual freedom will free the villagers from harmful, judgmental rules and social control. But in truth the village's success is not based on self-sufficiency, but rather is dependent upon people with surplus income. The authentic small-scale relationships so treasured by Madroids depend on the dominant economic system for survival just as does the rest of America. The artists and craftspeople would have no market for their products were it not for tourism and, increasingly, Internet connections. Even the most hardened back-to-the-lander maintains a vehicle of some kind in order to haul in fuel (wood, kerosene, or small propane tanks; only the better-off afford a large propane tank), and an equal number of people haul water for domestic use. Since there is no Laundromat, gas station, or larger grocery store in or near the village, a minimum of a twenty-mile round trip must be made just for gasoline and other necessities. As in the early days of resettlement, it is still common for one person in the family to have steady or part-time work in Santa Fe, and that money is spread around the local village economies. It is increasingly common for the aging population of Vietnam veterans to qualify for permanent Social Security disability, and some individuals use other government transfer payments or food stamp support systems to enable their "living lightly off the land." Even simple living, in other words, depends upon the outside world.

Other aspects of life in Madrid do approach the ideals of authenticity, honesty, and tolerance, yet once again we see the emphasis on self over community, although the pursuit of self-fulfillment is couched in terms of community. This aspect is illustrated in this quote from Roseanne, former professional from the East Coast and a later arrivee:

I think in the beginning in Madrid, I thought this was totally about the individual trip; you just come here to search yourself out. And nobody cared whether you were suffering or not. . . . [But] we need each other and I really enjoy the freedom of not having set rules about how I'm supposed to dress, how I am supposed to speak to you, what manners we are all playing by. . . . Another part of it is, being actually with the other. . . you and I in the bigger space. Just keep expanding it.

You know, I think there's a reason why lots of people can't live there for a long period of time. Because you are really up against yourself and it can be very uncomfortable. (interview 1999)

As Roseanne remarks, Madrid is a community where you are up against yourself a great deal of the time, and if you are not comfortable with yourself, nobody is going to help you with that. On the other hand, there is a certain undeniable freedom to dress and act just about any way you feel on a particular day. As many field researchers have found, I had to retrain myself to comb my hair and find suitable clothing before appearing in public after leaving Madrid, and I found the freedom to not care about such matters entirely refreshing. But the lack of consistency—not having set rules to play by—feeds into the community's lack of social solidarity. The villagers have not yet gotten past thinking of their community as this "bigger space" that is supposed to materialize from random social interactions. In fact, this same person remarked later in the interview that it was very difficult "doing community" in Madrid because it was always the same little group of people who did everything; one week it was a healing, another week a bead-working class or drumming session on someone's land, and truly including more people was hard because there was not enough communication between people.

In Madrid, each person is assumed to be responsible for her own space, physically and emotionally. This is also part of the counterculture's ideology of the individual—do not take responsibility for anyone other than yourself, or you risk entering into a judgmental "power trip" over someone else's life. Outsiders often miss this aspect of Madrid, and assume that because villagers are independent, nonconformist, and a bit oddball, that the people who live in Madrid ended up there because no one else would have them. While this is true for the walking wounded sheltered by Madrid, the vast majority of the villagers are there because they choose to be. Witness this conversation, again with Roseanne:

People think, how did this happen to you? [They're thinking] Oh,
you got fired from your job. No, it took a lot of courage to leave
what I had going and say, "I get exactly where it's going [my old
job]. I was going to make a lot of money and I'm going to be living
in a beautiful home . . . and have everything. Eat what I want to,
know all the players in my space—and I didn't want it. I'll go be
nobody. People will say, do you know who I was, and everyone
says, "Who cares?" I used to play the drums for Phil Collins, and
who cares? I used to be the head of the Human Resources for the
East Coast, who cares? Who are you now? (interview 1999)

"Who are you now?" is the ruling paradigm for Madrid residents, and the
majority of people interviewed or observed prefer this conjunction of needing each other while enjoying the freedom of not having set rules to live by,
and prefer being a nobody in Madrid to being a somebody in a consumer-
oriented society. But in Madrid, the need for each other translates into the
confirmation of individuality rather than into creating a gemeinschaft community, and not having a set of rules refers to suspending judgment about
others so the self is free—including being ostensibly free of the need to build
social solidarity.

I bring these aspects to the forefront here because Madrid conforms to
so few theoretical stereotypes of community and yet is still, in its fashion,
very much an identifiable community. Since the Industrial Revolution we
have theorized that good communities developed associations and institutions that protected individuals from the tyranny of the state while providing social support networks for their members. Madrid has little of either
attribute; furthermore, it is neither a gemeinschaft nor a gesellschaft society, as it more closely resembles a postmodern society of minimal social interaction with fluid, fragmented social obligations. The community is held
together by cultural attributes inherited from its counterculture founders:
defiant individualism, self-reliance, and the carefully controlled distance
people keep from each other. The community quickly weeds out those who
do not bring this particular set of characteristics with them, and likewise
rejects people who want something in return from the community or who
expect to be treated deferentially due to their status outside the village. In
this way, Madrid offers an opportunity to understand what a small-scale
community of choice might look like: a community in which people choose

to live according to lifestyle preference rather than the demands of work, and where there is neither a romantic return to pure agrarian living nor the compulsion to follow a charismatic leader, as was so often the case with communes and other experimental communities.

If Zablocki was right in his assessment that such communities appear whenever there are interstices in the monotonic march of modernity, then we need to understand a great deal more about how such communities reflect and respond to those interstices. Such understanding might lead to engendering more spaces in which individuals could experience some degree of autonomy and liberty in communities not dependent upon increasing consumption for self-definition and status. Furthermore, if America once more enters into a mode of intense surveillance of its civilian population and heavy-handed social control methods to deter dissidents, we may see another era of alternative community formation.

Theoretical Threads

Conflict over Consensus

Marx's concept that capitalism would provide the material base for a non-capitalist egalitarian society was one of the founding ideologies of the counterculture movements, and I have described how the outward rejection of the capitalist agenda forms a large part of counterculture defiant individualism, even while the community remains dependent on this material surplus. Using Marxist conflict theory, we would expect Madrid to have a relatively high level of community cohesiveness based on shared ideologies and the relative lack of material inequality; in fact, that is what I expected to find—at least among the resettlers. But the hegemony of counterculture beliefs in defiant individualism, tolerance, and anarchy prevents close associations from forming; and the continuance of the drug subculture works against building trust in the community. While there is a general sense that Madroids have common interests in maintaining their space, their freedoms, and their relative isolation, we have seen that these interests seldom mobilize the community into joint action, and villagers remain convinced that their anarchy will prevent any faction from taking over the town.

A divide has formed, however, between resettlers who participated in the rebuilding of the town and for whom Madrid is a good place to live, and those later arrivees who see the village as a good place to run a business. The resentment felt toward the latter group stems from the perception that the newcomers are thought to be much wealthier than others in the village and that they are exploiting the hard work of earlier settlers. But this divide has yet to result in creating greater cohesion or greater ability to mobilize resources within each of these groups, as the overall cultural inability to create frameworks for building social solidarity affects everyone in the community equally. Since conflict in Madrid has always been individual rather than collective, no permanent factions have yet emerged to permanently control scarce resources; since everyone considers themselves to be the authority on issues, there has been no emergence of a stable charismatic leader to act as an intermediary for organizing (with the exception of Tia, as we have seen). Without a clear and stable leadership structure that can initiate and carry out programs, organized resistance is left to whoever at that moment has the emotional energy to step onto the stage (Michels 1962).

Marxian theory does hold, I believe, part of the explanation for the relative lack of overt violence within the village. Outright predatory violence has usually occurred between "consenting adults," those deeply involved in various drug dealings. There has only been one documented death of an innocent person who was in the wrong place at the wrong time, when a young woman was killed as she accidentally got in the way of a gunfight between two men involved in settling a drug dispute at the tavern. For the most part, as the interviews have revealed, unless you were looking for trouble, Madrid was, and is, a good place to be. The underlying dynamic of diffusion rather than concentration of resources results in a relative lack of inter-group conflict since there are no meaningful organizations to garner emotional and material resources, thus the belief prevalent among Madroids that it is their disorganization that is their community's strength.

But this dynamic alone does not fully explain why a small community like Madrid does not more resemble the gemeinschaft communities theorized by Tonnies (1940 [1887]), or the post-capitalist lifestyles hinted at in Marx's works. Even Zablocki felt that the counterculture communities represented at least a partial return to gemeinschaft relationships. Madrid is a community where artisans, crafts production, and galleries are the predominant form of legitimate economic activity, and it is not an unreasonable assumption to expect to find more of a community of artists working in concert at the very least to protect their own investments. I would like to recall here Max Weber's understanding of the powerfully individualistic secular strands contained within capitalism. This secularization of the world reduced or even destroyed traditional ties to family and community, producing a centrality of materialism and a sense of individualism without spiritual or moral content. Even the counterculture communard movements were unsuccessful in stripping the secularism from individualism. While Madroids have so far avoided Weber's "dictatorship of the bureaucrats" (Bendix 1962, 458–59) and have not recreated the massive inequalities so prevalent in contemporary American society, they have also avoided building mechanisms for concerted social action. Thus the villagers have no avenues for protecting themselves from threats either from inside the community (as with Dizzy Doris and the two brothers) or from outside the village, as with growth issues.

In Madrid, the constant interplay of associative and dissociative forces at the micro level is a palpable force in the community; it is common to hear people in the bar or the coffee shop remarking about some event that should have elicited some kind of communal action but that, as usual, did not. This awareness leaves a residue of conflict over important issues such as Rachel and the death of baby Anna, but this residue seldom rises to the collective level of organized action. These types of micro conflicts are the everyday substance of life in Madrid, and can be understood analytically through the work of George Simmel.

Simmel saw social conflict arising from more than just economic interests, with forms of association and dissociation always operating together. He noted that conflict was part of the life force of the human species, that societies without conflict were not viable entities. For Simmel, conflict is inevitable but does not dictate social change, and, in fact, conflict can be the integrating force in a social system. The diffuse network of consensual relationships, which, I theorize, have kept the community from developing strong internal dissent as well as allowing for a fair degree of individual freedom, are also characterized by a relatively constant amount of low-level conflict—conflict that underlies the surface of life in the village and that can break through the surface over key issues—such as the beating Rudolph suffered after his involvement with Rachel. It is this tacit understanding that each individual brings to Madrid the potential for discommunity that forms its tentative unity. Instead of a unity of opposites, Madrid appears to thrive on the continual renewal of what Zablocki termed "the cultivation of the unfinished," where tensions arising from defiant individualism form an ever-changing landscape of always slightly problematic relationships, with meaning and synthesis being continually and individually negotiated. Unlike the communes, in the absence of formalized institutions for problem solving, it has been only the occasional emergence of a charismatic, transformative experience that brings the community together as a whole. It is in this sense that the unfinished, existentially focused interpersonal conflicts become a unifying process for the villagers, for it is part of "being present to what is happening" in the community. These types of fluid, temporary, and personally interpreted interactions expand Simmel's work on postmodernism.

Post-modernity and the Collective Conscience

Simmel is primarily a sociologist of postmodernity and the avant-garde. For Simmel, the modern liberal individual was an unfinished piece of work. Simmel rejected two myths of liberalism: (1) the myth of political liberalism, that individual freedom was synonymous with equality, and (2) the myth of economic liberalism, that self-interest was automatically synonymous with social interest. Simmel reconsidered the Enlightenment ideal of equality of the isolated individual, and theorized that this equality had gone in two different directions in the nineteenth century. Historically, two separate tendencies emerged: the socialist agenda of "equality without individuality" and the liberal capitalist thrust of "individuality without equality." For Simmel, human differences represent a moral demand—a requirement that every person has to realize a moral ideal by and in himself and that no two are the same (Leck 2000, 78). This is a new interpretation of the Kantian moral imperative; here Simmel is suggesting that each of us must realize our individuality by reuniting the two separated strands of individualism: equality and material gain.

Just how were we supposed to do this? By engaging in an aesthetic civics, by developing an "ethical will" that would transform the negative side of individualism arising from liberal capitalism into a "living and social constitution, which created a positive synthesis of the two types of individualism." This civic aestheticism was to be evolved through continual dialogue and investigation of the particular social and historical conditions as experienced by the individuals involved. This was not a task merely for the elites, but a moral imperative for everyone, working in their own social milieus (Leck 2000, 78–89).

This moral imperative in Simmel's work implies an unresolved tension between individual narcissism and the creation of a social ethic, for "genuine morality arose as an iconoclastic creation of the isolated individual who opposed the herd mentalities of the status quo," on the one hand, and the demand that "the erratic and multiform idiosyncrasies of individuated values undergo a thorough sociological evaluation to determine their validity as a civic ethics" (Leck 2000, 90). This individually conceived but sociologically expressed morality was required because a true social ethic could only be achieved through a critique of and an active moral resistance to the hegemony of the bourgeois ideology of the state and its liberal institutions. For Simmel, the money-church-state nexus had produced a society of liberated but ethically empty human beings, upon whom the state was all too ready to force a conformity of bourgeois liberalism without true recognition of individuality (or of the validity of social class differences), and through whom the twin processes of money and consumerism worked to level authentic and needed differences between individuals and groups. This situation resulted in massive civic indifference to the external realities of social life, as monetary exchange allowed for the removal of subjectivity from human interactions, and "products are sold without reference to an ethical examination of production and its consequences" (Leck 2000, 79–92, 93).

I apply this imperative directly to the question I raised earlier about the sincerity of the principled stands taken by the counterculture movement, and whether—if there were genuine ideals embedded in the movement—the resettlers of Madrid were capable stewards of these principles. I believe that there were principled stands taken by counterculture participants, among them: do not participate in exploitation of the earth or its peoples; to accomplish that, live simply and give back more than you take; make as many of your personal necessities as you can; buy socially just products that do not threaten the environment; and, as a corollary, interfere as little as possible with other people's agendas, for to do so implies judgmental, ego-driven power trips. Here is the core of what Simmel implied in his ethical will: liberal individualism—made possible by the material productivity of capitalism—was empty of human values because production was separated from the product; furthermore, consumption took place separate from production. The connection that tied humans to their resource base was broken and the true relationships of social and environmental exploitation could not be perceived once we became passive consumers.

This emptiness of ethical connections was quickly filled by the hegemony of bourgeois consumption patterns reinforced by state and religious ideologies that justified growing inequalities through impersonal markets controlled by those who benefited from them—not through those whose lives were impacted through their operation. This individuality without equality had not been successfully countered by socialism because socialism created equality but ignored the very real social class and ethnic differences that gave meaning to human life. The only way out of this modern dilemma was a "continual dialogue and investigation of the particular social and historical conditions as expressed by the individuals involved." This was the imperative: both individual narcissism and the leveling, homogenizing forces of modernity must be continually challenged and tempered through dialogue with and recognition of others in the shared social space. Only then could a meaningful form of individuality emerge that was grounded in a socially conscious ethic. Further, this was everyone's responsibility; this process could not be handed off to others for it must involve all the social actors if it was to represent the true differences between people. This is a key failing in Madrid: the dyslexical, highly personalized language each person speaks has created such a dispersive community that these shared social conversations do not happen. This dyslexia contrasts to the 1970s counterculture commune movement, in which individuals approached Simmel's ideal of intense communal questioning and seeking for more meaningful social categories through which to understand our lives.

We have evidence from the research on communes that this ethical communitarianism was the stated goal of the ideological work in which communards engaged in order to create and maintain the family—a family based on a subjectivity raised to the level of the social. But most of the communes dissipated because of dense network ties that threatened community solidarity. The advantage to a village over a commune is that those individuals who cannot stand "to be up against themselves" all the time leave without its being a crisis for the community; the disadvantage is that there are no negative sanctions for not participating in such intense work. In Madrid, Simmel's full aesthetic civics has only reached the level of concern for authenticity. There is a perception on the part of many residents—whether through their beliefs in environmental causes, astrological forecasts of needing to be more like the star children, or counterculture values of minimalism and post-consumerism, or just plain poverty—that authenticity means getting away from mediated images of our culture and actively engaging in a philosophy of simpler living. If that means hauling water, living "out on the land" with a bare minimum of necessities, and making do with whatever jobs and materials are at hand, those are the costs these folks have been willing to make to feel themselves free of subjugation to the dominant culture.

Madrid is not quite yet an example of a community of continually questing, ethically involved individuals. Madrid is, after all, a village that harbors outlaws along with counterculture advocates, a place where artistic creativity flourishes alongside sleazy characters who rip off local charity donations, and a place where the drug culture surfaces as a quasi-legitimate activity. The dominance of defiant individualism, which in part is a Simmelian critique of capitalism, has led to only a partial realization of an ethical communitarianism. The strengths of Madrid's stand against the hegemony of exploitative market-driven relationships and their attendant inequalities are partly unraveled by its equally heartfelt inability to join in mutual dialogue for the common good.

The greatest failures, however, of Madroids and other counterculture groups to live up to the ideals suggested by Simmel are the failure to curb narcissism along with the accompanying hedonistic pursuit of pleasure and the disengagement from political activity, as Peter Coyote documented. The continuance of the drug subculture from the hippie era in Madrid, with its paranoia, self-indulgence, and divisiveness, creates a major hurdle to community discourse of all kinds, as does the positing of community on various other *self*-interests. It is very seldom that the *self* part of nearly every equation in Madrid gets fused into a collective consciousness that could be the medium for the civic ethics Simmel envisioned. The disenchantment and disengagement with power—whether for the stated reason of not engaging in ego trips or due to fear of retribution—means that even if Madrid's residents did approach the level of intimate, intense ethical work engaged in by members of communes, the results would remain purely personal. The likelihood that such dialogues would result in positive collective action is even slimmer for Madroids than for communards. Such is the costs of dispersion and dyslexicality. That said, I think Madrid serves as a variant of an authentic, ethically grounded community, albeit an imperfect one.

In the choice to live simply and to pick your material possessions based on that ethic, the villagers engage in questioning and subverting the dominant bourgeois culture of late capitalism. But by opting for a loosely tied community instead of a communard situation, Madroids have further emphasized individualism, rather than containing it within a consensual moral compass. There is always the possibility, however, that as the more radical outlaws die off or if the drug subculture lessens its impact on the village, a civic ethics will emerge among a more cohesive and less distrustful cohort of residents. If accomplished through participatory discourse, this emergence could serve to protect the tolerance toward human differences and the respect for liberty that have been the hallmarks of the village since its resettlement.

In summary, the relative egalitarianism of Madrid and the genteel poverty cultivated by the majority of village inhabitants have enabled a culture of individualism to flourish without the development of deep community associations or structures. Diffusion of wealth and power over the social space appears to have prevented structures both of inequality and of social support. But no matter how well-nourished the ideologies of defiance, disaffection from authority, and commodification remain in Madrid, no community today is untouched by global forces of restructuring. To understand these forces and what Madrid has to offer as a case history of resistance to these processes, I turn to the work of contemporary theorists.

Themed Environments and Scripted Lives

The meshing of the micro world of individual social action and interaction with the dominant social forces and structures of the world of late capitalism is uniquely focused in a small community like Madrid. Scripted and themed environments designed for corporate profit now replace the religious and aesthetic core of human experience. Such scripts penetrate deeply into the private lives of individuals, controlling consumption and status possibilities (Giddens 1991; Gottdiener 1997). While our theoretical understanding of the globalization of the relationships of capitalism continues to develop, it is clear that the forms of association in Madrid have reflected these relationships from its beginnings. Even the pre-European contact period saw its share of inter-regional influences. Madrid was a showcase of industrial paternalism under Huber, and a picture of Walt Disney visiting with Oscar Huber in front of Madrid's Christmas displays in the 1930s has given rise to the local legend that Disney took inspiration from the Madrid Christmas pageants for Disneyland (Motto 1973). Madrid's reincarnation as a counterculture community participated in the global reaction to the spread of capitalist relations worldwide. Its next phase will certainly reflect these global forces as much as its previous forms.

In weaving together the threads of contemporary theories of the state, of capitalism, and of the polity, Gottdiener's *The Decline of Urban Politics* (1987) represents a comprehensive and synthetic revision to Marxist urban theories. This work synthesizes the Marxist position with the pluralists' views of voluntarism. In doing so, this theory of the local state moves beyond the reductionist and determinist position of many neo-Marxists while also recognizing the limitations of agency in a highly structured environment. The overall position taken by Gottdiener is one of complexity, with outcomes contingent upon the particular mix of structural elements and human decision makers in each unique setting. This combination of elements makes Gottdiener's work particularly useful for taking the understanding of Madrid's place in the study of communities beyond the simplistic stands of most of classic urban theory.

Because of the newness and synthetic nature of this emergent theory, a short description of Gottdiener's work in this area is necessary. In terms of local political institutions, local variations in public policy outcomes for individual communities can only be understood by taking a look at three sources of such variation: (1) the various forms of representation legitimized by the local state; (2) the administrative aspect of the state; and (3) the forms of actual intervention (including the intersection of policy with local street bureaucrats).

> Thus, the three sources of formal variation: forms of representation, administration, and intervention, combine with the contentious nature of social interests to produce political outcomes that are contingent and underdetermined by economic forces in an action-structure dialectic of considerable complexity. The outcomes of this process are functional for capital only in so far as they do not challenge the fundamental premises of accumulation itself, although they may explicitly aid that process in more direct ways. (216)

Modern forms of the state and of capital are complex, with competing agendas and interests within each element comprising "fractions" of the whole.

> The preceding discussion suggests that politics is underdetermined by economic relations. It argues for an approach to politics

representing a three-way struggle between capital, labor and the State, or, more voluntaristically conceived, between capitalists, workers and State managers along with all their fractions. The characteristic of politics is its contingent nature. Containing this clash are the imperatives of forces operating at the deep level—the impulse of power and its technological domination, the necessities and contradictions of the capitalist system of expropriation and the political system of expropriation. (219)

Rather than the deterministic view of productive relations underlying and determining both social and cultural relations, this view recognizes that state managers, representatives of labor, and capitalists themselves are not monolithic interest groups. Each sector contains fractions of competing interests while they simultaneously compete with the other sectors for legitimacy and hegemony. Power still lies with those who control the economic productive relations, and the state functions to legitimize and enforce this power, especially the expropriation of property through maintaining private property laws. Additionally, the interests of each sector are not mutually exclusive; for instance, fractions of state managers expropriate property in the interest of the state (the Arctic National Wildlife Refuge, as an example), and this expropriation is not necessarily coincident with the interests of capitalists. These overlapping and competing interests, coupled with the recognition of the voluntary role of individuals in maintaining legitimacy of existing regimes, prevent deterministic predictions. This understanding provides a new focus for the study of communities and their underlying web of relationships.

Part of the impetus for developing a more comprehensive theory of urban politics came from empirical studies documenting the decline of political participation at the local level. The rapid expansion and decentralization of regional settlement and work patterns after World War II created fragmented political entities in new growth areas while depopulating older city centers. Suburbs are now multifunctional centers for working, living, and limited forms of governance, while corporations decentralized their operations to metropolitan hinterlands or overseas. The effect on local politics has been to divorce the local geographical area of political influence from its population. In turn, local governments, finding themselves providing services without an expansive tax base, have turned increasingly to higher levels of government:

state and federal incentives in the form of tax breaks or block grants to finance local needs. Local governments (the local state) have also found themselves tied to growth coalitions—local or otherwise—that promised to bring in immediate revenue at whatever the cost to long-term sustainability of the community or the environment.

The pattern of urban sprawl so typical of American suburban and exurban areas is thus part of this complex picture of the local impact of the globalization of capital, the growth of the federal state, and the partly voluntaristic choices made by consumers of space. But while all this has been redefining the American landscape, it has left participation in local politics emasculated— lack of civic involvement and a tax base not bound by the geographic limits of local governments have left two main functions for the local state: regulation and social control. Local politics, as a result, has devolved into arguments about the dialectic issues of uncontrolled growth and quality of life, rather than the larger issues of the nature of democracy and the need to be involved in decision making.

What does all this have to do with Madrid, New Mexico? The pull of back-to-the-land movements and the push to get out of cities with their regulation and social control brought counterculture settlers to places like Madrid throughout the West during the early 1970s. At least in Madrid, the resettlers had already opted out of governance at all levels, local or otherwise. The quest for non-commodified, authentic relationships not based on exchange values was a principled stand taken by well over half of those interviewed for this study, and continues to be an important ideological position—forming part of the divide over growth issues in the village. The town remains unincorporated largely because of the ideologies of dispersion and decenteredness, coupled with the inability to delegate leadership (or take on leadership for fear of retribution). While it is unlikely that most Americans will trade their suburban and exurban lifestyles for off-the-grid subsistence living, Madrid's residents aptly illustrate that increasing consumption and "getting ahead" do not have to be part of a reasonably comfortable life.

If, as the new urban theory predicts, we continue to become increasingly disaffected from government, increasingly distanced from sources of powerful decision makers, and increasingly atomized, then Madrid is a living example of what such communities might look like. Madroids self-consciously chose to disconnect from state sources of power because as a generational cohort we believed the government and its policies were corrupt and unjust. The resettlers brought with them, and the community continues, the drug subculture as a lifestyle choice, increasing the atomization of defiant individualism. As there is no major source of employment in the village, and no compelling reason to stay outside of these lifestyle advantages, people who do not like this combination of lifestyles simply leave. To date, Madroids have been largely able to script their own lives. This independence is quite different from communities where people feel compelled to stay due to economic dependency, or where a drug subculture may be imposed by a small group of users and dealers, or where increasing individual isolation is due to the destruction of previously existing social institutions. Under conditions of coercion, elements similar to those at work in Madrid might well be at work, but would arrange themselves differently.

Regimes of Power

The present regimes of capital accumulation are rooted in the expropriation of nonrenewable energy sources, which has had devastating effects on the physical, social, and cultural realms. It is possible that within the foreseeable future new fractions of capital will appear—some of them exploiting more renewable energy sources that are already available such as solar, wind, and fuel cell technologies. The usefulness of the above theoretical scheme is that it allows for changes in the productive relations to have a myriad of unanticipated consequences in all the other relationships, including shifts of allegiances throughout the system that feed back to the resource base itself. If the capitalist base becomes fragmented along deep enough fissures, it may legitimize more affiliations concerned with addressing the tragedy of the commons—the inability of the present forms of capitalism to deal with the common good beyond the narrow self-interests of the elites. Such fissures—if they do develop—will be at the deepest level of economic and technological relationships, and point toward a severe crisis in management for the old regime if they are unsuccessful in gaining control over new resource bases.

The data presented here (chapter 2) clearly adds one additional bit of evidence that the judicial system, as seen from the U.S. Supreme Court decisions, is indeed directly tied to the source of power under the present relationships, and has been extremely reluctant to move in the direction of protecting the environment as communal property or communal good. It is indeed in the local level of state apparatus that we see legislation setting aside areas (such as the Madrid greenbelt and open space) restricted from private development. These have been accomplished by the formation of mobilized special-interest groups concerned with quality of life issues—sometimes with the quality of life for local inhabitants and sometimes for the earth itself. In the present research, it came from the local state itself working in concert with highly motivated interest groups. Such set-asides indicate that the state and its managers do exercise power that is not always coincident with that of the representatives of capitalism.

Even deep-level changes to productive relations, if Madrid is any example, do not necessarily bode well for reestablishing participant democracy, however. If disgust with agents of social control partly underlay the 1970s resettlement of places like Madrid, it is not likely that the current political climate of increasing domestic surveillance will encourage a movement of back-to-the-landers to become politically vocal. It is, it seems to me, much more likely that individuals similar to Madroids will choose to retreat even further from sources of state power, creating a void that (at least at the present writing, on the eve of a preemptive war with Iraq) appears to be filled by those afraid of loosening their grip on nonrenewable energy sources.

Today, ironically, retreating from centralized power is both more possible and less possible at the same time. Technologies allowing for a reasonably comfortable life using a minimal of nonrenewable resources are within the purchasing ability of modest income groups, and such technologies (solar and wind power) allow living without leaving heavy physical traces on the landscape, as discussed above. Yet the mobility achieved through the use of cell phones and laptop computers for telecommuting and selling of arts and crafts items—outside of drugs and other underground economies the most common form of employment in Madrid—leaves surveillance trails observable to remote sources of state power. Such technologies also require a great deal of time and physical monitoring by the user—another form of social control. Thus, some of the tools of perceived self-sufficiency are also scripts of power—not all of which emanate from the state, but that can be easily co-opted in the future.

A resurgence of state power, actuated at the federal level but implemented at the local, will have indeterminable effects in places like Madrid. Madrid's greatest threat is already from growth, albeit not from a new influx of counterculture folks. Sociologically, the greatest hope for change lies, as

Lyon suggests, at the community level but articulated back though the state apparatus, through political mobilization and new forms of legitimation. This is where Madrid's example should be a warning: folk who have self-consciously disconnected from voluntary civic involvement are unlikely to be in the forefront of active social change. The transformations through which Madrid's resettlers and other counterculture descendants have passed may be symptomatic of a far larger disconnect in American life. Merely preserving spaces like Madrid from uncontrolled growth, therefore, is not sufficient to allow the development of a true civic aesthetic.

Synthesis

> For meaningful alternatives to come into being, however, the
> dominance of surface over substance must be overcome. There
> must be a reconciliation of image and meaning, a reinvigoration
> of a politics of substance. Only then will people be able to
> ensure that the imagery of pleasure is joined to the experience
> of pleasure; that seductive images of the "good life" are rooted
> in the principles and practices of a human community; and
> that images of freedom, satisfaction, and social resistance are
> meaningfully engaged with the resources and real options
> available to us in the world we inhabit. (Ewen 1988, 201)

In his definitive study of the power of commodified images to shape our sense of reality, Stuart Ewen's *All Consuming Images* (quoted above) declares the necessity of retreating from artificially manufactured and superficial experiences, experiences that only bring more power to the producers of such images while emasculating the consumer's ability to understand and comprehend the underlying relationships of exploitation. The faction of my generation who participated in counterculture living was attempting to rejoin the substance of life with its outward expression; at our best and most principled, we were attempting to come to grips with the illusion of freedom created by bourgeois consumption compared to the reality of resource and human devastation caused by such consumption. We were seeking an authentic good life that confronted and resisted the hegemony of corporate and state bureaucracies—and we attempted this resistance not through political means but through living our beliefs in alternative community relationships.

Whether in urban enclaves, rural communes, or village sites like Madrid, we carried out agendas aimed at subverting the power structure by removing ourselves from its reach. In this, we were not much different from similar experimental communities stretching back to the early Christian era, save that we had no unifying, charismatic, systematic ideologies to sustain our experiments. Our solidarity—such as it was—came from shared cultural expressions: rock music, radical literature, and street theater, and the loose ties created by the ceaseless migrations of hippie families from site to site, all of which reinforced the legitimacy of defiant individualism as both personal fulfillment and rejection of all forms of authority.

Throughout this study of Madrid, I have referred to Peter Coyote's memoir as a legitimation of my own memories of this time in American history. Coyote wrote his memoir as a celebration of the accomplishments of our generation; I read it entirely against the text—that our generation's greatest failings, the incapacity to rein in the individualism and freedom we so cherished, confirm the power of capitalism to reduce human societies to atomistic actors stripped of supporting networks of social control and moral compass. In the pursuit of pleasure, were we any better than our bourgeois parents? Our parents pursued happiness through scripted consumption of commodities for status; we pursued pleasure through the unrestricted consumption of drugs. We genuinely thought our passive resistance would set examples that would expand to the general population, and that our own fringe communities would become the norm. But our pursuit of absolute freedom failed to generate new, creative forms of supportive relationships, leaving individuals vulnerable to vengeance and retaliation while simultaneously heightening the retreat from proactive involvement in social change.

Madrid exemplifies the best and the worst of my generation's experiments with alternative lifestyles as a form of resistance to modernity. Rebuilding a community from the abandoned refuse of the era of coal, Madrid's resettlers were as dependent upon an earlier generation's creation of wealth as the contemporary villagers are upon the excess wealth that spawns the tourist industry. Freedom from exploitative relationships was as illusory then as it is now, for tourism brings its own themes and scripts to which the villagers increasingly conform.

Who knows what the foreign tourists from Germany and Japan who fill the tour buses stopping in town think about Madrid; perhaps they think they have seen a bit of the old Wild West. In some ways, they have at least seen its latest reincarnation. Madrid's resettlers shared much with earlier frontier migrants, not the least of which was the hope for renewal and regeneration in the vast open spaces of the unsettled West. Again, the illusion did not match the reality, for the West has been invaded multiple times, with each migration adding its burden to the fragile landscape. And here is yet another illusion: the resources that wave after wave of settlers thought were inexhaustible in reality could barely sustain the populations that arrived here with the Spanish conquest, much less the massive Anglo expropriation of nonrenewable resources.

Madrid's resettlers had less impact on the fragility of the West's resources, but exploited their own human capital with the same ferocity that characterized the village as a coal camp. The legacy of the West as a space without the confining and debilitating fetters of civilization was congruent with the counterculture's desire to be in a free space, particularly a space free from authority—federal, state, local, and interpersonal. In creating a community with very few consensual moral constraints, they freed individuals from external social controls but simultaneously subjected themselves to the tyranny of individualism. This freedom was a temporary victory, however, as the history of the West has shown over and over again: No matter how self-sufficient and sustainable particular populations of migrants have been, the ability of extra-territorial forces to rescript the lives of the remotest peoples has never abated.

Within its own space, Madrid temporarily achieved some victories against the monotonic march of modernity, victories that are important to highlight because they show that some of the principled stands taken by counterculture participants were not illusory and could be sustained—at least in small communities. Chief among these is the ability to provide a meaningful life to folks who would be institutionalized elsewhere. Also critically important to a world running out of sustainable resources is the model of simple living and living lightly off the land, which are not mere slogans but a lived reality for the majority of Madrid's residents. Nor is this a simplicity born of necessity except for a few truly poor—this is a community largely made up of people who chose to live less resource-exploitative lives. Madrid's residents leave a positive legacy for other social movements such as anti-consumer movements, permaculture practitioners, and other simple living advocates worldwide.

But the difficulty of simple living in a semi-remote location adds to other legacies that the counterculture resettlers brought with them to Madrid. Tolerance toward individual idiosyncrasies was extended to all forms of deviance, and (when coupled with the distrust for any type of authority) allowed for an unfettered individualism to emerge that provides neither shelter for those times when individualism fails nor protection against its tyrannical excesses. The decision to disconnect from engagements in social control is probably my generation's greatest failure among the various experiments that we tried in alternative living, and this failure is particularly evident in Madrid, where the excesses of the drug subculture were allowed to undermine tentative experiments in building social solidarity. And this solidarity could have been modeled along the lines Simmel suggests—where individuality is allowed to flourish as a moral imperative but within a continual social dialectic curbing its excesses; it need not have repeated our parents' homogenized suburban experiences. This lack of solidarity leaves the village even more at the mercy of the very external forces its resettlers moved there to escape. With no cohesive voice of its own, Madrid must rely on the goodwill of street-level bureaucrats and local political functionaries to frame its future. This future is increasing insecure, as is the sustainability of all culturally unique places in the West, as the already greatly compromised resource base continues to be eroded by exurban population growth.

If this population growth were the only external threat to Madrid's continued existence as a site of resistance to modernity, the village might survive as an enclave surrounded by protected open space and greenbelts. But the much greater threat, as always in the region, is the action of remote decision-makers over whom local constituents have no control. These decision-makers are no longer warring nation-states, as in the first centuries of conquest in New Mexico; they are now multinational corporatists, intent on maximizing the rationality and efficiency of their organizations on a global scale. Local political institutions—indeed even national political institutions—are being realigned in conformance with these latest power brokers. No amount of local organizing and solidarity—at the moment—appears to be sufficient to counter these realignments.

Yet these old regimes of power based on nonrenewable energy sources may be threatened by upstarts with access to renewable energy sources— energy sources that may be able to resist monopolization by corporate behemoths. If there are rifts at this most basic level of power—control of energy resources and the political forms that legitimate such control—then unanticipated and unpredictable shifts in all the upper layers of power and subjugation will occur. Realignments at this most basic seat of power will pose grave problems of maintenance for the ancient regime, whose scripts have underwritten the development of Western culture since the Industrial Revolution, and it will not retreat from domination easily. But if enough cracks appear in this monotonic dialogue, there may yet be room for many good communities to emerge in the interstices of change. We may at least hope that such communities will affirm the best attributes of the counter-culture's ideals as expressed in Madrid, but avoid repeating our generation's tyranny of individualism over the common good.

References

Alderfer, E. G. 1985. *The Ephrata Commune: An Early American Counterculture*. Pittsburgh: University of Pennsylvania Press.

Allen, James B. 1966. *The Company Town in the American West*. Norman: University of Oklahoma Press.

Atencio, Tomas. 1989. "Welfare Reform in a Society in Transition: The Case of New Mexico." In *Reforming Welfare: Lessons, Limits, and Choices*, edited by Richard M. Coughlin, 225–49. Albuquerque: University of New Mexico Press.

Bailey, L. H. *Country Life Movement in America*. 1913. New York: Macmillan and Company.

Banfield, Edward. 1954. *The Moral Basis of a Backward Society*. New York: Free Press.

Bellah, Robert, Richard Madson, William Sullivan, Ann Swidler, and Steven Tipton. 1992. *The Good Society*. New York: Knopf.

Bendix, Reinhard. 1962. *Max Weber: An Intellectual Portrait*. New York. Anchor Books.

Berger, Bennett M. 1981. *The Survival of the Counterculture: Ideological Work and Everyday Life among Rural Communards*. Berkeley: University of California Press.

Binford, Henry C. 1985. *The First Suburbs: Residential Communities in the Boston Periphery, 1815–1860*. Chicago: University of Chicago Press.

Bowers, William L. 1974. *The Country Life Movement, 1900–1920*. Port Washington, NY: Kennikat Press.

Burns, Ken. 1999. *Lewis and Clark*. PBS video.

Callies, David L., Robert H. Freilich, and Thomas E. Roberts. 1994. *Cases and Materials on Land Use*. 2d ed. St. Paul, MN: West Publishing.

Cox, Craig. 1993. *Storefront Revolution: Food Coops and the Counterculture*. New Brunswick, NJ: Rutgers University Press.

Coyote, Peter. 1998. *Sleeping Where I Fall: A Chronicle*. Washington, DC: Counterpoint.

Davis, Mike. 1992. *City of Quartz*. New York: Vintage Books.

DeBuys, William. 1985. *Enchantment and Exploitation: The Life and Hard Times of a New Mexico Mountain Range*. Albuquerque: University of New Mexico Press.

Design and Planning Assistance Center. 1997. *Madrid Planning Study.* Albuquerque: School of Architecture and Planning, University of New Mexico.

Domingues, Joseph R., and Vicki Robin. 1992. *Your Money or Your Life: Transforming Your Relationship with Money and Achieving Financial Independence.* New York: Viking.

Downing, Andrew Jackson. 1841. *The Theory and Practice of Landscape Gardening.* New York: Wiley and Putnam.

Etzioni, Amitai. 1975. *A Comparative Analysis of Complex Organizations: On Power, Involvement and Their Consequences.* New York: Free Press.

Ewen, Stuart. 1988. *All Consuming Images.* New York: Basic Books.

Firestone, David. 1999. "Overrun." *Albuquerque Journal,* Wednesday, December 8, C1, 8.

Fodor, Eben. 1999. "The Twelve Big Myths of Growth." *Designer/Builder 6,* no. 4 (August): 13–18.

Friedenberg, Edgar Z., ed. 1971. *The Anti-American Generation.* Chicago: Aldine Press.

Gamson, William A. 1966. "Rancorous Conflict in Community Politics." *American Sociological Review* 31:71–81.

Gardner, John S. 1984. *The Model Company Town: Urban Design through Private Enterprise in Nineteenth-Century New England.* Amherst: University of Massachusetts Press.

Giddens, Anthony. 1991. *Modernity and Self-Identity: Self and Society in the Late Modern Age.* Stanford, CA: Stanford University Press.

Gordon, David M. 1996. *Fat and Mean: The Corporate Squeeze of Working Americans and the Myth of Managerial Downsizing.* New York: Martin Kessler Books.

Gottdiener, Mark. 1997. *The Theming of America: Dreams, Visions, and Commercial Spaces.* Boulder, CO: Westview Press.

Gottdiener, Mark. 1977. *Planned Sprawl: Public and Private Interests in Suburbia.* Beverly Hills, CA: Sage.

————. 1987. *The Decline of Urban Politics: Political Theory and the Crises of the Local State.* Newbury Park, CA: Sage Publications.

Granovetter, Mark S. 1972. "The Strength of Weak Ties." *American Journal of Sociology* 78, no. 6 (May): 1360–80.

Hahn, Stephen, and Jonathan Prude. 1985. *The Countryside in the Age of Capitalist Transformation.* Chapel Hill: University of North Carolina Press.

Harbottle, Garman, and Phil C. Weigand. 1992. "Turquoise in Pre-Columbian America." *Scientific American* 266, no. 2 (February): 78–85.

Harden, Garret. 1968. "Tragedy of the Commons." *Science* 162:1243–48.

Harvey, David. 1993. *Potter Addition: Poverty, Family, and Kinship in a Heartland Community.* New York: DeGruyter.

Hayden, Dolores. 1976. Seven American Utopias: The Architecture of Communitarian Socialism, 1790–1975. *Cambridge, MA: MIT Press.*

Hill, G. Richard, ed. 1993. *Regulatory Taking: The Limits of Land Use Controls.* Chicago, IL: American Bar Association.

Huber, Joe. 1963. *The Story of Madrid.* Albuquerque, NM: Southwest Printing Company.

Independent (Edgewood). "Edgewood Water Sale: Good News." Vol. 2, no. 55, August 30–September 5, p. 4.

Independent (Edgewood). "Ring around the Sandias: No Joke." Vol. 2, no. 55, August 30–September 5, p. 4.

Jankowski, Martin Sanchez. 1991. *Islands in the Street: Gangs and American Urban Society.* Berkeley: University of California Press.

Kagan, Paul. 1975. *New World Utopias: A Photographic History of the Search for Community.* New York: Penguin.

Kanter, Rosebeth. 1972. *Commitment and Community: Communes and Utopias in Sociological Perspective.* Cambridge, MA: Harvard University Press.

Kaufmann, Edgar Jr., ed. 1970. *The Rise of an American Architecture.* New York: Praeger Publishers.

Klett, Mark. 1992. *Revealing Territory: Photographs of the Southwest.* Albuquerque: University of New Mexico Press.

Lasn, Kalle. 1999. *Culture Jam: The Uncooling of America.* New York: Eagle Books.

Leck, Ralph M. 2000. *Georg Zimmel and Avant-garde Sociology: The Birth of Modernity, 1880–1920.* Amherst, NY: Humanity Books.

Leonard, Olen, and G. P. Loomis. 1941. *Culture of a Contemporary Rural Community: El Cerrito, New Mexico.* Rural Life Studies (1). Washington, DC: Bureau of Agricultural Economics, U.S. Department of Agriculture.

Limerick, Patricia Nelson. 2000. *Something in the Soil: Legacies and Reckonings in the New West.* New York: Norton.

Ludvigson, Teri. 2001. "Property Taxes." *Horsefly* 3, no. 9 (October 15): 10.

Lyon, Larry. 1987. *The Community in Urban Society.* Chicago: Dorsey Press.

Madrid, New Mexico, "Oldtimers List." Madrid Historical Society. Unpublished.

Madrid News. August 1978. Vol. 3, no. 7.

Madroid Tabloid. June 1999.

Madroid Tabloid. July 1999.

Madroid Tabloid. August 23, 1999.

Margolis, Eric. 1999. "Between Feast and Famine: Coal Communities in the American West." In *Community in the American West,* vol. 21, edited by Stephen Tchudi. Reno: Nevada Humanities Committee.

Maryanski, Alexandria, and Jonathon H. Turner. 1992. *The Social Cage: Human Nature and the Evolution of Society.* Stanford, CA: Stanford University Press.

McDonald, Johathan. 2001. "Report: Santa Fe Fifth from Bottom in Density." *Santa Fe New Mexican,* Wednesday, July 25, 2001, 1, 3.

McDowell, Steve. 1990. *The Persistence of Memory: New Mexico's Churches.* Santa Fe: Museum of New Mexico Press.

McHugh, Cathy. 1988. *Mill Family: The Labor System in the Southern Cotton Textile Industry, 1800–1915.* New York: Oxford University Press.

Melzer, Richard. 1976. *Madrid Revisited: Life and Labor in a New Mexico Mining Camp in the Years of the Great Depression.* Santa Fe: Lightening Tree Press.

Michels, Robert. 1962. *Political Parties: A Sociological Study of the Oligarchical Tendencies of Modern Democracy.* New York: Free Press.

Miller, Timothy. 1991. *The Hippies and American Values.* Knoxville: University of Tennessee Press.

Motto, Scytha. 1973. *Madrid and Christmas in New Mexico.* N.p.

Mulrooney, Margaret M. 1989. *A Legacy of Coal: The Coal Company Towns of Southwestern Pennsylvania.* Washington, DC: National Park Service, U.S. Department of the Interior.

Northrop, Stuart A. 1975. *Turquois and Spanish Mines in New Mexico.* Albuquerque: University of New Mexico Press.

Oregon Visions Project. 1992. *A Guide to Community Visioning: Hands-on Information for Local Communities.* Portland, OR: American Planning Association.

Padgett, Tim. 1999. "Saving Suburbia." *Time Magazine* 154, no. 7 (August 16): 50–51.

Pogue, Joseph E. 1970 [1915]. *Turquois.* Memoirs of the National Academy of Sciences. Vol. 12. Glorieta, NM: Rio Grande Press.

Polechla, Paul J. 2000. *Ecology of the River Otter and Other Wetland Furbearers in the Upper Rio Grande: Final Report.* Albuquerque: Museum of Southwestern Biology, University of New Mexico.

Rittenhouse, Jack D. 1975. "Southwest Imprints." *Book Talk* 4 (May): 4.

Roszak, Theodore. 1968. *The Making of a Counter Culture: Reflections on the Technocratic Society and Its Youthful Opposition*. New York: Doubleday.

Santa Fe County Planning Department. 1972. *Santa Fe County Reconnaissance Survey: Final Report*. Santa Fe, New Mexico.

————. 1975. *Santa Fe General Plan Report*. Santa Fe, New Mexico.

Schnatt, Peter J. 1969. *Back to Nature: The Arcadian Myth in Urban America*. New York: Oxford University Press.

Schor, Juliet B. 1991. *The Overworked American: The Unexpected Decline of Leisure*. New York: Basic Books.

————. 1998. *The Overspent American: Upscaling, Downshifting, and the New Consumer*. New York: Basic Books.

Scurlock, Dan. 1998. *From the Rio Grande to the Sierra: An Environmental History of the Middle Rio Grande Basin*. Fort Collins, CO: U.S. Department of Agriculture.

Simmons, Marc. 1988. *New Mexico: An Interpretive History*. Albuquerque: University of New Mexico Press.

Smith, William L. 1999. *Families and Communes: An Examination of Nontraditional Lifestyles*. Thousand Oaks, CA: Sage Publications.

Spurlock, John C. 1988. *Free Love: Marriage and Middle Class Radicalism in America, 1825–1860*. New York: University of New York Press.

Tonnies, Ferdinand. 1940 [1887]. *Gemeinschaft and Gesellschaft*. Translated by Charles P. Loomis. New York: American Book Company.

Truettner, William H., ed. 1991. *The West as America: Reinterpreting Images of the Frontier, 1820–1920*. Washington, DC: Smithsonian Institution Press.

Turner, Frederick Jackson. 1993 [1893]. "The Significance of the Frontier in American History." In *History, Frontier, and Section: Three Essays by Frederick Jackson Turner*. Albuquerque: University of New Mexico Press.

U.S. Department of Commerce. 2000. Census Bureau. "Quick Facts," http://factfinder.census.gov.

————. N.d.. "Population of Counties by Decennial Census, 1900–1990." http://factfinder.census.gov.

U.S. Senate. 1909. *Report of the Country Life Commission*. Washington, DC: Government Printing Office.

Varenne, Herve. 1972. *Individualism, Community and Love in a Small Midwestern Town: A Structural Analysis*. Chicago: University of Chicago Press.

Vidich, Arthur, and Joseph Bensman. 1968 [1958]. *Small Town in Mass Society: Class, Power, and Religion in a Rural Community*. Princeton, NJ: Princeton University Press.

Weber, Max. 1958 [1904–5]. *The Protestant Ethic and the Spirit of Capitalism*. New York: Scribner.

Westhues, M. 1972. *Society's Shadow: Studies in the Sociology of Countercultures*. New York: McGraw Hill.

White, Richard, and Patricia Nelson Limerick. 1994. *The Frontier in American Culture*. Berkeley: University of California Press.

Whitmer, Peter O. 1987. *Aquarius Revisited: Seven Who Created the Sixties Counterculture That Changed America*. New York: MacMillan.

Wilson, Chris. 1997. *The Myth of Santa Fe: Creating a Modern Regional Tradition*. Albuquerque: University of New Mexico Press.

Wooster, Ernest S. 1924. *Communities of the Past and Present*. New York: AMS Press.

Wrobel, David M., and Michael C. Steiner. 1997. *Many Wests: Place, Culture and Regional Identity*. Lawrence: University of Kansas Press.

Zablocki, Benjamin. 1980. *Alienation and Charisma: A Study of Contemporary American Communes*. New York: Free Press.

Zicklin, Gilbert. 1983. *Counterculture Communes: A Sociological Perspective*. Westport, CN: Greenwood Press.

Reference Bibliography for Community Studies and Other Relevant Works

⸺ ☙ ❧ ⸺

THE CHICAGO SCHOOL ERA AND RELATED STUDIES

Anderson, Nels. 1923. *The Hobo*. Chicago: University of Chicago Press.

Cressey, Paul G. 1932. *The Taxi Dance Hall*. Chicago: University of Chicago Press.

Galpin, Charles. 1924. *Rural Social Problems*. New York: Century.

Galpin, Charles. 1918. *Rural Life*. New York: Century.

Park, Robert E. 1952 [1929]. *Human Communities*. New York: Free Press.

Riis, Jacob. 1970 [1890]. *How the Other Half Lives*. New York: Garrett Press.

Shaw, Clifford. 1930. *The Jack-roller: A Delinquent Boy's Own Story*. Chicago: University of Chicago Press.

Thrasher, Frederick M. 1927. *The Gang*. Chicago: University of Chicago Press.

Zorbaugh, Harvey. 1929. *The Gold Coast and the Slum*. Chicago: University of Chicago Press.

THE ECOLOGICAL VIEWS

Hawley, Amos. 1981. *Urban Sociology: An Ecological Approach*. 2d ed. New York: John Wiley and Sons.

———. 1986. *Human Ecology: A Theoretical Essay*. Chicago: University of Chicago Press.

McKenzie, Roderick. 1925. "The Ecological Approach to the Study of the Human Community." In *The City*, by Robert E. Park et al. Chicago: University of Chicago Press.

Park, Robert E. 1952 [1929]. *Human Communities*. New York: Free Press

Park, Robert. E., et al. 1925. *The City*. Chicago: University of Chicago Press.

Wirth, Louis. 1938. "Urbanism as a Way of Life." *American Journal of Sociology* 44:8–20.

Wirth, Louis. 1928. *The Ghetto*. Chicago: University of Chicago Press.

POWER AND CONFLICT MODELS OF COMMUNITY

Castells, Manual. 1983. *The City and the Grassroots: A Cross-cultural Theory of Urban Social Movements*. Berkeley: University of California Press.

Davis, Mike. 1992. *City of Quartz*. New York: Vintage Books.

Fasenfest, David. 1986. "The Community, Politics, and Urban Redevelopment: Poletown, Detroit, and General Motors." *Urban Affairs Quarterly* 22:101–23.

Engels, Friedrich. 1969. *The Condition of the Working Class in England*. St. Albans, UK: Panther Books.

Feagin, Joe R. 1988. *Free Enterprise City: Houston in Political-economic Perspective*. New Brunswick, NJ: Rutgers University Press.

Harvey, David. 1973. *Social Justice and the City*. Baltimore: Johns Hopkins University Press.

Hunter, Floyd. 1958. *Community Power Structure*. Chapel Hill: University of North Carolina Press.

Hunter, L. 1993. "Local Knowledge and Local Power: Notes on the Ethnography of Local Community Elites." *Journal of Contemporary Ethnography* 32, no. 1:36–58.

Jacobs, Jane. 1961. *The Life and Death of Great American Cities*. New York: Vintage.

Jankowski, Martin Sanchez. 1991. *Islands in the Street: Gangs and American Urban Society*. Berkeley: University of California Press.

Kemmis, D. 1990. *Community and the Politics of Place*. Norman: University of Oklahoma Press.

Logan, John R., and Harvey L. Molotch. 1987. *Urban Fortunes: The Political Economy of Place*. Berkeley: University of California Press.

Lynd, Robert, and Helen Lynd. 1929. *Middletown: A Study in Contemporary American Culture*. New York: Harcourt, Brace.

———. 1937. *Middletown in Transition: A Study in Cultural Conflicts*. New York: Harcourt, Brace.

Mumford, Lewis. 1961. *The City in History: Its Origins, Its Transformations, and Its Prospects*. New York: Harcourt, Brace and World.

Sassen, Saskia. 1991. *The Global City*. New York: Princeton University Press.

Sibley, David. 1995. *Geographies of Exclusion*. New York: Routledge.

Suttles, Gerald D. 1990. *The Man-Made City: The Land Use Confidence Game in Chicago*. Chicago: University of Chicago Press.

Swartz, Marc. J. 1969. *Local-Level Politics: Social and Cultural Perspectives*. London: London University Press.

Warner, Sam Bass Jr. 1972. *The Urban Wilderness: A History of the American City*. New York: Harper and Row.

———. 1973. *Streetcar Suburbs: The Process of Growth in Boston, 1870–1900*. New York: Atheneum.

Weber, Max. 1958 [1904–5]. *The Protestant Ethic and the Spirit of Capitalism*. New York: Scribner.

Zukin, Sharon. 1991. *Landscapes of Power: From Detroit to Disney World*. Berkeley: University of California Press.

———. 1995. *The Cultures of Cities*. Cambridge, UK: Basil Blackwell.

NEIGHBORS AND NETWORKS

Allen, Irving Lews. 1983. *The Language of Ethnic Conflict: Social Organization and Lexical Culture*. New York: Columbia University Press.

———. 1983. *The Language of Ethnic Conflict: Social Organization and Lexical Culture*. New York: Columbia University Press.

Fischer, Claude. 1975. "Toward a Subcultural Theory of Urbanism." *American Journal of Sociology* 80:1319–41.

———. 1982. *To Dwell Among Friends: Personal Networks in Town and City*. Chicago: University of Chicago Press.

———. 1984. *The Urban Experience*. 2d ed. San Diego: Harcourt Brace Javonovich.

Gans, Herbert. 1962. *The Urban Villagers*. New York: Free Press.

———. 1967. *The Levittowners*. New York: Columbia University Press.

Johnstone, Barbara. 1990. *Stories, Community, and Place: Narratives from Middle America*. Bloomington: Indiana University Press.

Liebow, Elliot. 1967. *Tally's Corner*. Boston: Little, Brown.

Whyte, William Foote. 1943. *Street Corner Society*. Chicago: University of Chicago Press.

ETHNICITY AND/OR SHARED LIFEWORLDS

Berger, Bennett M. 1981. *The Survival of the Counterculture: Ideological Work and Everyday Life Among Rural Communards*. Berkeley: University of California Press.

Suttles, Gerald D. 1972. *The Social Construction of Communities*. Chicago: University of Chicago Press.

Warner, Sam Bass. 1972. *The Urban Wilderness: A History of the American City*. New York: Harper and Row.

THE CONFLICTUAL COMMUNITY

Banfield, Edward. 1954. *The Moral Basis of a Backward Society*. New York: Free Press.

Gamson, William A. 1966. "Rancorous Conflict in Community Politics." *American Sociological Review* 31:71-81.

Vidich, Arthur, and Joseph Bensman. 1968 [1958]. *Small Town in Mass Society: Class, Power, and Religion in a Rural Community*. Princeton, NJ: Princeton University Press.

THE POSTMODERN COMMUNITY

Giddens, Anthony. 1991. *Modernity and Self-Identity: Self and Society in the Late Modern Age*. Stanford, CA: Stanford University Press.

Gottdiener, Mark. 1997. *The Theming of America: Dreams, Visions, and Commercial Spaces*. Boulder, CO: Westview Press.

Index

Page numbers in **bold** type indicate photos.